D0141611

Weapons of Mass Psychological Destruction and the People Who Use Them

Weapons of Mass Psychological Destruction and the People Who Use Them

Larry C. James and Terry L. Oroszi, Editors

Practical and Applied Psychology
Judy Kuriansky, Series Editor

An Imprint of ABC-CLIO, LLC
Santa Barbara, California • Denver, Colorado

Library of Congress Cataloging-in-Publication Data

Names: James, Larry C., editor. | Oroszi, Terry Lynn, editor.
Title: Weapons of mass psychological destruction and the people who use them
   / edited by Larry C. James, Terry L. Oroszi.
Description: Santa Barbara : Praeger, 2016. | Series: Practical and applied
   psychology | Includes bibliographical references and index.
Identifiers: LCCN 2015028353 | ISBN 9781440837548 (hardback) | ISBN
   9781440837555 (ebook)
Subjects: LCSH: Terrorists—Psychology. | Terrorism—Prevention. | Weapons of
   mass destruction. | World politics—2005–2015. | BISAC: POLITICAL SCIENCE
   / Political Freedom & Security / Terrorism.
Classification: LCC HV6431 .W4143 2016 | DDC 363.325—dc23
LC record available at http://lccn.loc.gov/2015028353

ISBN: 978–1–4408–3754–8
EISBN: 978–1–4408–3755–5

20 19 18 17 16   1 2 3 4 5

This book is also available on the World Wide Web as an eBook.
Visit www.abc-clio.com for details.

Praeger
An Imprint of ABC-CLIO, LLC

ABC-CLIO, LLC
130 Cremona Drive, P.O. Box 1911
Santa Barbara, California 93116-1911

This book is printed on acid-free paper ∞

Manufactured in the United States of America

Contents

Series Foreword

Dirty bombs, mustard gas, nuclear fallout, agent orange. These may be words from the past when my generation studied about wars in school, or ducked under our desk in drills during the Cold War, but such dangers are still possible. In our present times, we hear more about techniques like shoe bombs, suicide bombings, and IEDs. And we are still reeling from large-scale terrorism attacks on 9/11 in New York and other countries like Spain and Bali, and from more up-close-and-personal attacks like that of the Tsarnaev brothers in the Boston Marathon bombing.

Are we securely safe on planes or trains, in buildings, or while running marathons?

Honestly, no. Any public place can be the target for terrorists. Our fear rises to as levels as alarming as the colors of the terror alert chart. Fortunately, many threats are thwarted, thanks to intelligence forces monitoring terrorist communications, but nevertheless, we live in an age of high alert.

Public fear is reasonable and warranted. As psychologists, we do our best to calm those fears whenever terror events happen, whether close to home or abroad. We must control our fears, trust our protectors, and yet be prepared.

Authors Larry James and Terry Oroszi make us very aware that education is key in that process. Educate us they do, in their book, *Weapons of Mass Psychological Destruction and the People Who Use Them*.

Their approach is brilliant and breakthrough. Many of us became very aware of the phrase "weapons of mass destruction" when the Bush administration justified the invasion of Iraq on the premise that terrorist Osama bin Laden was harboring and planning to use these. Now, James and Oroszi introduce us to an elaborated concept that is illuminating and helpful in understanding what we are facing in current times of terrorism: "Weapons of Psychological Mass Destruction" or WPMD.

Congratulations to co-author Terry Oroszi for "coining" the term during a discussion aiming to understand the intent and motivations of the Boston Marathon terrorist attack. It's a brilliant concept, one that threads through the chapters of this book, tying together fascinating facts about and insights into all aspects of the terrorism we face. This ranges from a psychological understanding of the nature of terrorists themselves and the acts they commit, to a factual and extensive comprehension of the actual agents.

The concept makes perfect sense. The WMD that terrorist use are meant to create mass psychological distress. Thus, expanding the concept to WPMD is an approach that should be known by all psychologists, as well as law enforcement, homeland security, politicians, policy makers, scientists, international relations experts, and students of related disciplines. In my role as Chair of the Psychology Coalition of NGOs at the United Nations, where our mission is to educate government and civil society representatives and other stakeholders about contributions of valuable important psychological science and practice to achieving the global agenda, James and Oroszi's concept of WPMD can be helpful to ensure one of the Sustainable Development Goals adopted for the next 15 years, from 2015 to 2030, to ensure peaceful societies.

I wish I had known this WPMD concept as I sat, some time ago, on a destroyed building step at the perimeter of the "pit" at Ground Zero created by the September 11 terrorist attacks on the World Trade Towers, talking to an FBI agent about what can be done to prevent future such attacks. I also wish I had the concept in mind when talking to the driver of the truck doing reconstruction at that scene, a driver who told me how traumatized he was by inadvertently driving over what turned out to be body parts. Now, I am armed with this valuable concept of WMPD when called upon to communicate about the psychological sequealae of such acts while addressing professionals about coping with terror.

The chapters of this volume that explore the motivations and psychological, family, and social dynamics of terrorists deepen my understanding, through analysis and extensive research citations. They add to my interest that started many years before, during a seminar by psychologist Raymond Hamden, and other presentations at the Middle East and North African Conference on Psychology in Dubai, U.A.E., when psychologists of various cultures came together to share even cultural views that influence these acts. Later, the Praeger book set on *The Psychology of Terrorism* by psychologist Chris Stout added more insight. Then I explored this issue in my own work on the psychosocial issues underlying the Israeli-Palestinian conflict, presenting psychological dynamics from each side, and research on the impact of proximity and other issues on emotional reactions, documented in Praeger volumes, *Terror in the Holy Land: Inside the Anguish of the Israeli-Palestinian Conflict* and *Beyond Bullets and Bombs: Grassroots Peacebuilding between Palestinians and Israelis*. Topics I touched on are greatly elucidated in this present volume, including the question of why women become suicide bombers.

I intend also to use the term WPMD, and what I have learned from reading James and Oroszi's book, when addressing terrorism acts on many media shows that seek me out as a commentator. The explanation of Weapons of

Psychological Mass Destruction will help clarify the fears of the public after events like the shootings at Sandy Hook, and on anniversaries of other terrorism attacks. Applying the principle of WPMD to understand how our home-grown youth angst can lead to such drastic and evil actions will be as helpful as learning about the motivations of foreign threats such as those of Al Qaeda or ISIS.

The media is understandably critiqued in a chapter in this volume for its role in heightening psychological terror. Yet I know from vast experience that the media can also be harnessed to communicate valuable healing messages, especially when communicated by psychological experts. I have written, done trainings, and given advice about this, related to coping with news about terrorism at home, in the Middle East, and elsewhere in the world. Using the concept of WPMD will be a valuable addition to this work.

In Part III of James and Oroszi's book, we learn about biological agents, including those we encounter in daily life and household solutions, like ammonia and chlorine. In these chapters, an extensive list of agents are presented, with their chemical composition and deleterious impact on people's physical and emotional states. I found it fascinating to learn about how those agents act, and why they might be chosen by terrorists.

The editors also heighten our awareness that technology constitutes the latest threat, as terrorists are more easily able to trigger our emotional sore spots, as well as to plan and carry out acts more easily with advances in technology, like hand-held devices delivering immediate posts on public internet sites to display beheadings inevitably causing widespread panic.

This volume's editors wisely know, too, that after recognizing dangers, we need solutions. Education and training, they suggest, are key. Educators can use this concept of WPMD in courses, to elucidate understanding about terrorism. Another important solution pointed out is community policing. And many reasonable policy recommendations are offered that should be immediately implemented.

I have long known Colonel Larry C. James, co-editor of this volume, through encounters at conferences of the American Psychological Association, and been interested in his career as an officer of the U.S. Army. James has had a distinguished career as a psychologist in the military, in positions including Chief of the Department of Psychology at Walter Reed Hospital, and Chief Psychologist for the Mental Health Task Force. His knowledge and insights into the issue of terrorism, as a way to protect us and prevent evil acts, as revealed in this volume, is irrefutable.

I read every word of *Weapons of Mass Psychological Destruction and the People Who Use Them*. I found it engaging, timely, and illuminating. I learned a lot. I believe that all readers will have a similar compelling experience, and appreciate this book, its principles, and content, for professional and personal edification given its relevance to our lives today and to the lives of our children and future generations.

Dr. Judy Kuriansky, Series Editor

Introduction

Larry C. James and Terry L. Oroszi

In 1763 the United States experienced its first recorded use of a biological WMD (weapon of mass destruction), the distribution of smallpox-laden blankets by British officers. The threat that terrorist pose with WMDs never felt as personal as it did on 9/11 and the anthrax attacks a month later. Whether the terrorists are domestic or foreign born, their intent is clear, to psychologically torture the public as well as to kill the innocent.

The innocence commonly associated with amateur running events such as the Boston Marathon was changed forever on April 15, 2013. On that day, two terrorists intent on inflicting psychological terror on the United States detonated two "dirty bombs" near the finish line of the Boston Marathon race. Three people were killed and more than 250 innocent people were injured. These bombs were strategically located and set to detonate later in the race. Several questions arise regarding this incident. Why did the terrorists not detonate the bomb at the start of the race when thousands of runners were squeezed into a small area? Hundreds of runners, race officials, and/or bystanders could have been either seriously injured or killed. Had the terrorists deliberately waited until most of the international runners completed the race to detonate the bomb? Were the terrorists motivated to kill or injure more Americans rather than runners from either Africa or the Middle East? Would this act cause more psychological harm to Americans viewing the race from their living rooms across the country?

In April 2013, shortly after the Boston Marathon bombing, the editors of this book were discussing all the events surrounding the bombing. Why would people do such a thing? How could someone be convinced to harm innocent people? What were their intent and/or motivations? Were the terrorists motivated by politics, religion, a mental disorder, or just plain hate? As the editors discussed, compared ideas, and challenged each hypothesis, Terry Oroszi coined the term "weapons of mass psychological destruction" (WMPDs).

Larry C. James, PhD, and Terry L. Oroszi, MS, editors of this book, have assembled experts within the field of terrorism to "push the envelope" and pioneer and expand what we know of as weapons of mass destruction as part of a paradigm shift to *weapons of mass psychological destruction*. The editors and contributors to this book will assist the reader in ascertaining how a terrorist attack such as the Boston Marathon bombing was intended to inflict mass psychological harm and emotionally terrorize the Americans watching the race on television. If Americans are killed or injured in the process, these terrorists view this as an added benefit, but most often it is not the targeted goal.

James and Oroszi begin the book with an excellent discussion of "what are weapons of mass psychological destruction (WMPDs)?" The authors will guide the reader to an understanding through case vignettes, to acquire a detailed understanding of WMPD. Moreover, through their discussion and analysis, the reader will become cognizant of the fact that often the goal of anthrax, ricin, or any CBRN (chemical, biological, radiological and nuclear) attack may be causing psychological damage or harm rather than to just kill in mass. In Chapters 3 and 4, we tell the reader critical information about terrorists. Through this discussion and analysis, authors will assist the reader in understanding why the psychology of terrorism is a major factor in WMPD.

Some have claimed that culture and religion are factors in the proliferation of terrorism around the world. In Part II of the book, authors will examine culture, political motivations, and how terrorists use the economy as a psychological weapon. Likewise, a senior marketing and communications executive George W. Heddleston in Chapter 4 will illustrate for the reader how terrorist employ the media to psychologically torture the public.

Part III will assist the readers in their understanding of the major CBRNE threats and the related medical and health consequences of exposure to these weapons. Kelley J. Williams discusses the types of psychological symptoms that can be expected with each WMD. We consider the question, "will biological weapons create more paranoia in the general population than the use of chemical, radiological or nuclear weapons?" The author also discusses the unique aspect of each WMD that will most likely increase psychological trauma if citizens are exposed to it.

Often, the goal of a terrorist is to shape or alter the policies of his or her nation. Part IV of our book examines prevention policy and strategies to prevent WMPDs and serves as a guide for law and policy makers.

Part II of the book offers future considerations in the area of WMPDs. For example, Chapter 8 explains the use of the suicide bomber as a WMPD. As of this publication, suicide bombings have not yet affected the United States. In this chapter, the authors discuss the demographics, intent, goals, and the psychology of the suicide bomber terrorist. In addition, the chapter authors provide case examples of how female suicide bombers, in particular, can be deployed as a WMPD.

Finally, Chapter 14 examines specific terrorist group and how these groups may use WMPDs in the future to inflict terror upon communities and nations. The psychology of the terrorist is where the void in our understanding rests at this time. Thus, a book such as *Weapons of Mass Psychological Destruction and the People Who Use Them* will greatly assist us all in furthering our understanding of why and how a terrorist will be motivated to kill innocent people and destroy lives.

Part I

Defining Weapons of Mass Destruction and Weapons of Mass Psychological Destruction

1

Defining Weapons of Mass Psychological Destruction

Larry C. James and Terry L. Oroszi

On April 19, 1995, U.S. citizens Timothy McVeigh and Terry Nichols drove a white van loaded with homemade explosives, and parked the vehicle in front of the Alfred P. Murrah Federal Building in downtown Oklahoma City, Oklahoma. The car bomb made of common products was detonated, killing 168 people and wounding another 680 people. Three hundred and forty-two buildings in a 16-block radius were destroyed or damaged, and the total cost of the damage from the terrorist attack equaled $652 million (FBI, 2015b). Was this homemade bomb a weapon of mass destruction (WMD)?

In April 2013 Hayden and Wadman (2013) published an article in *Nature* entitled "US Ricin Attacks Are More Scary Than Harmful." According to the U.S. Federal Bureau of Investigation, a suspect was detained in connection with three apparent ricin-contaminated letters sent to American politicians. The agency confirmed the discovery of a letter addressed to U.S. president Barack Obama, one day after Congress's Capitol Police quarantined a letter sent to a Republican senator. A third letter was delivered to an unnamed government official in Mississippi. According to experts the risk associated with ricin is comparatively low; although minute amounts of ricin can be lethal, it is difficult to process raw materials into the toxin's most dangerous form, a readily inhaled fine powder. Ricin is unlikely to cause mass casualties, in spite of the availability of the castor bean recipes offered on the Internet.

Ten years prior to that incident ricin-tainted mail was retrieved from South Carolina and Washington, D.C.; both tested positive for the toxin. However, few such incidents result in deaths, says Raymond Zilinskas, director of chemical and biological weapons nonproliferation at the Monterrey Institute of International Studies in California. Zilinskas believes the latest scare is unlikely to cause serious harm. Is ricin a WMD? Is ricin a WMPD (weapon of mass psychological destruction)? First, we must consider what constitutes a WMD. Moreover, what are the criteria for a WMPD?

DEFINING WEAPONS OF MASS DESTRUCTION

The Department of Defense defines "weapons of mass destruction" as "chemical, biological, radiological, or nuclear weapons capable of a high order of destruction or causing mass casualties, and excluding the means of transporting or propelling the weapon where such means is a separable and divisible part from the weapon." The Federal Bureau of Investigation further defines a "weapon of mass destruction" as "any destructive device as defined in section 921, to include: any explosive, incendiary, or poison gas, bomb, and grenade." There is continued debate on the definition of WMD, and as technology expands, this definition will do so as well. Technology's role in WMD has never been as clear as it is now, with cyber terror and computer viruses as WMDs. Death and destruction can occur with such infections, and can cause mass panic. This book contains a section dedicated to chemical, biological, radiological, nuclear, and explosive (CBRNE) warfare; below you will find a brief summary of each.

Chemical WMDs

Schneider (2014a) provides historical data of when chemical weapons were used as WMDs. Schneider posited that "[c]hemical weapons did not become true weapons of mass destruction (WMD) until World War I (1914–1918). Upon conclusion of WWI an estimated 1,300,000 casualties, including 91,000 fatalities were a direct result of chemical warfare. One-third of all U.S. casualties in World War I was from mustard and other chemical gases."

There are examples of more modern-day chemicals being used as WMDs.

Warrick (2013), in a *Washington Post* article, describes a chemical attack in Syria that killed 1,400 people. Johnston (2015) provides a detailed spreadsheet of chemical and biological attacks dating back to 1994 and how chemical and biological agents were used as WMDs.

Biological Weapons

According to Schneider (2014b), "biologic weapon, also called germ weapon, or any of a number of disease-producing agents that may be utilized as weapons against humans, animals, or plants. The direct use of infectious agents and poisons against enemy personnel is an ancient practice in warfare. Indeed, in many conflicts, diseases have been responsible for more deaths than all the employed combat arms combined, even when they have not consciously been used as weapons."

History provides us with many examples of biological weapons being used to kill or injure thousands of people. Biological agents such as anthrax, the plague, or others have destroyed thousands of lives. In the fall of 2001, letters laced with anthrax were mailed to the Senate office buildings in Washington, D.C., as well as to the downtown District of Columbia postal mail processing center. A total of five people died. ABC7 News (2011) has chronicled in detail the anthrax attacks of 2001.

At the same time, as the United States prepared for the Gulf war, concern among the U.S. forces was widespread in regard to the use of an antibiotic or the Anthrax Vaccine Adsorbed (AVA) vaccine as preventative care. Soldiers, sailors, and Marines from across the country were concerned about the adverse effects of the AVA vaccine. The increased fear due to preventative treatment of anthrax was not predicted; the fear of an anthrax attack was. In 2003, Garamone reported that Iraq may have had 15,000 to 24,000 liters of anthrax prepared to use as biological weapon if the United States invaded the country.

Radiological Agents

A radiological dispersal device (RDD) is any nuclear material used in medicine, weapons, naval vessels, and power plants. A "dirty bomb" is one type of a radiological dispersal device that combines conventional explosives with radioactive material. Most RDDs would not release enough radiation to kill people or cause severe illness; the conventional explosive itself would be more harmful to individuals than the radioactive material. An RDD explosion does create fear and contaminate property and can be costly to clean up. Use of the media to ensure accurate information is available to the public will help alleviate fear. A dirty bomb is often referred to as a weapon of mass disruption, where contamination and anxiety are the terrorists' major objectives.

Nuclear WMD Agents

In 2003 the United States invaded Iraq based on questionable information regarding the manufacturing of nuclear weapons. Perhaps the psychological fear and reminders from the United States' use of the world's first deployed atomic bomb over the Japan during WWII was a motivating factor that led the Western alliance of nations to invade Iraq out of fear. An atomic bomb works by splitting large atomic nuclei (fission) such as uranium or plutonium. Hydrogen bombs use an atomic force to ignite a nuclear fusion. No other nation, since the atomic bombs were dropped, than Japan has seen such widespread devastation. Thousands of human beings were killed in that atomic blast and the nuclear fallout lasted for decades. Nuclear WMDs hold the largest threat to kill or destroy. The psychological threat of nuclear weapons as a potential is a common military defense tactic.

Explosives

The attacks at the Pentagon and the New York Twin Towers have led the U.S. government to now conceptualize explosives or powerful bombs as an unconventional WMD. On September 11, 2001, terrorists attacked the United States, killing approximately 3,000 people. Boeing airplanes, full of jet fuel, served as WMDs, the largest terrorist attack in history on American soil. In meeting the threshold for a WMD, the act must have as part of its goal to shape a political, social, or economic outcome. The drivers behind the September 11, 2001, attacks used these deadly explosives (airplanes) to alter American foreign policy.

The motive of the terrorists can be questioned. The death of thousands of Americans on 9/11 was traumatic; the fear of a similar incident still haunts Americans to this day, more than a decade later. For the first time in the history of the United States, an enemy used a WMD as a psychological torture tool against the American people.

THE PSYCHOLOGY OF WMDS

Dr. Larry James, the first author of this chapter, served as the chief, Department of Psychology, Walter Reed Army Medical Center, during the Washington, D.C., anthrax attacks, and the September 11 attack on the Pentagon (2001–2002). It was during these experiences that Dr. James saw firsthand the psychological effects of a WMD attack.

The anthrax attacks coupled with the 9/11 bombing forced a functional and psychological change in the everyday life of Americans. Fear of attack, domestic or international, is now at the forefront of everyone's mind when traveling for business or pleasure. Unattended baggage, profiling, and stress have made Americans more vigilant, at times to the detriment of other innocent passengers. Terrorists have gained entry into the minds of Americans, forcing them to make lifestyle changes. Numerous Americans began to see their country as a dangerous place, a target for terrorists, and were determined to protect themselves. Nationwide sales of guns increased by 21 percent as citizens began to view their surroundings as hazardous despite lack of imminent threat.

The 2001 anthrax attacks in the United States occurred one week after the September 11 attacks. Letters containing anthrax spores were mailed to several news offices and two U.S. senators, killing 5 people and infecting 17. Two letters went through Washington D.C.'s mail processing facility; a small number of employees were treated at local hospitals and released. Unfortunately, one employee of the mail processing center inhaled anthrax and as a result died.

Following the incident HAZMAT (teams used to clean up environmental, chemical, nuclear, biological, or radiological accidents or attacks) teams cleaned up the center and deemed it safe. Regardless of the facts several U.S. postal employees refused to return to work, and the mail processing center had to be relocated to another facility. The responsible party successfully used the media to insert into the psyche of the Washington, D.C., citizens a sense of paranoia.

Although the mail processing center was clean, hundreds of people in the DC metro area refused to touch their mail for fear of death. In fact, any substance slightly resembling anthrax (e.g., baking powder or baby powder) caused hysteria in the workplace throughout the city even though the actual physical hazard was over.

Less than 2 percent of all terrorist attacks in the European Union since 2010 have been "religiously motivated." Religious motivations constitute a slightly larger percentage of terrorist attacks in the United States. Dr. Charles Kurzman (2013), professor of sociology at the University of North Carolina, stated that Muslim Americans are "a minuscule threat to the public." Yet racial profiling has been on the rise since 9/11.

James (2008) and Banks and James (2006) eloquently described the mind of the terrorist as one motivated to paralyze the victim with fear: a fear that is unseen, cannot be touched, and is psychological in nature. To this end, terrorist cells will boldly broadcast a beheading or a hanging of innocent people repeatedly in an effort to control, alter, and/or deter a government and the citizens of a nation.

WEAPONS OF MASS PSYCHOLOGICAL DESTRUCTION

"WMD is often referred to by the collection of modalities that make up the set of weapons: chemical, biological, radiological, nuclear, and explosive (CBRNE). These are weapons that have a relatively large-scale impact on people, property, and/or infrastructure" (FBI, 2015b).

"How do WMPDs differ from WMDs?" Do WMPDs require the death of 100 or more people or involve a CBRNE device? Or, could a single firearm such as the pistol and rifle used in the Fort Hood shootings be conceptualized as a WMPD?

The authors of this chapter have modified the definition of a WMD to include a specific intent to cause psychological and/or physical harm through the use of CBRNE devices. A WMPD is any destructive device designed to cause death, serious bodily injury, or intense psychological harm through the release, dissemination, or impact of the CBRNE weapons.

GUIDELINES FOR ASSESSING A WMPD

The verdict is still out on the consensus definition for a WMD. Inclusion of firearms or other non-CBRNE weapons is up for debate, and will continue to be so, as we move forward. One may question if a death number defines it as a WMD, asking if mass destruction equates to death or damage with specific numbers or dollar amounts. We propose the inclusion of psychological damage in connection with mass destruction. For an act to be classified a WMPD event, it need not involve an agent capable of large death numbers, or property damage.

The pivotal question is "does an act, even if the loss of life or property is low, have the potential to also cause long-term, intense psychological harm to the masses, and if so should it be declared a WMD/WMPD?"

The following case examples describe WMPD that may, or may not, be considered WMD.

Case One: Anthrax

Over a decade ago, anthrax spores were delivered in letters that eventually killed 5 people, injured 17, and changed how the U.S. Postal Service thinks about mail safety. In 2010 Jay Stuart DeVaughn pleaded guilty to sending 26 letters containing white powder to President Obama, private citizens, and foreign embassies, with a note saying "take a whiff." The 2001 anthrax letters sparked the fear that Jay DeVaughn anticipated when he delivered his innocuous letters.

Case Two: Bombing

The Boston Marathon bombing, which left 3 people dead and 264 injured, as a WMD is debated; the psychological impact it had on the citizens of Boston, the running community, and the nation is not. Although the homemade explosive devices were not designed to kill thousands of people, the attack continues to have a psychological effect on many people. Even though race participation has returned to its normal levels, security levels are elevated all across the country, requiring more time, people, and expense to launch running events. The terrorists, although one is deceased and the other currently incarcerated, would view their efforts as successful; they adversely altered the way of life for thousands.

Case Three: Terrorism by Plane, D.C.

Tourists who visited Washington, D.C., frequently included the Pentagon, a historic site. After September 11, 2001, the facility no longer allows tourists. Prior to 9/11 attack, the Pentagon had an easy access subway metro rail station inside of the Pentagon. There was never a need to leave the station and walk outside in inclement weather. The Pentagon metro rail stop no longer exists. Moreover, all bags are searched and all Pentagon employees and visitors are screened via metal detectors. These are significant departures from the untroubled days prior to 9/11. All 22,000 employees, even those not present in 2001, are now mindful of the last terrorist attack at the Pentagon because of increased security levels. Dr. Larry James was appointed the chief psychologist for the medical task force that responded to provide disaster mental health counseling. Named Operation Solace, the mission was to deliver comprehensive behavioral health services to the 22,000 military and civilian Pentagon employees. The behavioral health task force remained at the Pentagon for months after the bombing and its staff eventually began to return to their normal duties across town at Walter Reed Army Medical Center. But, even at six months after the bombing, hundreds of employees had either not returned to work, took unpaid leave of absences, or exhausted every minute of sick time even though the Pentagon building was declared safe by a team of engineers.

Case Four: Terrorism by Plane, NYC

New York City, September 11, 2001. Nearly every American knew someone, or personally affected by the Twin Towers destruction, which left 3,000 dead and 300 million psychologically affected.

Case Five: Handgun

On November 9, 2009, while participating in the mobilization process to deploy, Army Major Nidal Hasan shot and killed 13 of his fellow soldiers and wounded another 30 with a pistol. Hasan's last words were "Allahu Akbar"—the Muslim exhortation "God is great." Can this be conceptualized as a WMPD? Although Hasan was fueled by religion and political causes, his vehicle of death or harm was a handgun, rather than a typical WMD. If one examines the negative psychological impact this had across the Unites States and army soldiers worldwide, it becomes easier to contextualize this act as a WMPD. This evil act on November 9, 2009, may have killed 13 people at Fort Hood, Texas, but Major Hasan's intent to psychologically harm affected millions of Americans.

Guidelines

The following guidelines will assist in determining if an act of terror or event is simply a horrible crime, a WMD event, or a WMPD act or event.

1. Was the act of terror politically motivated? Terrorists are often motivated to change a government. The IRA is an example of a terrorist group; but members of IRA see themselves as freedom fighters, not terrorists.
2. Do the attackers want to impose their religious beliefs upon a particular group of people? Although religious fanatics are a minority, they tend create more fear than political dissidents involved in terrorism. Their use of social and news media exaggerate their presence.
3. Does the act destroy significant property related to one's health or survival? The nation's water supply is a primary target for terrorism. U.S. water systems are set up to deal with contaminants. A terrorist using chemical or biological agents in the water supply is unlikely to be successful. Contamination with a biological agent would not likely produce a large risk to the public because of the dilution effect.

4. Is the act of terror public? A common goal of terrorists is for the killing, physical or destruction, to be very public and for the news sources to broadcast the event over and over to a nation to inflict psychological harm.
5. Does the killing or act involve women, children, or the elderly? Terrorists are cognizant of the fact that the killing or harming of children, women, or the elderly increases the effect and psychological impact of their terrorist actions. The act of beheading a young mother will cause great psychological harm to anyone viewing this evil act of terror.
6. Is a chemical, biological, radiological, or nuclear (CBRN) agent used? Most commonly and perhaps easier to understand and view an act as a WMPD would be the attacks that involve CBRN agents. Terrorist attacks (or the threat of an attack) using a CBRN substance have been well documented in the last few decades.
7. Did the act or event involve a firearm(s)? Earlier in this chapter an introduction to the use of firearms as a WMPD, with the Fort Hood shooting as an example, was provided.
8. Does the act involve an explosive device? The "E" for explosives has been added to the FBI's understanding and definition of a WMD. The Oklahoma City bombing, the Pentagon attack, and the 9/11 bombing of the New York Twin Towers involved airplanes as explosive devices rather than just a CBRN agent. These are clear examples of how an unconventional explosive device (such as a plane) can be used as a large scale WMPD.

REFERENCES

ABC7 News. (October 21, 2011). 2001 Anthrax Attacks Timeline: Five Die after Letters Mailed. Retrieved from http://www.wjla.com/articles/2011/10/2001-anthrax-attacks -timeline-five-die-after-letters-mailed-68155.html

Banks, L. M. & James, L. C. (2006). Warfare, Terrorism & Psychology. In Bongar, B., Brown, L., Beutler, L., Breckenridge, J., & Zimbardo, P. (Eds.) The Psychology of Terrorism. pp. 216–224. New York, NY: Oxford University Press.

Federal Bureau of Investigation. (2015b). Definition of Weapons of Mass Destruction. Retrieved from http://www.fbi.gov/about-us/investigate/terrorism/wmd/wmd_faqs

Garamone, J. (January 27, 2003). Iraq and Biological Warfare Agents. DOD News. Retrieved from http://www.defense.gov/news/newsarticle.aspx?id=29525

Hayden, E. C. & Wadman, M. (April 18, 2013). U.S. Ricin Attacks Are More Scary than Harmful. Retrieved from http://www.nature.com/news/us-ricin-attacks-are-more -scary-than-harmful-1.12834

James, L. (2008). Fixing Hell: An Army Psychologist Confronts Abu Ghraib. New York: Grand Central Press.

Johnston, W. R. (March 15, 2015). Summary of Chemical & Biological WMD Attacks. Retrieved from http://www.johnstonsarchive.net/terrorism/chembioattacks.html

Kurzman, C. (2013). Muslim-American Terrorism: Declining Further. Triangle Center on Terrorism and Homeland Security, February, 1.

Schneider, B. R. (January 1, 2014a). Chemical Weapons of Mass Destruction. Retrieved from http://www.britannica.com/EBchecked/topic/108951/chemical-weapon/ 274179/Weapons-of-mass-destruction

Schneider, B. R. (January 1, 2014b). Biological Weapons of Mass Destruction. Retrieved from http://www.britannica.com/EBchecked/topic/938340/biological-weapon

Warrick, J. (August 30, 2013). More than 1,400 Killed in Syrian Chemical Attack. Retrieved from http://www.washingtonpost.com/world/national-security/nearly -1500-killed-in-syrian-chemical-weapons-attack-us-says/2013/08/30/b2864662-1196 -11e3-85b6-d27422650fd

2

Who Becomes a Terrorist?

Michelle Holman, Timothy Shaw, Larry C. James,
and Terry L. Oroszi

Who becomes a terrorist in today's world, and why? What motivates a human being to kill an innocent bystander—or thousands of them—for political gain? Is the root cause really political, or can mental illness be the principal driving force? Here we discuss and review the existing body of literature to address those questions and many others posited by rational persons aiming to understand who becomes a terrorist. We examine average age, education, socioeconomic class, psychological and physical traits, gender, marital status, political influences, and common motivations. James (2008, 2015) and others (Hudson, 1999, 2002; Jenkins, 2001; Navarro, 2015; Simon, 2013) inform us on both the psychology of the terrorist and the common demographics. Also, as a brief case study, we examine the workings of the Irish Republican Army (IRA). Much can be learned about terrorists from the more than 50 years of activity by the IRA. Although Ireland's location, culture, and demographics differ from those of other countries, valuable insights can be gleaned from the IRA's terrorist patterns. IRA's cause differs from those of terrorists in other nations, especially domestic terrorists in the United States, but many IRA patterns including recruiting, indoctrination, weapons usage, and use of psychological warfare are very similar to those incorporated by terrorists in the United States and worldwide.

AGE, EDUCATION, AND SOCIOECONOMIC CLASS

One particular demographic of interest is age and its importance in recruitment into terrorist groups. Hudson (1999) asserted that it is likely that age contributes to the group because it is necessary to have younger, very fit individuals to carry out particular missions. Keeping this in mind, it is no surprise that the majority of active terrorist members are usually between 22 and 25 years old

(Hudson, 2002). These ages are accurate for Palestinian, German, and Japanese groups. However, there is a significant difference for Arab and Iranian groups, which are more likely to recruit boys between 14 and 15 years old for their dangerous missions. Younger members are less likely to question orders or to attract attention, thus making them ideal candidates for terrorism.

The leaders of said groups are seldom significantly older than the members they recruit. In the big picture, terrorist leaders are found to be anywhere between 35 and 60 years old. There is an obvious difference between the ages of "operators" and their leaders; however, it is important to remember that work as a terrorist is physically demanding. Therefore, as James (2015) asserted, a terrorist operator will need to be a younger individual to be capable of completing missions. The leadership of terrorist groups focuses more on planning, financing sources, recruiting, and tactical strategy.

Authors such as James (2008, 2015), Seager (2012), and Simon (2013) have examined motivation(s) questions and driving forces for domestic and international terrorists. Hudson (1999, 2002) holds that one common factor found in extremists in the least developed countries is lack of education. Terrorists from a developed country are typically more educated than those from developing countries; however, in general, terrorist members have more than an average education. It has been proposed that approximately two-thirds of terrorist group members have some form of university education. Often, highly educated recruits are promoted into leadership positions.

A preponderance of senior group leaders was found to be professionals such as doctors, bankers, lawyers, engineers, journalists, and university professors, as well as mid-level government executives. These professions mask their involvement within a terrorist group, because outsiders assume terrorist members are not exceedingly valued in society. Highly skilled professionals are effective in obtaining funding for terrorist groups. Not only do these high-paid specialists offer funding to their organizations personally, but they also acquire associations with equally high-paid individuals who have the ability to fund the terrorist group.

Generally, terrorist members continue to practice their legitimate professions and take up the calling of a terrorist only when they receive orders to carry out a mission. This practice is one of the reasons the IRA has successfully maintained anonymity in its group. Anarchist groups are more infamous, and can be spotted by Interpol or on police's most-wanted posters. A typical anarchist group member is in hiding, stressed, and in fear of capture, making him unable to function in a normal workforce.

The majority of terrorist members within the IRA are drawn from the laboring class (BBC, 2015; Coogan, 2002; TRAC, 2015). Often, paramilitary groups, like the IRA, are not university educated. Arab terrorist organizations recruit members from poor and homeless refugees; however, their leaders originate from the middle and upper socioeconomic classes (Hudson, 1999, 2002).

It is common for international and domestic terrorists to be angry individuals who feel isolated from society. They target their anger toward either their government or a foreign regime (Hudson, 1999, 2002; James, 2008, 2015). They often have a grievance, or see themselves as victims of some kind of injustice within society. Recruits from developed countries are uneducated, leaving school prior to graduation, giving them something in common with their lesser developed country counterparts. Terrorists do not see their deeds as criminal. Their violent actions are instigated because of a commitment to a cause, whether it be political or religious, so they believe they are making a difference. Extremist members are very loyal to each other; however, when one of the members acts in a disloyal manner that member is handled more harshly than enemies outside the group.

New recruits are regularly expected to execute an armed robbery or commit murder to show allegiance to the group, to bind themselves with the criminal activity in an attempt to be accepted. This is similar to gang orientation in the United States and elsewhere. These members and recruits will not show fear, pity, or remorse for anything outside of the mission. There are many levels of sophistication, or technology "savvy," within terrorist groups, depending on the financial resources, and context of the actions, the organization takes. The more sophisticated the group, the more likely it will be dangerous, and that it can carry out larger strategic attacks.

Members of these groups are trained to use a large variety of weapons, vehicles, and communication equipment, and are familiarized with their physical environment, anything from a Boeing 767-200ER, used in 9/11, to a national courthouse. If it is essential to carry out the mission, they will gain the skill needed to cause death and destruction. Terrorists are unlikely to operate in large groups, unless it is an operation that necessitates taking over a large building or the like. By functioning in smaller groups they can easily blend into the environment (PBS, 2015).

PSYCHOLOGICAL TRAITS, PHYSICAL TRAITS, GENDER, AND MARITAL STATUS

There are some psychological traits that are conventional to right-wing (conservative) terrorist groups. These traits are as follows: ambivalence toward authority, poor defective insight, adherence to conventional behavioral patterns, emotional detachment from the consequences of their actions, magical and stereotyped thinking, hetero- and auto-destructiveness, low-level education reference patterns, and adherence to violent subcultural norms. These traits are what Francesco Bruno—criminologist, psychiatrist, professor, teacher at the University of Salerno and La Sapienza, Rome—calls an "authoritarian-extremist personality." It has been concluded by some that right-wing terrorism may be more dangerous than left-wing (reformist) terrorism because within the right-wing terrorism, the individuals are frequently psychopathological and the ideology is empty.

Generally, terrorist members will be healthy and strong; however, they strive to be undistinguished in their appearance and manner. Some may have enhanced physical fitness if they have had extensive military-style training. They are likely to have a medium build and height in order to easily blend into a crowd. These individuals are unlikely to have abnormal characteristics or any peculiar features, genetic or acquired, which could draw attention to them or single them out of a group. Their hair and dress will depend on the environment in which they are in. In addition to their ordinary appearance, they will talk and act like the typical person. Some may even resort to plastic surgery if their identity is made public knowledge or if their photos are on police's wanted posters (Hudson, 1999, 2002; PBS, 2015).

Throughout history, well over 80 percent of terrorist groups and terrorist operations have been led, directed, and executed by males (Hudson, 1999, 2002). Females have never been as prolific as males in terrorist groups; however, there is a significant likelihood that female membership in terrorist groups will continue to grow. Although urban terrorism remains a predominantly male phenomenon, with women functioning mainly in secondary support roles, other areas are seeing a growth in the number of females working at an operational level. Many individuals underestimate the active, operational role played by women in Latin American and West European terrorist organizations.

Leftist terrorist groups and operations have frequently been led by women. Out of the eight individuals on Germany's wanted terrorists list of 1991, five were women. In the same year, 13 of the 22 terrorists being hunted by German police were women. While some groups will continue to only use women in secondary roles, leftist groups continue to expand their use of women as terrorists. Many theories have been postulated to explain why German women have been so drawn to violent groups. One theory speculates that they are more emancipated and liberated than women in other European countries.

Before taking up the terrorist path, many Irish women moved from small or medium-sized communities they were raised in to large cities. Their occupations prior to their involvement in terrorist activity broke down as follows: 35 percent were students; 20 percent were teachers; and 23 percent held white-collar jobs as clerks, secretaries, technicians, and nurses. A small number of them were affiliates of a political party or trade union organization, whereas 80 percent were a part of leftist extra-parliamentary movements. Another prevalent theory regarding the women is that are inclined to join a terrorist group as a result of a family decision (BBC, 2015; TRAC, 2015).

Women revolutionaries tend to have an absolute practicality, indicating they work well under pressure. Female terrorists possess a levelheadedness, which is one of the most important qualities needed in these groups. According to Christian Lochte, director of the Hamburg State office for the Protection of the Constitution, women are more capable of keeping things together during war-time. Women can fly under the radar because the general public is less likely to equate women to terror. Rather, individuals see a woman as a mother figure, nonviolent, fragile, or even victimlike, making them easier to pass through scrutiny by security forces. They also believe women to be more capable of with-standing suffering. Some consider female terrorists to be even stronger, more dedicated, and faster, as well as more ruthless than their male counterparts.

Eileen MacDonald (1992), author of *Shoot the Women First*, has said, since the late 1960s, women have begun replacing imprisoned or interned male IRA members as active participants. IRA women's terrorist role against both the British troop protestant paramilitary units, and the British public has increased dramatically over the years (Ozeren, Gunes, & Al-Badayneh, 2007). This time frame also includes the time the IRA merged its separate women's section into the IRA.

MacDonald has interviewed a few of the female members within the IRA. She described them as all seeming ordinary. Some were friendlier than others. Most of the females were unmarried teenagers or in their early twenties when they joined the terrorist group. Not one of them were recruited by a boyfriend or partner. When MacDonald asked why they joined the terrorist group, they replied with "how could they not." Each woman MacDonald spoke with shared the same hatred for the British troops and a total belief that the violence they used was justified.

Female terrorists have also been found to be more dangerous than men because of their ability to be single-mindedly focused on the goal or mission at hand. Women also tend to hesitate less when the need to shoot someone is required to complete their mission. Bloom (2011), James (2015), and others (Hafez, 2007; Skaine, 2006; U.S. Army War College, 2015) assert that female terrorists may be more dangerous than male terrorists. The reasons for these views have complex underpinnings. These researchers believe that female terrorists may feel the need to prove themselves capable of being more ruthless than the men. That need the women feel, a need to prove their worth, gives the appearance of greater dedication to the cause than their male counterparts.

It is also possible that since women tend to be more idealistic than men, they could be more driven to perpetrate terrorist activities in response to a failure to achieve the desired change, or the experience of a death or injury of a loved one. The promise of power or glory they would receive appears to appeal to women as much as, if not more than, it does to men. It may also be the attractiveness of a promise for a better life for their children, as well as the desire to meet people's needs, which is a driving force.

In the past, most terrorist members have been unmarried. Several researchers (Hudson, 2002; Jenkins, 2001; PBS, 2015; Seager, 2012; TRAC, 2015) demonstrate that 75 to 80 percent of terrorists in various regions in the late 1970s were single and never married. The remaining 20 percent of foreign terrorist group membership consisted of married couples. It is likely that terrorist members remain single because of the household responsibilities, which are generally precluded by requirements for mobility, flexibility, initiative, security, and total commitment to a revolutionary movement. The demands on the terrorist make married or family life virtually impossible. Depending on the sophistication of the group, and the cause they are trying to serve, many terrorists do not return home once their mission is complete. There is, nonetheless, a belief popular in some organizations that having a family or a spouse grounds the terrorist enough so he or she will not make irrational decisions, and will be more likely to follow orders that are made by their terrorist leaders.

U.S. RESEARCH NEEDED

A true understanding of domestic terrorists within the United States remains unclear. Researchers such as Jenkins (2001), Navarro (2015), Seagar (2012), and Simon (2013) have suggested that American terrorists share some common traits with international groups. Yet, little is known about how exactly American terrorists are radicalized to extreme violence against the United States and civilians in America. Many sound logical arguments can be postulated as to why foreign nationals turn to terrorism. Arguments such as political oppression, poverty, lack of education, and the murder and/or imprisonment of one's family members are just a few rational reasons why foreign youths turn to terrorism. Within the United States, these motivations are far more rare. Thus, research that examines domestic terrorists to ascertain the cause is clearly needed.

REFERENCES

Bloom, M. (2011). *Bombshell: Women and terrorism*. New York, NY: Random House.
British Broadcasting Company. (2015). The Search for Peace: The IRA Continuity. http://news.bbc.co.uk/hi/english/static/northern_ireland/understanding/parties_paramilitaries/continuity_ira.stm
Coogan, T. P. (2002). *The IRA*. New York, NY: Palgrave Macmillan Trade Press.
Hafez, M. (2007). *Female Suicide Bombers: The Strategy and Ideology of Martydom*. Washington, DC: United States Institute of Peace.
Hudson, R. (1999). *The Sociology & Psychology of Terrorism: Who Becomes a Terrorist & Why?* Washington, DC: The Library of Congress.
Hudson, R. (2002). *Who Becomes a Terrorist and Why?* New York, NY: The Lyons Press.
James, L. (2008). *Fixing Hell: An Army Psychologist Confronts Abu Ghraib*. New York: Grand Central Press.
James, L. (2015). Domestic, Radicalized, Terrorism in the United States. A paper presented at the Middletown Chamber of Commerce. Middletown, Ohio.

Jenkins, B. (2001). *Stray Dogs & Virtual Arms: Radicalization to Jihadist Terrorism in the United States*. Washington, DC: Rand Corporation.

MacDonald, E. (1992). *Shoot the Women First*. New York, NY: Random House.

Navarro, B. (2015). *Acts of Terrorism in the United States*. Scotts Valley, CA: Creative Space Publishing.

Ozeren, S., Gunes, I. D., & Al-Badayneh, D. M. (Eds.). (2007). *Understanding Terrorism: Analysis of Sociological and Psychological Aspects (Vol. 22)*. Amsterdam, The Netherlands: IOS Press.

Public Broadcast Station. (2015). America and the Conflict. http://www.pbs.org/wgbh/pages/frontline/shows/ira/reports/america.html

Seager, W. (2012). *Bureau of Counterterrorism Report on Terrorism in the United States*. Washington, DC.

Simon, R. (2013). *Lone Wolf Terrorism and the Great Threat*. New York, NY: Prometheus Press.

Skaine, R. (2006). *Female Suicide Bombers*. Jefferson, NC: MacFarland & Company.

Terrorism, Research & Analysis Consortium. (2015). http://www.trackingterrorism.org/

U.S. Army War College. (2015). *Female Suicide Bombers*. Carlisle Barracks, PA: Create Space Independent Publishing Platform.

Part II

The Psychological, Cultural, and Economic Issues Related to Who Becomes a WMPD Terrorist and Why

3

Terrorist Recruiting for Weapons of Mass Psychological Destruction*

Lewis M. Pulley

Many factors contribute to people eventually becoming terrorists, and terrorist groups' appeal is usually multifaceted (Ozeran, Murat, Yilmaz, & Sozer, 2014). Recruitment rationales vary to some degree (Smelser, 2007). While no single profile or personality exists, common themes exist (Bos, 2013; Daymon, 2014; Jacques & Taylor, 2009; Smelser, 2007). In view of this, successful terrorist recruiting adapts to the particular audience and region. Processes used in one area may differ noticeably from those used elsewhere. Consequently, no lone recruiting approach exists. In addition, the methods used will change over time in order to stay effective (Gerwehr & Daly, 2012).

Spitaletta, Newton, Bos, Crosett, and Leonhard (2013) noted that data examining terrorist recruitment encompass numerous different cells, people groups, and regions. Despite that tendency, research on Islamic terrorist recruits from numerous countries and terrorist affiliations indicated recurring patterns. Overall, individuals joined for a variety of reasons, and often no particular motive stood apart from others. The sum of the motives is what drew recruits.

Idiosyncratic (particular to the individual) and situational motives also played a collective role. Propaganda and individual incentives were effective when used in conjunction with personal and situational motives. Coercion was also found to be highly effective, but only when it was mixed with additional affirmative factors (Spitaletta et al., 2013) Some variables apply to a variety of individuals while others are more applicable to persons in particular regions or in other circumstances. When possible, those differences are delineated in this chapter.

As an introductory note, this chapter examines recruitment from a broad perspective. The term *terrorists* applies to persons aligned with an extremist

*The views expressed in this chapter are the author's alone and do not represent the views of Eglin Air Force Base or the U.S. Air Force.

organization centered on using ideology and purposeful violence to enact its policies for a variety of potential gains. Consequently, the terrorist recruits described herein include persons planning to engage in terrorist activities, such as bombings. At times, it also includes insurgencies planned to overthrow governments or install an Islamic caliphate using military arms, improvised explosive devices, or other similar means. While there may be some technical delineation between these groupings, their overall goals and means are collectively similar.

Gerwehr and Daly (2012) observed that there is a paucity of empirical literature on what makes people susceptible to being recruited. While it exists within intelligence agencies, that data are chiefly categorized into demographic factors due to the associated ease of collection and organization. Psychographic and state variables may be better indicators of recruiting potential. Psychographic variables include the recruit's perceptions, biases, stereotypes, and emotions. State variables include factors such as depressive or anxious symptoms or results of poverty, such as malnutrition and ill health.

Ramswell (2014) identified four factors that contribute to terrorist recruitment. They are socioeconomic forces, political climates, religious extremism, and cultural issues. Similarly, some individuals join due to their proximity to problematic locations. Ozeran et al. (2014) described those areas as having socioeconomic disparities, poverty, high population density, ethnic factors, and state laws. Those conditions can contribute to individuals being marginalized in society and consequently make them more open to terrorist ideology or influence.

Additional influences may be as simple as extremist organizations fulfilling social needs such as creating a feeling of belonging to a seemingly exclusive group or being valued as an individual. This appeal can also establish a sense of purpose. For example, recruits may have opportunities to offer their solutions to problems and therefore deepen their camaraderie and contributions to the group (Mendelsohn, 2011; Ozeran et al., 2014).

SOCIAL AND DEMOGRAPHIC FACTORS

Smelser (2007) observed that terrorist recruits often lived in a country that differed from their place of origin. It is common for recruits to be unemployed before recruitment (Sageman, 2004; Smelser, 2007). Those factors could infer they lacked strong affiliation and may have felt like outcasts. Bos (2013) reported that marginalization due to ethnicity, religion, tribe, or ideology may be the most powerful contributor to persons being open to terrorist recruiting. Similarly, Piazza (2006) observed that areas with greater ethnic, economic, and religious divisions tended to have higher incidents of terrorist activity when they existed in countries with complex multiparty political structures. He proposed that these factors formed weak (broadly divisive) political climates that established an environment that was more amenable to terrorist activity.

GRIEVANCE AND RECRUITMENT

Numerous sources found that skilled terrorist recruiters know how to manipulate actual or supposed grievances to draw recruits. Recruiters also know which topics might detract from their efforts. Common themes include injustice, unfairness, and inequality. Recruiters place a particular focus on socioeconomic, political, religious, and even cultural arenas to draw recruits (Ramswell, 2014). Taarnby (2005) noted that recruiting is closely tied to persons who feel marginalized, are searching for an identity, are inclined to Islamic extremism beliefs, and have strong political grievances. Appealing to this sense of injustice (real or inflated) encourages some prospective terrorists to seek vengeance from their perceived oppressors.

Terrorist organizations consequently seek people from locations with problematic social and demographic factors. Those factors include socioeconomic disparity, poverty, high population density, low education, age (youth or younger adults), ethnic background, and a tumultuous political climate. These conditions may isolate potential recruits from the general surrounding population and indirectly make them susceptible to engaging in terrorist activity (Ozeran et al., 2014).

Other grievances stem from perceived injustices, and dissonant political policies, which are used to fuel recruitment. These include anger against the West due to the belief that it is waging war against Muslims. Recruiters therefore preach that Muslims are persecuted in order to draw new adherents (Ryan, 2007). Ramswell (2014) noted that recruiters are knowledgeable of preconceived grudges in their audiences and use negative emotions to entice their prospects. Limited education may further contribute to the exploitation of prejudices or ignorance.

Recruiters further utilize envy to spur allegiance to their cause. One such tactic involves claiming that "infidels" immorally acquire wealth and influence. They then use current events, such as bombings in Syria or other locations, to illustrate the alleged projection of that immorality. Jihad (terrorism) then offers a seemingly justified solution.

SOCIOECONOMIC FORCES

Bos (2013) speculates that poverty indirectly influences the climates from which extremist organizations draw adherents. Relative deprivation or perceived economic differences promulgate dissatisfaction more than the actual economic degree of deprivation. In other words, the appearance of the disparity is more important than the actual value of the difference, and that perspective makes individuals more susceptible to terrorist influence. This difference is again tied to the belief that wealthier individuals necessarily acquired their finances through immoral means. It is hypothesized that some persons in these circumstances believe they have few alternative options or little to lose, which increases the allure of terrorist activity (Ozeran et al., 2014). This susceptibility is best viewed as a risk factor and not a single contributing cause.

FINANCIAL INCENTIVE

Amble and Meleagrou-Hitchens (2014) determined that financial incentive draws some to join terrorist causes. For example, recruits to al-Shabaab in Africa were promised 4 to 20 times the typical monthly wage. Recruiters routinely sought recruits in indigent areas to capitalize upon the appeal of this tactic. This approach has a particular allure in impoverished regions with few employment options. As an aside, the organizations promising such high wages failed to pay anything in several instances. In response, some individuals fled the associated group, which implies that financial incentives are a motivating force in some instances.

Recruiters further appeal to the belief that the government is not interested in addressing poverty or unemployment (Amble & Meleagrou-Hitchens, 2014). This belief legitimizes joining an extremist group in that they are fighting a government entity supposedly uninterested in their welfare. Marrying that notion with religious ideology suggests that joining the organization is not only permissible but also noble.

POLITICAL CLIMATES

As previously suggested, political factors play directly in extremist recruitment. Anderson (2014) remarked that jihadist leaders know how to capitalize on political unhappiness to draw recruits. Governments viewed as illegitimate or uncaring serve as incubators for recruiting (Bos, 2013). As previously noted, countries with numerous large political parties are more inclined to terrorist activity when they simultaneously have ethnic and economic divides (Piazza, 2006). This may contribute to individuals from marginalized and underrepresented people groups being more open to terrorist network associations. That condition alone does not cause people to join terrorist networks; however, it may have that effect when combined with other themes.

THE ROLE OF RELIGIOUS EXTREMISM

Numerous sub-motivations exist under the umbrella of Muslim extremist ideology. This version of Islam purports that adherents are pious followers rather than apostates. Indeed, practitioners consider themselves to be the true Muslims (Ryan, 2007).

Religious ideology further plays a predisposing role to terrorist recruitment in that persons typically became demonstrably more religious before joining terrorist groups (Smelser, 2007). Similarly, Leonhard and Conley (2013) remarked that terrorist recruiters focus on persons already inclined toward Muslim extremism beliefs. This inclination toward terrorist groups is important; however, having personal connections to others with similar beliefs is the key factor that usually leads individuals to join.

Fair (2004) reported that terrorist networks control or influence mosques in areas of Pakistan and potentially Afghanistan as well. The imams (religious leaders) may encourage parents to send their children to those facilities for intense religious study. That education is tailored toward specific ends. It also purposely creates exposure to recruiters, who encourage youths to attend terrorist training camps.

Mosques may further facilitate recruiting efforts. Inviting particular speakers to discuss certain topics allows many potential recruits to be exposed to ideology at a single time. Additional meetings, often in more private settings, address other topics related to the group's interests. Further meetings become more specific and eventually allow attendees to join the extremist cause (Fair, 2004).

Islamic terrorists often marry religious ideology with alleged injustice. They purport their actions as attempts to correct those perceived wrongs. The terrorists then label their cause as one sanctioned by Allah since their targets seemingly oppose principles in the Koran. Extremists emphasize the importance of Sharia (fundamentalist) law. They then demonize those who do not adhere to their dogma and justify jihad as a result. This technique is particularly effective in recruiting youth. This ideological coupling yields young individuals willing to engage in a variety of violent activities and emboldens them in a seemingly religious (justified) quest (Ramswell, 2014). Religion-based recruitment is effective in some countries (such as Pakistan) whose youths seek religious organizations to provide solutions for their grievances (Fair, 2004).

While religious extremism permeates all elements of all Islamic terror groups, there are different interpretations and applications of it. For example, Muslims from one region of Africa were encouraged to fight Muslims from another area for any number of supposedly religious reasons (Amble & Meleagrou-Hitchens, 2014). Similarly, rhetoric for or against Sunni or Shiite branches of Islam is used by respective terror groups (Zelin, 2014). This leads to the conclusion that practitioners of these beliefs have interests other than purely religious; however, terrorist recruiters and leaders understand the draw and the power of such beliefs in attracting recruits.

TERRORISM AS AN ALTERNATIVE TO ALIENATION

Numerous factors and predispositions contribute to individuals joining terrorist organizations. Moghaddam (2005) described the progression that leads recruits to that decision. He noted that numerous people experience mistreatment and deprivation, yet they do not seek recourse in terrorism. Those who join the ranks often feel entirely forsaken by society and lack a sense of belonging. They are particularly open to the sense of community that terrorist cells possess and ripe for indoctrination. The cells capitalize upon the sense of alienation while simultaneously demonizing the associated people groups or society at large. Populations are labeled as immoral by the organization. Terrorist leaders then have the simplified task of convincing recruits that the terrorist organization is virtuous and its acts are therefore justified and righteous. Terrorism is framed as the punishment or cure for society's ills.

SPECIFIC POPULATIONS: RECRUITING YOUTH

Multiple sources suggest that youths are particularly susceptible to joining terrorist networks. Involvement stems from the allure of adventure, camaraderie, battlefield exploits, or an opportunity to travel to a foreign land to fight for a "just" cause (Mendelsohn, 2011). Additional rationale ranges from opposing the violence of a particular political regime (Bashar al-Assad in Syria, for example) to countering America's alleged immorality—U.S. Coalition airstrikes killing Muslims—becoming a martyr (Daymon, 2014), or using an opportunity to rebel (Leonhard & Conley, 2013).

Other variables can influence young adults to join extremist groups. Youths (15–24 years of age) are more predisposed to acts of violence when three conditions exist. First, unemployment, underemployment, or limited economic options are generally the greatest force contributing to youths' inclination toward violence as a remedy. This in turn makes them more open to terrorist recruiting. A high population of young males (16–30 years of age) often increases that risk even further provided the previous factors coexists. Third, youths can be more inclined to act out against perceived injustices or dissatisfaction as compared to those who are older. This may be particularly true in youths who are otherwise unattached. These variables are particularly salient for terrorist activity in the Middle East as well as portions of Africa (Bos, 2013).

Hope Cheong and Halverson (2010) investigated Al Qaeda–affiliated terrorists' worldwide efforts to recruit youth. As previously described, many potential recruits come from impoverished backgrounds. In addition, they again often live in areas with little political representation or recourse. Furthermore, suspicion if not outright dislike of Western ways and America was not uncommon. They identified a three-pronged approach to describe the formation of a jihadist youth identity. As that identity was forged and fostered, it could then be exploited for terrorist purposes.

First, youths were extolled as a virtuous special class with high value. Youths were said they personify values such as wholesomeness, allegiance, and zeal. Proponents used elements of the Koran to laud youths' potential to right wrongs in society and the world while practicing "pure" Islam. This led directly to their second approach, which involved forging a youth identity to exploit for terrorism.

More specifically, that second youth-recruiting prong entailed labeling extremist youths as true Muslim believers. Terrorist groups build this belief system based on an extreme version of Islam. Terrorist organizations delineate themselves from non-jihadists by painting others as uncommitted, influenced by the West, or immoral "apostates." Extremist groups preach the necessity of creating an environment of "true Islam" where the perceived evils and grievances against them do not exist. Consequently, establishing a caliphate, or Islamic state, based upon Sharia law is an end goal of those beliefs (Hope Cheong & Halverson, 2010).

Finally, terrorist recruiters and leaders idealize jihadist warriors who sacrifice their lives for a supposedly noble cause. This approach hinges off of well-known historical, religious figures in Islam, many of whom were young when they performed their acts of devotion. Terrorist cells laud those acts and encourage the young to forsake pursuing an education or careers in order to pursue jihad. In doing so, advocates say that youths are following in the footsteps of the previous saints and pursuing a more noble effort. Radicalized youths who concede and become operational are extolled for their devotion. Al Qaeda leaders then further hail fallen jihadists as role models for youths to follow (Hope Cheong & Halverson, 2010).

THE MENTALLY ILL

Persons with mental illness are documented to have been associated with terrorist activities (James, 2008; McCauley & Moskalenko, 2008). This is particularly true of individuals with severe psychopathology such as psychosis. While psychopathology occurs in some candidates, there is little data to suggest that recruiters usually seek out such individuals. Popular lore may suggest that many terrorists are "crazy"; however, terrorist operations usually necessitate persons of at least average competence to execute them. Consequently, the notion that the mentally ill are routinely recruited is unfounded.

RECRUITING WOMEN

Overall, women are less involved per capita in terrorist activity than men. While no lone variable influences women to join these groups, common motivations exist. Typical consensus states that women join extremist groups for individual reasons that differ from men. These may include the death of a family member, rape, and influence from a romantic partner (husband, boyfriend). On the other hand, Cunningham (2003) stated those motivations often mirror their male counterparts, and that is particularly true when the rationale includes political or social elements. She further noted that organizations are increasingly recruiting women because females are viewed as less dangerous, which lends itself to less visibility. Women consequently provide greater stealth to activities that require a low signature in order to succeed. Organizations also take advantage of feminine considerations such as pregnancy, which afford women less scrutiny in certain situations ("pat downs" or physical searches of the body, for example).

In contrast to Cunningham's conclusions above, Jacques and Taylor (2009) compared 30 male and 30 female suicide bombers. Both data sets were coded equivalently in terms of recruitment style, motivation, and results of the bombing. The results determined that female suicide terrorists were in fact more greatly influenced by personal events. For example, revenge motivated women to engage in terrorism-related violence significantly more than men. Males were more influenced by religion and sociopolitical factors. Women were far less likely to join terrorist activities due to religious beliefs or religious peer groups. Both genders were motivated by general peer pressure, exploitation, or self-interest.

RECRUITMENT METHODS

Recruiting efforts can be lengthy and may even take years to reach fruition for an individual. Potential recruits are observed and evaluated for their loyalty and potential abilities over an indeterminate period of time. Seemingly harmless or even benevolent organizations often serve as initial recruiting pools. These include student groups, athletic clubs, religious societies, political marches, or ideological groups. They are particularly useful in that the initial recruiting agency is legal and innocuous. They also offer a recruitment pool that is at least mildly in line with certain terrorist beliefs (Leonhard & Conley, 2013).

RECRUITMENT MODELS

Gerwehr and Daly (2012) researched common terrorist recruiting models. They determined that recruiters employ four general models, which include the net, the funnel, the infection, and the seed crystal. They noted that the models are not all encompassing. Instead, they portray the different approaches that recruiters typically utilize. Gerwehr and Daly further recommend that the models be viewed as flexible starting points for gathering data on terrorist recruitment rather than entrenched, nonadaptable approaches. Each is briefly described below.

The Net

The net approach targets a fairly homogenous group. The group is predetermined to possess recruitment potential and exist in an area with little opposition to aspects of the recruitment message. An example of this approach is members of a particular mosque led by a radical-minded imam being given the same DVD. Potential recruits are already familiar with aspects of the rationale. While some will ignore the effort, others stand a strong likelihood of responding. As a point of reference, this model stands the best chance of being successful in an area such as Pakistan's Northwest Frontier Province due to its popular support of Al Qaeda.

The Funnel

The funnel method is useful when a particular group possesses the recruitment potential, yet it lacks a common motive or identity with the terrorist cause. Consequently, the recruiter utilizes a gradual recruitment effort with associated phases to shape the pool of potentials. Shaping activities begin with less intensity (such as identity-building) and eventually work toward executing violence. The funnel makes use of techniques from social, clinical, and cognitive psychology. The "funnel" necessarily implies that some initial attractants will drop out; however, even when this occurs, their initial attraction may contribute to subsequent persons entering the funnel. At a minimum, it increases familiarity with and openness to the terrorist cause.

The Infection

The infection, as the name implies, occurs in environments that are not particularly amenable to terrorist notions as a whole. The "virus" therefore works by searching out individuals within that population who are susceptible due to a grievance or dissatisfaction. Three elements are important for the recruiter using the infection approach. The recruiter must appear credible, the recruiter empathizes with prospects' grudges and proposes terrorism as a potential remedy, and the recruiter is highly selective about who is approached. Due to the individual focus of the appeal, time is a particular consideration for this approach. Once the group recruits a sufficient number of people, it can then use its size to encourage a type of peer pressure to join. The infection recruiting approach may be utilized in regions such as Kenya or Tanzania, where most of the population is opposed to terrorist groups, but disgruntled persons may be open to influence.

Gerwehr and Daly (2012) further observed that this approach may be used in military or police organizations with disenfranchised persons. While the authors do not propose this assertion, it could provide groups access to intelligence or other resources from the military or law enforcement. Furthermore, it could garnish access to targets that are unreachable without someone on the inside to facilitate their attack. The Pakistani military is another example of this approach as it is known to harbor terrorist sympathizers.

The Seed Crystal

This method differs from the other approaches. It is utilized either in remote locations or by those not amenable to the direct influence of a recruiter. Instead, efforts are created to facilitate self-recruitment. It is inferred that once a sufficient number of self-recruits occur, then this approach morphs into one akin to the infection. The seed crystal may be incorporated in populations where efforts must be highly covert or largely untraceable. Internet radicalization is an implementation of this approach.

THE INTERNET AND TERRORIST RECRUITMENT

While the Internet plays a role in recruiting, its effectiveness varies by location and outcome. It facilitates drawing individuals from a worldwide pool, but it is not always used by organizations to fill their ranks. The Internet is limited in its power to vet prospective recruits (Mendelsohn, 2011). It stands in contrast with face-to-face recruiting. This often occurs through personal contacts (such as friends or family), which provide an increased degree of security for the recruiting organization (McCauley & Moskalenko, 2008).

While the Internet has facilitated persons joining jihadist terrorist organizations, there are also instances in which those efforts did not reach fruition. As an example, individuals who self-radicalized via the Internet attempted to join an extremist group by traveling to another country. They were subsequently denied access due to suspicion that they might be infiltrators from intelligence or other agencies (Mendelsohn, 2011). As a result, potential recruits are typically contacted face-to-face by someone skilled in evaluating individuals personally. Despite that limitation, social media such as Facebook and Twitter serve as initial recruiting outlets in some instances. Interested parties can "friend" or "follow" sites with similar interests, which can eventually lead to them joining extremist groups (Zelin, 2014). This indirect method of recruiting is represented considerably less in the literature than its alternative.

THEMES AND ATTRIBUTES OF RECRUITED TERRORISTS

Age

Jenkins (2011) acquired biographical details for 176 persons who were indicted in connection to terrorist activity from 2002 to 2010. The median age was 27, and the mean age was 32. He noted that those taking more operational roles (training for and then executing terrorist acts) were approximately seven years older than individuals filling logistical roles.

Origin

Over 50 percent of the 176 persons included in Jenkins's (2011) study were of Somali origin. The remaining countries of origin were predominantly Pakistan, Egypt, Morocco, Palestine, the Dominican Republic, and Australia. Twenty-five percent of individuals in the study were native-born Americans, and most of them were converts to Islam. Others in the study had their origins in Somalia, Pakistan, North Africa, the Middle East, South Asia, or the Balkans. The over-representation of recruits from Somalia and Pakistan infers that individuals who emigrated from war zones may be more susceptible to joining terrorist organizations. In addition, those countries are often more accepting of terrorist ideology. Similarities exist in Europe also. Extremists hailing from Somalia, Algeria, or Pakistan migrating to Europe are overrepresented in the study.

INTERNAL MOTIVATIONS

Cottee and Hayward (2011) identified three internal motivations for people becoming involved in terrorism. They include a desire for excitement, for finding purpose in their lives, and for esteem or notoriety. This conceptualization states that terrorist activity stands as a type of proxy when like-minded individuals cannot fulfill those needs through a legitimate (rational) channel. In several instances, groups of unemployed younger men pursued terrorist activity as a way of finding meaning in their lives. These groups lived in non-Muslim countries, and it appears that their Muslim extremist beliefs helped to create a sense of familiarity. Moreover, involvement with terror groups created a sense of stability and attachment to their previous culture (Sageman, 2004).

Sageman's (2004) analysis of 150 known terrorists determined that 68 percent of them joined as a group of friends. If one broadens that scope to include family members' influence on recruitment, then social relationships influenced approximately 75 percent of jihadists to become involved in terrorist activities. In view of that data, he proposed a three-step process for his study cohort becoming radicalized. This includes individuals joining via some type of social bond whether through family ties or through friendships. Next, those persons' religious beliefs become increasingly extreme, and they strongly identify with a jihadist ideology. Finally, those beliefs culminate in the group formally linking itself with another active terrorist organization or attempting a terrorist attack of their own.

Ahmad (2014) drew similar conclusions while investigating how social networks influenced college-aged young adults in Pakistan to join extremist Islamic organizations. It is important to note that the organizations in his study were not terrorist groups; however, their sympathies largely aligned with jihadist groups, and leaders were known to support terrorist ideals. As was previously stated, this type of entity can serve as a conduit for extremist cells. The organizations used informal social influences to gather recruits. Greater familiarity with a recruiter fostered friendships, which led the recruiter to invite the new friend(s) to group meetings. Further contact with the friend led to increased exposure to the organization, and individuals eventually joined even if their particular views did not align with the more stringent beliefs of the group. Some students' views eventually moved more in line with that of the groups, while others' did not. Regardless of the final outcome, the initial informal, personal contact led to subsequent invitations to group meetings and an increase in group members. Consequently, there appears to be some additional support for Sageman's hypothesis that individuals are susceptible to joining terrorist groups due to social influence and a need to belong.

Other recruitment builds off of related ideas. Daymon (2014) noted that individuals join extremist groups in order to become part of a larger cause and join others in a divine effort. Shrewd recruiters sometimes use this notion to spur individuals to join their cause by insinuating that only select persons are suited to their group. This elitist approach is particularly appealing to individuals searching for a sense of belonging or meaning. It also offers a form of redemption for those haunted by failure or rejection. Furthermore, some recruiters paint nearly mythical descriptions of jihad to further lure susceptible persons. Again, this selling point is nearly irresistible to those predisposed to terrorist recruitment who are searching for purpose, meaning, or significance.

INTERNAL ATTRIBUTES

Psychographic and state variables were briefly mentioned at the beginning of this chapter. These concepts dovetail with other information known about recruits, but from a different perspective. Five variables can make individuals more inclined to recruitment. The first is intense unhappiness and angst for one's present circumstances. The second variable is an unfulfilled cultural identity in someone attempting to find a sense of belonging. Next, is an unestablished moral or religious belief. A fourth predisposing factor is family dysfunction. Finally, a lack of self-efficacy and reliance upon others may serve as fertile ground for recruiters' influence (Gerwehr & Daly, 2012). It is probable that adept recruiters are able to identify these potential areas of vulnerability and exploit them to gain personnel.

GENERAL ATTRIBUTES

Ozeran et al. (2014) identified the elements as individual factors that contributed to people joining terror groups. Again, the interaction of these elements contributed to recruitment rather than a single, isolated factor. While their research studied Kurdish terrorist organizations, the elements are similar to those identified elsewhere in the literature. The first factor was family problems, which was further broken down into three sub-elements. They include a coerced marriage or prohibition from marrying the partner of choice, severing ties with family authority, and experiencing domestic physical or psychological violence.

Second, kinship effect plays a significant role in the acquisition of new members. Having relatives in a terrorist organization greatly facilitates other family members' acceptance into the group. Similarly, those ties themselves enhance the interest of prospective recruits.

Friendship and romantic influences further encouraged individuals to join. These personal connections could be romantic or platonic relationships. McCauley and Moskalenko (2008) echoed this assertion noting the influence of camaraderie and romance. Fourth, Ozeran et al. (2014) noted that legal problems led some to seek terrorist groups as a way of fleeing authorities. Ethnicity and nationalistic beliefs comprise the fifth individual factor encouraging prospects to join the organization. As was previously stated, recruiters are skilled in applying their knowledge of political, ethnic, and nationalistic perspectives to draw recruits. Unemployment and financial strain were further identified as factors.

Seeking vengeance, seeking status, and fleeing personal problems are the final recruitment factors described by Ozeran et al. (2014). Enacting revenge against the government or other forces draws new adherents to terrorism as does an opportunity for acceptance, approval, and the potential for fame. Finally, those with deep personal problems can find terrorism as an option because they have little to lose and may find some personal benefit from such activities.

ADDITIONAL THEMES

As previously mentioned, it is not unusual for members of terrorist cells to have engaged in criminal activity prior to recruitment. The crimes ranged from theft and robbery, to dealing drugs (Gautheir-Villars, Landauro, & Parkinson, 2015; Sageman, 2004). Leonhard and Conley (2013) stated that more mature organizations may entice prospects with provisions, drugs, money, or even medical care.

Conscription and coercion account for a small number of individuals joining jihadist causes. Terrorist insurgencies in parts of Africa have used an aggressive form of a "draft" to increase their numbers. They travelled to villages and conscripted one son per family. They may also employ more sophisticated methods to secure specific personnel skills or to acquire otherwise restricted access. For example, these organizations use blackmail and bribery to influence financial personnel, chemists, government workers, or other people with specialized skills or access (Leonhard & Conley, 2013). While these methods are used, they are not predominant means of acquiring additional terrorist personnel.

COUNTERMEASURES FOR TERRORIST RECRUITING

There are numerous instances of thwarted terrorist plots, yet proven methods of successfully stopping terrorist recruiting are scarce. Moreover, empirical literature contains some recommendations for potential interventions, but proven enactments of those efforts are difficult to find. In view of these realities, and this chapter's primary intended focus on recruitment efforts at large, key ideas from several sources follow.

Counter-Recruitment Principles

As previously observed, terrorist recruiting is fluid and evolving. Correspondingly, effective countermeasures must be flexible and adapt to changing enemies. Counter-recruitment should therefore use precise and area-focused strategies rather than general notions previously applied elsewhere. In other words, interventions cannot simply be exported from one area and imported to another. Haphazard or generalist approaches are unlikely to succeed, and they may even exacerbate the situation (Gerwehr & Daly, 2012).

Moghaddam (2005) clarified that terrorism is a moral issue that hinges on psychological factors. He keenly noted that technology-based efforts alone will not thwart problems in human society. To borrow a phrase from military jargon, efforts must "take the long view" and use multidisciplinary interventions to address aspects of the terrorist appeal. In keeping with multiple themes addressed throughout this chapter, he recommended seeking solutions to fundamental problems (sociopolitical and extremist ideology) by pursuing democratically based solutions that are compatible with the associated people groups. While these notions are a bit vague and perhaps even philosophical, they provide a meaningful contrast to be solely focused on military and technology-based solutions.

CONCLUSION

Multiple factors contribute to individuals joining terrorist groups. Recurrent themes include socioeconomic conditions, political environment, Islamic religious extremism, demographic variables, individual characteristics, interpersonal affiliations, and personal grievances. Common traits amongst terrorists in various contexts were also examined. The sum of these aspects usually moved people to the culminating point in which potential adherents transitioned to actual recruits. Proven countermeasures to terrorist recruitment are essentially absent; however, a thorough understanding of terrorist recruiting themes will contribute to future efforts.

REFERENCES

Ahmad, A. (2014). The Role of Social Networks in the Recruitment of Youth in an Islamist Organization in Pakistan. *Sociological Spectrum: Mid-South Sociological Association, 34*(6), 469–488. doi: 10.1080/02732173.2014.947450

Amble, J. C., & Meleagrou-Hitchens, A. (2014). Jihadist Radicalization in East Africa: Two Case Studies. *Studies in Conflict & Terrorism, 37*(6), 523–540. doi: 10.1080/1057610X.2014.893406

Anderson, G. (2014). Abu Bakr al-Baghdadi and the Theory and Practice of Jihad. *Small Wars Journal*. Retrieved from http://smallwarsjournal.com/jrnl/art/abu-bakr-al-baghdadi-and-the-theory-and-practice-jihad

Bos, N. (2013). Underlying Causes of Violence. In P. Tomkins, & N. Bos (Eds.), *Human Factors Considerations of Undergrounds in Insurgencies* (2nd ed., pp. 11–28). Fort Bragg, North Carolina: The United States Army Special Operations Command.

Cottee, S., & Hayward, K. (2011). Terrorist (E)motives: The Existential Attractions of Terrorism. *Studies in Conflict & Terrorism, 34*(12), 963–986. doi: 10.1080/1057610X.2011.621116

Cunningham, K. J. (2003). Cross-Regional Trends in Female Terrorism. *Studies in Conflict & Terrorism, 26*(3), 171–195. doi: 10.1080/10576100390211419

Daymon, C. (2014). A Ticket to Turkey and a Desire to Fight: Why Some Foreign Fighters Travel to Syria. *Small Wars Journal*. Retrieved from http://smallwarsjournal.com/print/17447

Fair, C. C. (2004). Militant Recruitment in Pakistan: Implications for Al Qaeda and Other Organizations. *Studies in Conflict & Terrorism, 27*(6), 489–504. doi: 10.1080/10576100490513675

Gautheir-Villars, DR., Landauro, I., & Parkinson, J. (January 14, 2015). French Terrorist had History of Police-run-ins, Setbacks. *The Wall Street Journal*, p. A8.

Gerwehr, S., & Daly, S. (2012). Al-Qaida: Terrorist Selection and Recruitment. In D. Kamien (Ed.), *The McGraw-Hill Homeland Security Handbook* (pp. 73–89). Retrieved from http://www.rand.org/pubs/reprints/RP1214.html

Hope Cheong, P. & Halverson, J. R. (2010). Youths in Violent Extremist Discourse: Mediated Identifications and Interventions. *Studies in Conflict & Terrorism, 33*(12), 1104–1123. doi: 10.1080/1057610X.2010.523862

Jacques, K., & Taylor, P. J. (2009). Female Terrorism: A Review. *Terrorism and Political Violence, 21*(3), 499–515.

James, L. C. (2008). *Fixing Hell*. New York, NY: Grand Central Publishing.

Jenkins, B. M. (2011). *Stray Dogs and Virtual Armies: Radicalization and Recruitment to Jihadist Terrorism in the United States Since 9/11* (Occasional Paper No. 343). Retrieved from http://www.rand.org/pubs/occasional_papers/OP343.html

Leonhard, R., & Conley, J. M. (2013). Recruiting. In P. Tomkins, & Leonhard, R. (Eds.), *Undergrounds in Insurgent, Revolutionary, and Resistance Warfare* (2nd ed., pp. 19–39). Fort Bragg, North Carolina: The United States Army Special Operations Command.

McCauley, C., & Moskalenko, S. (2008). Mechanisms of Political Radicalization: Pathways Toward Terrorism. *Terrorism and Political Violence, 20*(3), 415–433. doi: 10.1080/09546550802073367

Mendelsohn, B. (2011). Foreign Fighters—Recent Trends. *Orbis, 55*(2), 189–202. doi: 10.1016/j.orbis.2011.01.002

Moghaddam, F. M. (2005). The Staircase to Terrorism: A Psychological Exploration. *American Psychologist, 60*(2), 161–169. doi: 10.1037/0003-066X.60.2.161

Ozeran, S., Murat, S., Yilmaz, K., & Sozer, A. (2014). Whom Do They Recruit?: Profiling and Recruitment in the PKK/KCK. *Studies in Conflict and Terrorism, 37*(4), 322–347. doi: 10.1080/1057610X.2014.879381

Piazza, J. A. (2006). Rooted in Poverty?: Terrorism, Poor Economic Development, and Social Cleavages. *Terrorism and Political Violence, 18*, 159–177. doi: 10.1080/095465590944578

Ramswell, P. (2014). The Utilization and Leveraging of Grievance as a Recruitment Tool and Justification for Terrorist Acts Committed by Islamic Extremists. *Small Wars Journal*. Retrieved from http://smallwarsjournal.com/jrnl/art/the-utilization-and-leveraging-of-grievance-as-a-recruitment-tool-and-justification-for-ter

Ryan, J. (2007). The Four P-Words of Militant Islamist Radicalization and Recruitment: Persecution, Precedent, Piety, and Perseverance. *Studies in Conflict & Terrorism, 30*(11), 985–1011. doi: 10.1080/10576100701611296

Sageman, M. (2004). *Understanding Terror Networks*. Philadelphia, PA: University of Philadelphia Press.

Smelser, N. J. (2007). *The Faces of Terrorism: Social and Psychological Dimensions*. Princeton, NJ: Princeton University Press.

Spitaletta, J. A., Newton, S. D., Bos, N. D., Crosett, C. W., & Leonhard, R. R. (2013). Historical Lessons on Intelligence Support to Countering Undergrounds in Insurgencies. *Inteligencia y Seguridad: Revista de Análisis y Prospectiva, 2013*(13).

Taarnby, M. (2005). *Recruitment of Islamist Terrorists in Europe: Trends and Perspectives*. Aarhus, Denmark: Danish Ministry of Justice.

Zelin, A. Y. (2014). *The Radicalization of Syria: Jihadist Rivalries in the Levant could Threaten Europe*. Retrieved from The Washington Institute website: http://www.washingtoninstitute.org/policy-analysis/view/the-radicalization-of-syria

4

The Use of the Media as a Weapon of Mass Psychological Destruction

George W. Heddleston

Since September 11, 2001, the world has not been the same as a result of the attacks on the U.S. Pentagon and New York City's Twin Towers. Not only have the physical and safety threats become a concern in the minds of millions in the United States, but also at times the psychology of these attacks has paralyzed thousands of people by forcing them to alter their daily routines. How have these terrorists controlled the minds of so many without ever touching each and every American? Why has the farmer in Idaho changed his routine even though that farmer was thousands of miles away from either the Pentagon or the Twin Towers on 9/11? Why are so many Americans worried or more cautious now when they fly compared to before 9/11? This chapter will address these questions, as well as others, to assist in ascertaining how terrorists use the media to psychologically terrorize and torture millions, even though the innocent bystander is often thousands of miles away from the terrorists' actual target. In addition, the author of this chapter will provide suggestions for media executives on how to circumvent the terrorists' use of the media as a psychological tool and offer suggestions for coping with these continued national security threats.

In this book James and Oroszi (2015) have defined the concept of weapons of mass psychological destruction. The authors provided several case illustrations of how terrorists harm the public even though few people have been physically harmed or killed.

On March 4, 2015, while locked in his county jail cell, Christopher Cornell, age 20, called the Cincinnati, Ohio, Fox News 19 television station for an hour-long phone interview. He had been arrested on January 20, 2015, by the FBI after leaving a gun store with 600 rounds of ammunition and rifles. He had allegedly made terrorist threats against the United States and President Obama. During the phone interview from his jail cell, he asserted that he wants to shoot the president in the head (Macke et al., 2015) and do harm to the United States. Why?

Cornell was very mindful that he most likely would be incarcerated for the next 15 to 30 years; thus, he would not be a direct threat to the millions of Americans who heard his chilling phone interview. What were his motivations? Cornell was motivated to manipulate the media into allowing him to use Fox News as a platform to spew his hate to and psychologically torture thousands of people throughout the Midwest. Unfortunately, the television station aired the interview over and over and over. Additionally, radio, television news, and newspapers "picked up the story." As a result, the community was gripped with fear of an imminent terrorist attack after Cornell asserted that "there will be more attacks." For the moment, many Ohio citizens altered their way of life, changed their routine, or decided to simply "stay home" because of a pending terrorist attack. The attacks never happened!

On September 11, 2001, more than 2,000 innocent Americans lost their lives in the New York City Twin Towers bombing and the attack on the Pentagon. Millions of people in the United States and around the world were psychologically traumatized and their lives were negatively affected. Their behavior became changed forever, even though these individuals were not present at either site the terrorist attacked. Why so traumatized? The statement below by a news personality laments the sentiments of thousands of people in what has become today's reality.

> It's impossible for me to feel any joy when terrorists are psychologically impacting our well-being. When people are being burned or beheaded, or the thought that a terrorist group may eventually obtain weapons of mass destruction, these matters make my daily outlook bleak, depressed. I am part of the media that report these events, and believe me, no matter how good my personal life is living here in the greatest country in the world, it's hard for me to feel good about anything when there is such fear of mass destruction. (Hannity, 2009)

A Quinnipac University survey (2014) concluded that "It's a chilling and troubling thought: half of Americans think a terror attack on the Winter Olympic Games in Sochi, Russia, is either likely or very likely," said Tim Malloy, assistant director of the Quinnipiac University Polling Institute.

This chapter explores the phenomenon of how terror attacks that include weapons of mass destruction (WMDs) or other "devices of terror," when reported by the news media, become *weapons of mass psychological destruction* (WMPDs) that terrorists use to their advantage.

Do terrorists cause psychological harm to the public? What would motivate a terrorist to deliberately broadcast his intentions to kill innocent human beings or destroy property? Banks and James (2007), in their discussion of the psychology of terrorism, described that the goal of terrorists is to impose their will on a government, an organization, or a group of people. From 2010 to 2015 the world witnessed a stark increase in innocent people being held hostage by a terrorist group, and executions, such as beheadings or hangings, are shown via television to the world. As a result, these terrorist groups have been able to persuade nations, governments, and/or parents and loved ones to pay ransoms or participate in a prisoner swap. The United States, a nation that once asserted that it would not negotiate with terrorists, has done so.

When the news media reports to the public that a terrorist operation has sought out, obtained, or manufactured WMDs we cannot conclude that the activities psychologically affect everyone, but we can say that having this effect on many is one of the primary goals of terrorism. Individuals who believe in staying informed about terror operations worldwide will likely believe they have cause for concern; however, those less informed or less interested will feel more insulated from terror attacks. Throughout the United States millions living in small towns or rural communities, because of their location, cannot imagine that a terrorist attack will reach them; however, the same group of people harbor less security if the terrorists are in possession of WMDs.

Mass psychological destruction has been a part of our nightmares since the United States created and delivered the atomic bombs on Hiroshima and Nagasaki, Japan, in 1945. One can conclude that virtually all American adults living today who were not alive in 1945 nonetheless carry a feeling of dread that a similar occurrence of mass destruction could happen on American soil. So perhaps *psychologically* terrorists with WMD are a fearsome thought to ponder, even for people whose daily psyche is mostly unaffected by such thoughts.

THE PSYCHOLOGICAL IMPACT OF NEWS COVERAGE OF TERROR ATTACKS

In France and throughout most of Europe, citizens were on high alert after a terrorist attack in Paris in January 2015 left 17 people killed. Worldwide news coverage was dominated for weeks by the event in Paris. Ordinary citizens of Europe were distracted and nervous about further terrorist attacks. To those populations, the anxiety of a potential WMD attack caused psychological damage, albeit temporary. One indicator of the psychological effect after the Paris attack was the decline of tourism in Paris (Adamson, 2015; Ifgiferdiam, 2011).

Media reports incite fear and help terrorist organizations in their recruiting efforts. The media offers a platform for terror groups to spread their message globally. Osama bin Laden knew early in his terrorist planning days that even crude videos, sometimes taped in barren settings with poor lighting, could ignite one of the most primal human emotions—fear. Purveyors of terror continue to use the media to their advantage.

Numerous people worldwide refuse to be paralyzed by fear, and they are taking steps to counter terrorist activities. At the Islamic Center of Pittsburgh in western Pennsylvania volunteers place themselves at booths in the downstairs social hall, asking people to sign up to lead children's activities in order to prepare children, teens, and young adults to become more involved in the mosque in order to learn "true Islam" and counter what they say are murderous distortions purveyed by the terrorists around the globe where terror and psychological terror has struck, like Boko Haram in Nigeria, Islamic State in Iraq and Syria (ISIS), and various Al Qaeda and ISIS groups carrying out their own reigns of terror.

Tanielian and Stein (2006) of the Rand Corporation summarized the definition of "terrorism" and its psychological impact:

1. Terrorism is the illegal use or threatened use of force or violence; it is an intent to coerce societies or governments by inducing fear in their populations, typically with ideological and political motives and justifications; it is an act of an "extra societal" element, either "outside" society in the case of domestic terrorism or "foreign" in the case of international terrorism.
2. The purpose of terrorism is not the single act of wanton destruction, it is the reaction it seeks to provoke: economic collapse, the backlash, the hatred, the division, the elimination of tolerance, until societies cease to reconcile their differences and become defined by them (Blair, 2003). The *purpose* of terrorism can have a powerful psychological impact.

The authors explained that what the above definitions have in common is recognition that beyond the physical damage caused by the terrorism event itself—whether destructive attacks, chemical or bioterrorism attacks, or terrorism by WMDs—the very act is intended to have a psychological bearing. From the impact of an attack (e.g., destruction and death) and the consequences associated with the response (e.g., economic loss and disruption) to the impact of preparedness and counterterrorism themselves (e.g., behavioral and social ramifications of new security procedures), there is an urgent need for the development of effective intervention and tools for assessing and predicting psychological, behavioral, and social responses.

Two-thirds of the people directly affected by acts of terrorism, either as a victim or as a relative, are psychologically impaired (e.g., posttraumatic stress disorder, or PTSD) to some degree (Beaton & Murphy, 2002).

Such acts, when chronicled by the media, make widespread the negative psychological impact and often call for professional assistance (e.g., psychological counseling). Comfort can come to some affected people when victimized nations respond with force and a detailed plan of counterattack intended to eliminate WMD and the terrorists who deploy them. Such plans, again, are reported by the media.

In the United States, reducing vulnerabilities to WMDs is a topic of great importance to the nation's security. Actions to prevent attacks are high priority for the U.S. government and the Department of Defense. The United States faced the potential of massive destruction from nuclear weapons from the former Soviet Union for nearly half a century during the Cold War. Although people emotionally feared a worldwide nuclear holocaust, intellectually they did not live their daily lives in fear of such. However, today, because of "instant worldwide" media coverage, we now know that small groups of individuals have the ability to deliver devastating harm to the United States, both physically and psychologically. Such power in the past could only be delivered by nation-states with large economic, political, industrial, military, and social resources.

We can conclude that today, when individuals and small groups possess the technology to psychologically terrorize anywhere in the world, there is a greater psychological fear of terrorists—stoked by media coverage—than the moments of dread that struck Americans during the years of the Cold War.

Terrorists are cognizant that terrorism comes in many forms. One form of such treachery is food poisoning. In fact, the first and the single largest bioterrorist attack in the U.S. history took place in a remote region, Antelope, Oregon, located southeast of the Mount Hood National Forest and approximately 160 miles from Portland, Oregon. It is a rural area with a population of just 47 people in 2012. Antelope was briefly named Rajneesh in the mid-1980s, when followers of Bhagwan Shree Rajneesh (a.k.a. Osho) moved into the city from nearby Rajneeshpuram, Oregon, and voted for the name change. Bioterrorism was on the minds of Osho and his followers (Fitch, 2010).

Known as the Rajneeshee bioterror attack, the unlawful event revolved around the food poisoning of 751 individuals in Dalles, the county seat of Wasco County, Oregon, a county that includes Antelope and Rajneeshpuram. Dalles was originally a U.S. Army settlement on the banks of the Columbia River. Dalles, a Native American trading center, is famous as the original end-of-the-trail location of the pioneer-traveled Oregon Trail. Today Dalles is much more of a town (than rural area) in terms of size, schools, activities, and numerous business establishments with some 16,000 people residing there.

In 1984 the followers of Rajneesh deliberately contaminated salad bars in local restaurants by "spritzing" salmonella on them in 10 Dalles restaurants. Of the 700 people subsequently infected with salmonella, none died, but there were 45 people hospitalized. Osho and his group's motive was to incapacitate the voting population, so their own Rajneeshee candidates would win the 1984 Wasco County elections, which Osho believed would enable him to rule the county and spread his beliefs.

The attack became one of only two confirmed terrorist uses of biological weapons to harm humans between 1945 and 1984. Having previously gained political control of Antelope, Osho's followers sought election to two of the three seats on the Wasco County Circuit Court that were up for election in November 1984. Their efforts failed and agents of the contamination were discovered and prosecuted in 1985 when a sample of bacteria matching the contaminant that had sickened the town residents was found in a Rajneesh-puram medical laboratory. Two leading Rajneeshpuram officials were convicted on charges of attempted murder and served 29 months of 20-year sentences in a minimum-security federal prison.

The psychological affect these events had on scores of Oregon citizens was primarily a fear of filling their plates at local restaurant salad bars. It was a fear born of terrorism nonetheless. The chosen biological agent was *Salmonella enter-ica*, which, prior to the salad bar effort, was first delivered through glasses of water served to two Wasco County commissioners.

The larger point of this small-scale terror event, now just a footnote in Oregon's history and mostly forgotten, is that the events of Dalles, Oregon, clearly illustrate the psychological fear everyday citizens endure in the face of bioterror attacks, WMD attacks, and other mostly obscure, but deadly, vehicle attacks used by terrorists, whether purveyors of terror are acting alone or in groups. The psychology of terrorism is, in its most basic form, about fear and the media is most often used as the vehicle of the terrorists to spread the fear.

Sinclair and Antonius (2012), in their book *The Psychology of Terrorism Fears*, explain that terrorism is fundamentally about fear. The authors describe how our society has changed as a result of terrorism, and specifically, how our own systems for managing terrorism may in fact contribute to fear. Earlier psychological teachings did not ponder the effects of WMD terror like it must today.

Managing the psychological consequences of a terrorist event can require intervention beyond what is offered by the professionally trained participants. Teachers, workplace supervisors, and faith-based organizations all can contribute to lessening the residual fear of a terrorist attack. A post-9/11 survey has shown that the clergy called upon to counsel people in New York City, Washington, D.C., Western Pennsylvania, and nationwide were found to be one of the most frequently sought sources of help. Schools are in a unique position to provide grief counseling, reassure students about their safety, and monitor students with severe stress reactions (Dobelli, 2010). It takes all of the professionals discussed here, as well as community leaders and religious organizations, regardless of cat-egory or affiliation, to aid the masses against the psychological fallout of terror threats and real events.

The terrorist group ISIS, the Jihadist militants from Islamic State, is now endeavoring to expand its operations beyond the Middle East and use the media worldwide to further its cause. ISIS in fact has its own Hollywood-level video production company and professional publicists. It is when these terrorists pull on their orange jumpsuits and subsequently behead or burn to death other humans in the name of, and supposedly at the behest of, Prophet Muhammad while videotaping and publishing the entire event that they cause psychological fear to the world's masses. Their videos sent across the Internet informing the world of such murderous crimes strike everyone who is paying attention that there is genuine fear to be realized by such psychologically intended acts. News of this kind of violence has a psychological impact parallel to stories of WMDs' use. To most, these acts are just unimaginable to comprehend.

The use of mass weapons, reported in detail by the news media, can be viewed in the context of a quest to achieve political objectives that underlie military intervention and its threat (IBPP, 1998). Whether used for political or religious reasons, or both, WMDs usually have nuclear, chemical, and biological formats, and a shattering impact on people. Besides the force consequences, there are psychological bases as well. When the news media presents the WMD's force and counterforce consequences, the psychological functions of cognitive, emotional, motivational, and behavioral processes can range from neurotransmitter imbalances to gastrointestinal distress in people. WMDs can so powerfully affect a person that the psychological affect may interact with such processes as self-esteem, self-efficacy, ideology, and even motivation to comply with authorities. In summary, a news report about WMDs can affect psychological and physical functioning.

How can we mitigate against WMDs' noxious consequences? Public information about actions of prevention can somewhat lessen the fear caused by media reports, but a more powerful anecdote is the belief in mobilizing combat troops and military weaponry and force to halt WMDs and those who may hold them. People need a reason to believe that terror can be overcome, and here is where the news media can become an ally. Operations such as Desert Storm/Desert Shield were undertaken, in part, because of the threat of noxious WMD consequences. As various levels of success by allied forces were reported, the media reduced the fear by reporting the outcomes almost instantaneously. The U.S. military included in its combat missions the staffing and coordination of all politico-military initiatives that resulted in reporting through the news media successful combat strategies and tactics. Reported as public information, these reports not only served to gain public support and approval, but lessened fear and psychological trauma (IBPP, 1998).

The media will always see its role as providers of the facts, particularly in the United States. In their best intentions, members of the media believe they uphold free speech in America with their reporting of world events. Reporting on terrorism and those terrorists who obtain WMDs has become a part of the media landscape in the United States. How individuals react to such news, on a daily basis or at times when terror possibilities seem closer to home, has become part of modern-day life.

This new paradigm is not going to go away. Terrorism, and how we respond to it, now rests with our leadership and those of us who care enough to educate the masses, because this psychological attack on our senses cannot be allowed to become never-ending fear mongering.

SOME RECOMMENDATIONS FOR THE MEDIA

Reporting the news on terrorism presents a paradox to journalists, whose responsibility is to inform the public objectively and accurately, and most people understand that. But, is there a more productive manner for terrorism news to be reported, including news about weapons deployed by terrorists, or human burnings and beheadings? A way that is less stressful, yet still informative? Media scholars struggle with accusations that the media serve as accomplices to the aims of terrorists, magnifying the threat and fear. In their efforts to report the news fairly and objectively, we conclude that, in fact, the media does aid the terrorist agenda.

Television appears to be in a "no-win" trap because the lifeblood of television programming, especially its news reporting, is to increase viewers. In an anti-essay that appeared online in Emerging Media (2015) entitled "Media Bring More Harm," the author asserts that everything has changed so rapidly, including technology, which makes media reporting much more scintillating today. Most of mass media now use the advantages of technology for their essential role in getting audience attention to increase income, such as formulating some features in order to increase audience interest. The media wants to show an attractive performance and style, which is made easier by technology. It can beautify the features of the screen, attract the audience with a beautiful voice, and so on. The electronic media will use any strategy to compete in "dominating the market" (Ifgiferdiam, 2011).

Newspapers, magazines, and other printed pieces have a different rating system—provide the news that sells in order to stay relevant (and in business). Unfortunately, there are times when what the media presents to the public is distorted, trivialized, exaggerated, or inaccurate. Deadlines always put pressure on news rooms. Delivering the news to the public first is every editor's goal. To the news decision makers, terrorism is akin to good theater, and the news media, for their part, are unable to resist a good story. So they obligingly provide extensive coverage of terrorist bombings, hijacks, kidnapping, and assassinations, according to Abraham Miller (1982), who calls such coverage "the media's stepchild, a stepchild, which the media, unfortunately, can neither completely ignore nor deny." Terrorists know the conventions and news-gathering routine of the media, and so to achieve their objective of drawing attention to themselves and gain notoriety, they deliberately organize their actions to fit the key news values of drama, violence, and unexpectedness (Crelinsten & Schmid, 1993).

Two core principles of many media executives are that the news be significant, and dramatic. If not, violent news would be presented much differently. Below we have listed guidelines to reduce the likelihood that the media would be manipulated by terrorist group to expand news into psychological terror:

1. The media consider new ways to evaluate quick-breaking, terrorism-related news and either present it more cautiously or post content warnings to viewers and readers. Ask yourself: When was the last time you saw a newspaper, for example, provide an editor's note that cautions readers about a story's toxic content? Warnings are given frequently ahead of graphic television reports, which is laudable.

2. Gerald P. Koocher, past president of the American Psychological Association, suggests that psychologists become more actively involved as contributors to news reports. Koocher believes it is useful to society when psychologists are more actively involved in the media since they can serve the public by providing more precise information about human behavior. Unfortunately, too often the media believes it has to choose a quick format, which typically eliminates using a psychology expert and provides information that borders more on the sensational and does little to reassure the public's anxiety.

3. Media CEOs strengthen censorship policies to not just provide graphic image warnings, but eliminate many of the graphic images themselves, particularly in daytime and primetime reporting hours. Illuminating the graphic images in daytime/primetime would at least prevent the possibility of traumatizing children. There is abundant research available regarding events such as the 9/11 terrorist attacks and the 1995 bombing of the Alfred P. Murrah Federal Building in Oklahoma City and how these events exposed children to trauma-related coverage that affected the young as strongly as news about natural disasters, sexual abuse, community violence, and so on. Essays (2013) posed that in the case of electronic media channels, limiting graphic news reports in daytime/primetime would show some responsibility, and it would respect the emotions and sentiments of the public viewing such events.

4. The media should attempt and avoid eyewitness reports since they can be very traumatizing for citizens, and once again, especially children.

5. Limit the reprinting or replaying of images on the anniversaries of terrorism events. National magazines often reprint photos of the most grisly world events. Along with TV replays, replaying these stories may re-create trauma or increases the possibility of viewers re-experiencing the event.

A consensus on the complex issue of how the media should report on terrorism or destruction on a small or large scale may never be reached. We know that that the theatrical and dramatic ways the media report terrorist acts encourage further violence. Perhaps this is nothing more than a matter of media members displaying overconfidence in judging readers' and viewers' need-to-know-and-view destruction that results from terror?

Overconfidence is not the providence of members of the media. Everyday life is riddled with examples of overconfidence: drivers overestimate their driving skills; students, their test scores; couples their likelihood of staying married; employees, their chances of promotion; and managers, their investment and merger strategies.

Interviews with parents and teachers have been conducted to investigate observable changes in behavior that occur as an aftermath of a terrorist activity.

As caretakers of children, opinions from these interviews offer a better understanding of the situation. These findings will form the basis of further research on the intensity of these effects and how to minimize and overcome the negative impacts of the media coverage of terrorism (Essays, 2013).

REFERENCES

Adamson, T. (January 18, 2015). Tourist Numbers Drop in Paris After Terror Attacks. Retrieved from http://news.yahoo.com/tourist-numbers-paris-drop-following-terror-attacks-002040346.html

Beaton, R. & Murphy, S. (2002). Psychosocial Responses to Biological and Chemical Terrorist Threats and Events: Implications for the Workplace. *Journal of the American Association of Occupational Health Nurses, 50*(4), 182–189.

Banks, L. M., & James, L. C. (2007). Warfare, Terrorism, and Psychology. *Psychology of Terrorism*, 216.

Blair, T. (July 17, 2003). *Speech to Joint Session, U.S. Congress.* Washington, DC. Retrieved from http://www.cnn.com/2003/us/07/17/blair.transcript

Crelinsten, R. & Schmid, A. (1993). *Western Responses to Terrorism.* New York, NY: Routledge Press.

Dobelli, R. (2010). Avoid News: Towards a Healthy News Diet. Retrieved from http://dobelli.com/wp-content/uploads/2010/08/Avoid_News_Part1_TEXT.pdf

Emerging Media. (2015). Media Brings More Harm. http://emergingmedia360.org/2015/04/21/anonymous-more-harm-than-good/

Essays, UK. (2013). The Psychological Impact Resulting from the Media Coverage Psychology Essay. Retrieved from http://www.ukessays.com/essays/psychology/the-psychological-impact-resulting-from-the-media-coverage-psychology-essay.php?cref=1

Fitch, B. (2010). Good Decisions: Tips & Strategies for Avoiding Psychological Traps. Retrieved from https://www2.fbi.gov/publications/leb/2010/june2010/decisions_feature.htm

Hannity, S. (2009). *Deliver Us from Evil.* Harper Collins. http://en.wikipedia.org/wiki/1984_Rajneeshee_bioterror_attack

IBPP Online. (1998). Weapons of Mass Destruction: A Commentary. Retrieved from http://security.pr.erau.edu/read.php?kind=html&article_volume=4&article_issue=6&article_title=Weapons%20of%20Mass%20Destruction%3A%20A%20Psychological%20Commentary

Ifgiferdiam, R. (November 7, 2011). Media Bring Moreharm. Retrived from: www.antiessays.com/free-essays/Media-Bring-More-Harm-125979.htm

James, L., & Oroszi, T. (Eds.). (2015). *Weapons of Mass Psychological Destruction and the People that Use Them.* Santa Barbara, CA: Praeger. (In Press).

Macke, T., et al. (March 9, 2015). http://www.fox19.com/story/28284966/cornell-the-planned-attack-against-the-united-states-capitol-the-event-in-which-I-planned-was-but-a-reaction-to-the-continued-American-aggression

Miller, A. H. (1982). Terrorism, the Media and the Law. Retrieved from https://www.ncjrs.gov/App/publications/abstract.aspx?ID=86143

Quinnipac University Survey. (2014). www.quinnipiac.edu/.../quinnipiac-university
-poll/...

Sinclair, S. J. & Antonius, D. (2012). *The Psychology of Terrorism Fears.* New York, NY:
Oxford University Press.

Tanielian, T. L. & Stein, B. D. (2006). Understanding & Preparing for the Psychological
Consequences of Terrorism. Retrieved from http://www.rand.org/content/dam/rand/
pubs/reprints/2006/RAND_RP1217.pdf

5

Cultural Factors Concerning Weapons of Mass Psychological Destruction*

Mark A. Staal

This chapter will ascertain the complex cultural issues related to terrorist and how culture plays a role in the psychological aspects of weapons of mass destruction (WMDs). The reality is that individuals who conduct terrorist activities and those who ascribe to extreme ideologies are a diverse and complex lot. They come from all walks of life and across ethnic lines and cultural groups. Therefore, whenever we attempt to understand an individual's behavior, seeing that behavior in context is critical. Context includes many different variables such as religious, economic, political, social, psychological, and even geographical realities.

While the focus of this chapter will restrict its attention to cultural variables, it should be noted that culture encompasses many of the factors mentioned above. Militant extremism and terrorism are a pancultural phenomenon (Saucier, Akers, Shen-Miller, Knezevic, & Stankov, 2009). While there may be a focus on particular cultural groups in this chapter due to the current state of the world, it is not my intention to erroneously link one cultural group or ideological position to militant extremism over another. It is the intention of this chapter to explore what evidence and scientific models are in the extant literature that would help us better understand the role and impact of culture and cultural influences on extremist ideology and terrorist acts.

WHAT IS CULTURE?

Culture has been defined in many different ways. Cultural experts have contended that culture is a belief system and value orientation that impacts social norms, customs, and practices (Fiske, Kitayama, Markus, & Nisbett, 1998). The American Psychological Association has published guidelines concerning

---

*The views expressed in this chapter are those of the author and do not necessarily reflect the official policy of the Department of Defense or other departments of the U.S. government.

cultural awareness, competence, and multiculturalism and has posited that culture is, "the embodiment of a worldview through learned and transmitted beliefs, values, and practices, including religious and spiritual traditions" (APA, 2014). Put more simply, culture consists of "meanings and practices that are shared by a social group and constitute of a way of life" (Christopher, Wendt, Marecek, & Goodman, 2014).

TOWARD UNDERSTANDING CULTURAL CONTEXT

In addition to understanding the larger construct, it is important to identify and define a number of key terms associated with culture and multiculturalism. These concepts are particularly relevant whenever individuals from outside a given culture are trying to understand a culture that is not their own—even more so when judgments about members of that culture are being made, such as its potential influence on behavior. Traditionally, the two terms have been used to describe how we understand an individual's behavior in the context of cultural influences. *Emics* are those things that are specific to cultures, so they vary from place to place, depending on what cultural values and practices are present. In contrast, *etics* are those things that are assumed to be universal across people and people groups. Conflict and cultural bias can occur when we mistakenly apply etics onto emics—for example, when we mistakenly apply our own cultural lens (behavior, values, beliefs, practices, etc.) onto another that does not share our cultural perspective or experience. Similarly, we may make assumptions about cultural explanations that are actually attributable to noncultural factors, such as socioeconomic status and gender. This type of error is known as the *cultural attribution fallacy* (Hardin, Robitschek, Flores, Navarro, & Ashton, 2014).

A common example of cultural bias can be found in conflicts between the *moral visions* of two different individuals or people groups. Moral visions are often culturally bound and consist of values or beliefs concerning areas of social change, economic development, or social reform (Christopher et al., 2014). For instance, Western perspectives and moral judgments find many of the following sociocultural practices repugnant: child marriage, forced headscarves, and female circumcision. However, such practices are not uncommon in many contemporary cultures in Africa and the Middle East. In contrast, values promoting educational opportunities for girls, universal human rights, the decriminalization of homosexuality, and condemnation of suicide-bombers and martyrdom are all common place among Western societies (Obeid, Chang, & Ginges, 2010). These differences spark fierce debate among researchers concerning whether such practices represent the state of cultural difference and appropriate social norming or, instead, violations of universal human liberty, international law, and moral dignity. In such circumstances does one culture's moral code, worldview, religious belief, or normative practice hold weight over another?

While the answers to such questions are unlikely be answered here, these are questions worth asking and concepts worth debating as we seek for a thoughtful approach to multiculturalism and cross-cultural interpretation of behavior.

Hermeneutic cultural awareness is an additional approach to understanding individual and group behavior from within a cultural context. Hermeneutics relates to interpretation. In the context of cultural awareness, this approach involves a practice of interpretive understanding as it relates to everyday experience. From this perspective, the individuals and the context of their culture are inseparable. To understand the behavior of given individuals, we must first understand their culture and its influence on their experience (Christopher et al., 2014).

Additional concepts relevant to any discussion about culture and multiculturalism must include acculturation, cultural awareness, and cultural competence. *Acculturation* is a measure of the degree to which an individual's experience is aligned with a given cultural group. Individuals from within a given cultural group can best evaluate and interpret another individual's behavior when doing so from within that individual's cultural context based on their own degree of shared experience. *Cultural awareness* speaks to an individual's sensitivity toward an understanding of members of other ethnic groups. In other words, there is an awareness of a gap in understanding and a lack of shared experience between the individual and the subject or group being considered. Finally, *cultural competence* references the ability to effectively operate within different cultural contexts. Typically, competence correlates with the degree of acculturation achieved by the individual in reference to the identified group.

THE RELATIONSHIP BETWEEN CULTURE, EXTREMISM, AND TERRORISM

Recent attention has been directed toward the preconditions of terrorism and extremist behavior. Culture has been at the forefront of that examination as it sets contextual conditions that all individuals must work within. Growing evidence suggests that there are a number of culture-specific factors that are associated with terrorist acts and extremism. Gelfand, LaFree, Fahey, and Feinberg (2013) analyzed nearly four decades of terrorist acts across 21 countries and identified a number of promising connections between culture and extremist acts of terror. These researchers found several cultural variables that were associated with a greater frequency, and in some instances lethality, of extremist behavior and terrorism. These include cultures that incorporate a strong sense of fatalism, those that are socially or normatively tight, and those in which high male dominance and low gender egalitarianism are present. These variables predicted terrorist acts and extremism even when accounting for economic and religious factors. Cultures in which these dimensions played a prominent role appear to be fertile ground for the rise and spread of terrorism. A brief description of each of these dimensions as they relate to cultural factors is described below.

Fatalism

Fatalism relates to the belief that one's destiny or "fate" is predetermined and controlled by outside or external forces. In this context, individuals' lives, choices, and personal outcomes rest in the hand of a divine God who exercises His will over their daily experience (both personally and corporately). Similarly, fatalistic individuals may rely on some other construct of fate such as chance, luck, or Karma. Leung and Bond (2004) have found a number of troubling national and societal outcomes related to highly fatalistic cultural groups, including: lower life expectancy, lower environmental sustainability, lower gross domestic product per capita, lower voter turnout rates, and high rates of suicide and heart disease. In contrast, societies that are lower in fatalism tend to view themselves as responsible for their own actions and corporate destiny. Nonfatalistic cultures also tend to believe in internal control over their behavior and the outcome of their efforts. The good and bad that happen to a given individual is perceived as resulting from that person's decision—actions that direct the course of their own lives and work to accomplish goals and overcome challenges. In terms of fatalism's relationship with terrorism and extremist behavior, fatalistic perceptions may "decrease a sense of personal responsibility and increase risk-taking" (Gelfand, LaFree, Fahey, & Feinberg, 2013, 499). Furthermore, extreme behavior and destructive acts against others may be seen in foresight and/or hindsight as preordained and morally justified.

Tight Social Norming

Societies constructed with greater social closeness and those described as more tight-knit were found to be at greater risk for terrorist acts and produced acts of greater lethality. The degree of tightness found in a culture seems to relate to the pervasiveness and clarity of its social norms. Intolerance for violations of these norms is also an important element in socially tight cultures (Triandis, 1989). Researchers have found correlations between high "tight" societies such as Japan and Pakistan, who provide their citizens with clear normative expectations, pervasive monitoring mechanisms, and strong punitive systems for norm violations, and a demand within those cultures for conformity, obedience, and discipline (Gelfand, 2013). Evidence suggests that socially tight cultures are more prone to terrorist activities and extremism because they tend to be more ethnocentric and intolerant of group differences. Moreover, this intolerance and high-within-group orientation may incline members to perceive that their way of life is threatened by external forces or outside group pressures. Such views have been used to justify violence against deviations from the norm, particularly when considering moral deviations like homosexuality, prostitution, or divorce (Gelfand et al., 2011).

Gender Egalitarianism

The roles that men and women play in society are largely determined by the cultural proscription for each group. Societies with lower egalitarian gender roles tend to have fewer women in positions of leadership, are less likely to support higher education opportunities for women, are less likely to support men and women working in a shared space, and have fewer women engaged in daily decision-making roles in their families (House, Hanges, Javidan, Dorfman, & Gupta, 2004). The opposite is true for cultures with egalitarian gender roles. In addition, egalitarian societies are also associated with greater longevity and human development. As a risk factor for terrorism and extremist ideology, cultures proscribing low egalitarian gender roles reinforce the notion that women require protection from outside influences that may influence their thinking and their sexual purity, or in some other way upset the balance of power already established. Low gender egalitarian cultures often emphasize stereotypically masculine values such as aggressiveness and competitiveness while diminishing feminine values such as compassion, nurturance, and cooperation. In doing so, these cultures set conditions that often play out with an intolerance of gender norm violation, resulting in an expression of violence toward women.

Other Cultural Considerations

The research literature has also yielded a number of interesting findings concerning cultural factors and the preconditions necessary for extremist ideology and terrorist activity. Atran and others have pointed to the presence of closely held sacred values among a cultural group as tied to motivation for terrorism (Atran, Axelrod, & Davis, 2007; Atran & Ginges, 2012; Ginges & Atran, 2009). One of the most widely identified cultural group differences concerns individualistic versus collectivistic cultures. Collectivistic cultures tend to be interdependent with a strong distinction of in-group versus out-group identity. Furthermore, they socialize their members with a greater sense of self-sacrifice in favor of the needs of the larger group. As such, there are strict penalties imposed upon members who deviate from their group. In collectivistic cultures individual and group goals merge (Wenzlaff, 2004). Triandis (1989) asserted a number of connections between terrorist involvement and collective cultures. These potential risk factors include distinctions between in-group and out-group morality, intolerance for violations of in-group moral truths, and a sense of moral superiority as perceived by the in-group culture. Similarly, groups with greater cohesion around a shared belief system have been connected with a willingness to justify violence toward others outside of their group (Kruglanski, Chen, Dechesne, Fishman, & Orehek, 2009).

Individualistic cultures promote independence in thought, word, and deed. There is a general acceptance and promotion of debate and dissension. Protest and defiance are typically prized examples of liberty, freedom, and critical thinking. They are not seen as a threat to group cohesion, but rather an expression of democratic ideals and individualism.

Saucier et al. (2009) conducted a systematic study of militant extremist groups across geographical regions and cultures. Their analysis identified 16 themes associated with a militant extremist mind-set, many of which align with Gelfand et al.'s (2013) cultural findings. Tight social norming, religious or ideological justifications, and intolerance for norm violations are but a few themes identified across regional and cultural groups.

Post and Sheffer (2007) assessed terrorist risks among countries with large Muslim diasporic communities. Such countries were found to be at greater risk for self-radicalization among their Muslim populations. In fact, they reported that 80 percent of Salafist recruits come from these communities that are often alienated by their host countries. In closer examination of how diasporas approach their integration into the host country, the authors articulated six strategies: (1) *integration*—learning how to operate and be successful in the host culture while still maintaining some level of separation, (2) *acculturation*—blending into the host culture, (3) *communalism*—maintaining the integrity and separation of their own cultural group, (4) *corporatism*—possessing recognized host culture representation within government and political systems, (5) *autonomism*—remaining true to their culture of origin in social norms and political and economic pursuits while existing among host culture systems, and (6) *isolation*—living apart from their host culture and their culture of origin. Post and Sheffer (2007) found that the majority of ethnonational diasporic communities tended to choose either the communalist or autonomist approach to integration into their host cultures. Research has proposed that acculturation and culture integration into host countries may be easier for some individuals based on the culture they come from. Oyserman (1993) found Arab Israelis struggled to integrate into Western culture as compared to Jewish Israelis based on the level of collectivism in their cultural backgrounds.

Risks associated with extremism among collectivistic, socially tight diasporas may validate previous observations by Hogg (2000) and Castano, Yzerbyt, and Bourguignon (2003) who asserted that group entitativity boosts in-group extremism. *Entitativity* is the extent to which members of a given group perceive similarity, common fate, salience, and boundedness among the group's membership. These researchers found that greater in-group entitativity was associated with greater in-group identity and greater in-group favor, and the perception that a particular in-group behavior and beliefs were superior to those outside of the group.

ARABISM, ISLAMIST IDEOLOGY, AND TERRORISM

The culture question has never been stronger since the advent of 9/11. Over the last two decades much of the conversation has centered on Huntington's (1996) infamous, *Clash of Civilizations* and the idea that rising ideological and religious differences between Islam and the West make the two cultures incompatible (Khomeini, 1979; Mamdani, 2002; Maududi, 1975). One side of the debate has focused on alarmist questions concerning a looming Armageddon and a repeat of medieval crusades while the other side appears naïve to current events, contending that Islam is a religion of peace and that terrorism has no place among its faithful following. While neither extreme position appears likely, it raises the question, what is the relationship between the Arab world, Islamic ideology, and terrorism? To aid in our understanding of this relationship, it is important to first address some of the differences in culture and worldview between the Middle East or Arab experience and that of most Westerners. This discussion is not designed to be comprehensive, but it should sufficiently illustrate the point that there are significant differences between these two people groups. While these differences do not rise to the level of incompatibility, they do help explain why our two cultures have struggled throughout history to translate shared goals into shared realities.

MIDDLE EASTERN AND ARAB WORLDVIEW

Following the events of 9/11 there was an explosion of books and articles written in an attempt to increase Western understanding of Middle Eastern and Arab culture as well as Islamic ideology and religious belief (Clark, 2003; Lewis, 2002; Nydell, 2002). Many of these resources claimed an "Arab mind" or coherent framework of Arab personality to include interpersonal style and motivation. However, it may be more accurate to say that the majority of Arabs (living in the Middle East) are members of a sociocultural mosaic with a variety of normative, ideological, and individual traditions. While there is no "Arab personality," a number of common elements emerge from their worldview (Staal, 2012). Some of the most prominent are articulated below and many are consistent with previous literature describing the influence of Arab culture in shaping individual behavior (Lawrence, 1926, 1927; Lewis, 2002; Maxwell, 1994; Nydell, 2002; Patai, 1973; Thesiger, 1964).

Time: Monochronic versus Polychronic

In Western society, time tends to be viewed as a tangible entity (it can be spent and lost) and events are seen as occurring in chronological sequence. Time acts as a framework within which cause-and-effect relationships exist (e.g., events one and two occurred and three was the outcome). As expected, our lives are built around this sequence of events and we tend to pride ourselves on punctuality, strict schedules, and detailed and rigid planning. Most of our orientation is for the present and the future that we project in advance. This is in contrast to much of the Middle Eastern Arab world whose time orientation is polychronic. In this context time is intangible, fluid, and flexible. While there is structure, it is not nearly as defined or rigid as it is in the West and therefore schedules and appointment times are tentative (often relying on "inshallah" or God's divine will). Events evolve and unfold in a much less predictable manner, and there is a much greater orientation to the present and past (Al-Krenawi & Graham, 2000; Haboush, 2007).

Self-Identity: Individualism versus Collectivism

We Westerners value our individual self-expression, and we talk of self-actualizing. We see ourselves as the "masters of our own destiny" and hold up the belief in self-determination over other social conventions. Most important to us in the West are our individual rights and sense of personal responsibility. In psychological terms we tend to hold an internal locus of control. These values are in sharp contrast to the collectivistic approach more common among Arab culture. Group identification and intragroup cooperation are essential. A sense of belongingness, group status, and the lifelong development of a social network is important. Holding to an external locus of control, Arab culture promotes an emphasis on saving face, showing and maintaining respect and dignity, and upholding the family honor (Bierbrauer, 1992; Dwairy & Van Sickle, 1996; Haboush, 2007; Oyserman, 1993).

Guilt versus Shame

"Confession is good for the soul" is an expression that resonates well in the West. In a guilt-based society with internalized standards of conduct, this tendency to demand that individuals take responsibility for their actions makes sense. From this perspective, one's guilt and the feelings associated with it could last forever if left covered. Accordingly, sharing that information with others is a way to "get it off one's chest" and is encouraged since it tends to relieve the emotional pain associated with the guilty feeling. However, in a culture that is shame-based, the act of acknowledging one's violation is in essence inviting shame and negative feelings (not reducing them). To do so threatens one's group status, and the honor that one works hard to protect (Bierbrauer, 1992; Haboush, 2007). Instead, various defensive strategies tend to be employed in order to maintain these elements, including denial, rationalization, and diffusion of responsibility.

Communication: Low Context versus High Context

All communication is contextual; however, depending on your cultural values that context may have a high or low impact on the meaning of the communication. Within the Arab culture, meaning is highly contextualized and it is always embedded within the relationship of the communicators. There is much less emphasis placed on the explicit message. In contrast, Western audiences place greater value on the words expressed and the burden of meaning tends to rest on the sender.

Communication: Direct versus Indirect

Similarly, communications in the West tend to be more direct, effectively neutral, and factually based, with value placed in the precision and specificity of the message. In Arab culture, communications are often indirect, evoking affect, imagery, shared experience, and employing a much higher frequency of metaphor and symbolism. Communications also tend to be much more nonlinear in Arab culture, adhering to fewer unitary themes, with less chronological emphasis, and less "beginning to end" framing.

Objectivity versus Subjectivity

Westerners value logical, objective, and empirically based arguments. Effort is made to avoid interjecting emotion into decision making, and in fact, emotional arguments are often viewed as weak. In general, clarity, accuracy, and understatement "win the day" among Western communicators. In contrast, Arab culture prizes a more balanced blending of logic with emotional appeal.

ARAB CULTURE AND ITS RELATIONSHIP WITH ISLAM

Culture and religion are not synonyms. However, as previously discussed, culture does tend to include particular religious practices, ideologies, and social norms that are informed by a moral code. Islam is unique in some ways in that its practice is built into the daily experience of the society and culture in many, if not most, Islamic countries. It is often considered the de facto state religion and in many Middle Eastern countries it is illegal to promote any other religious faith. Among the Islamic community of nations, Islam is the prescribed practice in the daily experience of citizens in a manner that makes it an inextricable part of the cultural fabric (dietary restrictions, daily prayers, mosque attendance, religious festivals, etc.). As such, it is a distinctive part of the culture and cannot be separated. Many similar arguments could be made about Judaism and the degree to which this belief system is inherent in the culture and the identity of Jews or Israelis (Oyserman, 1993). While there are many nominal believers in Islamic countries, and what happens in the personal lives of Muslims varies as it does among any religious community, Islam also imposes many public rules to constrain the behavior of its members and to encourage conformity and obedience to Islamic law and moral codes.

Of course, not all Muslims are from the Middle East or of Arab descent; however, it is the origin of the faith system, it carries with it most of its religious scholarship and teaching traditions (the Sunna, the Hadith, Sharia), and lastly, the holy book of the Koran is written in Arabic. Many traditional Muslims assert that any translation away from the original Arabic is heretical and that true Koranic scripture can only be understood in its original form (Maududi, 1960). In fact, in many Islamic countries, believers may have much of the Koran memorized yet not be able to read the language or interpret its meaning.

In comparison, Western societies have typically distanced their political and social systems from religious practices. The separation of church and state is a 500-year-old reaction to the Protestant Reformation, the separation from Catholicism, and the forming of the United States. Most Americans and Westerners are very sensitive to the connection between government and private life and the idea of nationalizing religion or a particular religious practice is an anathema. Many Americans would recall that such separation and personal expression are part of what the founding fathers of this country fought to protect (Rossiter, 1999).

A CLASH OF CULTURES FROM WITHIN

While it has been popular to focus on the differences between the West and the East and to pit Christianity against Islam, it may be more useful to look within the Arab world and Islam itself. Mamdani (2002) posits, as others have, that the class of civilizations is not between cultures but within cultures. One example of this within-culture conflict concerns a disturbing shift in traditional Islamic teaching and ideology. This shift, occurring gradually over the last century, has facilitated a meaningful change among ideological concepts that has been seized upon by extremist teachers and Islamic ideologues (El Fadl, 2005; Knapp, 2002). The rise of the *Muslim Brotherhood* in Egypt initiated some of this shift, but it was consolidated by a number of Islamic scholars over the convening decades (Khomeini, 1979; Maududi, 1947, 1960, 1975, 1976; Qutb, 1964). This shift can be explained by a number of factors, including (1) Western policies pushing global democratization, (2) spreading Western cultural influences, (3) perceived decadence and excess among Western countries, (4) the perception of the West's negative influence on traditionally conservative Islamic populations, and (5) a growing awareness of hypocrisy and apostasy among the leaders of Islamic counties (as perceived by fundamental religious followers within the region). Some of the more notable examples of this shift in traditional Islamic ideology have been briefly described below.

Jihad: Akbar versus Asgar

Perhaps the single-most misused and poorly understood concept in Islamic teaching is that of jihad. Traditionally, Islamic scholars have distinguished between the *jihad akbar* (the greater jihad) and the *jihad asgar* (the lesser jihad). "Jihad" means "struggle" or "striving" (typically in the way of God) or to work for something with determination; it does not, however, mean "holy war" (war in Arabic is *harb* and fighting is *qital*). Jihad akbar has traditionally been interpreted by Muslims as an internal struggle against personal weakness while the lesser jihad has been a proscription for self-defense and self-preservation (Bonner, 2006; Mamdani, 2002; Peters, 1996). In the Koran, "jihad" is used to describe "fighting in the path of God" (*jihad fi sabil Allah*); or warfare against the enemies of the Muslim community. Jihad cannot imply an Islamic conversion by force, since the Koran states that "There is no compulsion in religion" (Pickthall, 2002, 2:256). However, historically there have been challenges to this interpretation, and twentieth-century Islamist extremists have rallied against the consensus view of a restricted, defensive version of jihad based on the early writings of Taqi al-Din Ahmad Ibn Taymiyya, a thirteenth-century Muslim legal philosopher known today as the father of Salifism (Al-Banna, 1978; Bonner, 2006; Maududi, 1960, 1975; Peters, 1996; Qutb, 1964).

> Islam wants to employ all forces and means that can be employed for bringing about a universal all-embracing revolution. This far-reaching struggle that continuously exhausts all forces and this employment of all possible means are called jihad. (Sayyid Abu'l A'la Maududi, 1995, pp. 9–10)

Takfir: Kafir, Kufr, and Jahiliyya

Traditionally, individuals given the label of *kufr* are considered as unbelievers. They do not adhere to the Islamic faith and are not Muslim. They live lives in a state of ignorance concerning the truth regarding God (Caner & Caner, 2002; Maududi, 1960). Such individuals represented the *jahiliyya* or community of people, outside of the *dar al-Islam* (community of believers) who through their own pagan ignorance are not Muslim. It may be that they have never been exposed to the truth or that they are believers of another faith, but they have not rejected Islamic teaching per se. In contrast, *kafiri* are individuals who reject the belief in Islam, those who are born Muslim but choose of their own free will to reject this position and live as a nonbeliever.

Islam teaches that it is not right to accuse another of wrongdoing or disbelief: "A man does not accuse another of being a transgressor (*fasiq*), nor does he accuse him of being a kafir (*disbeliever*)" (Ali, 2001, Hadith, Bukhari Sura 78:44). Moreover, it is forbidden for believers to fight against each other, seeing as both are members of the faithful: "When two Muslims meet each other with their swords, both of them are in the fire" (Ali, 2001, Hadith, Bukhari Sura 2:21). However, turning again to Ibn Taymiyya's writing in the thirteenth century, he strongly advocated jihad as warfare against the Crusaders and Mongols who then occupied parts of the dar al-Islam. His teaching broke with the mainstream ideology of his day by asserting that a professing Muslim who does not live by the faith is an unbeliever (an apostate or takfir). In doing so, Ibn Taymiyya justified attacks against other Muslims by essentially denying them their status as a Muslim (Khan, 1973; Taymiyya, 2001). Moreover, he extended the argument against Muslim governments, providing written authority for jihad against "un-Islamic" states (Qutb, 1964). He advocated for government that supported governance by God (*hakimiyya*) and not a sovereignty of man over man. Twentieth-century Islamic ideologues have taken this fringe teaching and capitalized on its message. They have expounded on Ibn Taymiyya's writings and have used these ideas to push jihad against various governments and state actors, to include those within the Islamic and Middle Eastern communities (Maududi, 1975; Qutb, 1964).

> [T]he whole world is steeped in Jahiliyya, which takes the form of claiming that the right to create values, to legislate rules of collective behavior, and to choose any way of life rests with men, without regard to what God has prescribed. The result of this rebellion against the authority of God is the oppression of His creatures... The foremost duty of Islam in this world is to depose Jahiliyyah from the leadership of man. (Sayyid Qutb, 1964, p. 11)

Hijra versus Jahili

The *hijra* describes Muhammad's movement of the community of believers from Mecca to Medina under the duress of attack and harassment by the Quraishite tribe of his origin (Maududi, 1940). The forced move was a migration from one area to another in order to avoid persecution. In contrast, the concept of *jahili* traditionally referenced a moral and, in some instances, physical separation from unbelieving society. The idea was one of separation for purification (Qutb, 1964). Over the last century, Islamist extremists have co-opted these two terms to supplant the traditional use of jahili with that of the hijra in order to bolster calls for requirements among true believers to separate themselves from their unbelieving societies and seek a consolidation of pure faithful followers. This type of disconnection and disenfranchisement has a number of potential risks for extremist indoctrination, within-group intolerance for norm violation, and control.

> Islam is a revolutionary doctrine and system that overturns governments. It seeks to overturn the whole universal social order ... It is not satisfied by a piece of land, but demands the whole universe...Islamic Jihad is at the same time offensive and defensive ... The Islamic party does not hesitate to utilize the means of war to implement its goal. (Sayyid Abu'l A'la Maududi, 1995)

Shahadat versus Istishad/Intihar

Martyrdom is not unique to terrorist groups within the Middle East. Historically, there have been a number of martyr-like groups—individuals who have sacrificed their own lives in the service of their country or the ideology of their group. The Jewish Sicarii zealots of the first century, the Hindi "thugs" of the seventh century, and the Islamic Nizari Ismailis or "hashishiyyin" of the eleventh through thirteenth centuries are some examples (Bloom, 2005). One could even argue that Japanese kamikazes of the last century were a form of suicidal terrorists, although this group has some distinct differences from the previous historical examples identified above.

Among the traditional Islamic teaching, a *shahadat* is an individual who gives his life in conventional combat as a Muslim. In contrast, an *istishad* is a martyr-like jihadi who dies in the name of Allah, but does so in nonconventional warfare. Lastly, *intihars* are individuals who take their own life and commit suicide, something that is forbidden by Islamic teaching (Shiqaqi, 2002; Victor, 2003). These three descriptors clearly denote three different types of individuals, and yet, recent Islamic extremist teaching has gradually displaced earlier notions of what it means to be a shahadat, a conventional solider who dies on the battlefield (Qutb, 1964). As the modern battlefield has been reinterpreted as anywhere jihad takes place, so too the individual dying for their cause has been recast as an Islamic soldier fighting for the community of the faithful.

As a result of this shift in traditional Islamic teaching, there remain a number of contemporary concepts in dispute among the moderate and extreme elements of the Muslim community. What does "jihad" really mean and encompass and how do we understand the implementation of the greater and lesser forms of struggle? What is the responsibility of the Muslim community or Middle Eastern community in speaking or acting out against this "hijacking" of traditional Islamic ideology? How does this requirement fit into a culture that is collectivistic in nature and fatalistic in belief? Such actions, if they occur or do not, are regarded as ultimately directed by God, not by individual free will (Knapp, 2002).

While some may say that this chapter has unfairly focused on Islamic terrorism, I would argue that it has brought upon itself otherwise inordinate attention based on current events and recent terrorist activities across the globe (Caner & Caner, 2002). As the editor of the London daily, *Al-Sharq Al-Awsat*, and general manager of the Arab satellite network, Al Arabiya, observed, "Obviously not all Muslims are terrorists, but, regrettably, the majority of the terrorists in the world are Muslims" (Arab and Muslim Reactions to the Terrorist Attack in Beslan, Russia, 2004).

CULTURAL FACTORS THAT INCREASE RISK FOR WMD ATTACKS

According to Hoffman (1998) and Harari (2005), in terrorist groups that are fueled by religious ideology, violence is a sacramental act or a divine duty. It allows for unrestrained action. In other words, such groups are not bound by political, moral, or social constraints, and therefore, the use of weapons of mass destruction (WMDs) by such groups is more likely.

Nonreligious or nonideological terror groups are less likely to use WMDs for several reasons: (1) the use of such weapons is likely to result in wide condemnation, (2) such weapons are difficult to keep from negatively impacting their own constituency, and (3) WMD use represents a breach of constraint that would risk jeopardizing the support of the population needed by the terrorist group for their survival (Harari, 2005).

In contrast, terrorist groups willing to use WMD tend to be religious or ideologically motivated. They see the world as divided between two groups: "us" and "them." These divisions often fall along their religious fault lines. There is no reason to negotiate terms or hold peace talks because, as one extremist put it, "God does not negotiate or engage in discussion." In 1995 religious groups perpetrated 25 percent of all terrorist acts, yet accounted for 58 percent of all resulting fatalities (Hoffman, 1998). Groups willing to engage in WMD terrorist acts find justification for their violence through various forms of moral disengagement: (1) *Moral justification*—They often perceive themselves as the saviors of a constituency threatened by a great evil. They believe their way of life or community is threatened, and they believe they have a religious duty to protect that community at all costs. (2) *Displacement of responsibility* —They portray themselves as functionaries who are "just following orders." Authority to act is often provided by the group's leader or a religious conduit to that leader who is perceived as a divine authority, bolstering their belief that such extreme action is not only permissible, but required. (3) *Minimization*—They insulate themselves from their moral anxieties by distance and a focus on their identified enemy's reactions, and not toward civilian causalities. Moreover, in many instances, there is a perception that there are no neutral actors. In other words, even civilians are in league with their enemies, if not actively then passively. (4) *Dehumanization*—Many groups indoctrinate their members by referring to the enemy as "infidel," "pig," "dogs," or "the great Satan." Such monikers create a useful emotional distance, and disdain, and reinforce a justification of violence (Bandura, 1986).

While there is psychological conditioning used to prepare terror group members for their external engagements, life on the inside of a terrorist group can be much different. Groups often provide their members with many personal and sociocultural experiences that are otherwise missing from these individuals' lives. In the case of members of a diaspora, it may be that they have not found fulfillment of such needs due to the lack of integration, acculturation, and/or acceptance among their host nation. Among these groups there may be a sense of invulnerability, excessive optimism and encouragement to take risks, a presumption of the group's morality, one-dimensional perceptions of the enemy, intolerance to the challenges of the group's shared beliefs, a tendency toward "groupthink," and peer pressure or strong group solidarity that makes compliance and conformity nearly certain.

CULTURAL PROTECTIVE FACTORS AGAINST EXTREMISM AND TERRORIST ACTS

Very little has been explored to date on what protects societies from extremism and terrorist acts. We are just starting to learn more about the ways in which individuals self-radicalize and become a potential threat. However, it has been proposed that nations and people groups can set conditions that will preventatively protect them against terrorism and the rise of extremist ideology (Post & Sheffer, 2007; Rynning, 2003). Several considerations to this end have been identified for further exploration.

Respect for Cultural Differences

Host cultures must attempt to accommodate some degree of cultural practices and differences in worldview, while facilitating acculturation by diasporic groups. By valuing diversity and seeing it as strength, host cultures are more likely to find balance between effective assimilation of a diaspora and its members' need to remain connected to their homeland and heritage. As a recent case example, Muslim girls living in France were forced to comply with French law and were prohibited from wearing their traditional headscarves (the *hijab*) while attending school. The inflexibility and intolerance of the French government in this regard resulted in a backlash by a number of angry, largely unemployed but well-educated Muslim men. This incident served to highlight a very poorly integrated Muslim community in France (BBC, 2014).

INTEGRATION OF REFUGEES AND IMMIGRANT POPULATIONS

Encouraging and even incentivizing acculturation and integration with the host culture while honoring the heritage and contributions of each member's cultural background is recommended. The speed and ease in which diasporic members integrate may be an indicator of their level of risk for exploitation and receptivity to extremist ideology (precursors for terrorist acts).

Community-Based Interventions

Programs must identify the most at-risk émigré populations and implement interventions within these communities that respect the cultural integrity of each. Host community celebrations of diaspora culture and culture-specific heritage are examples of how host cultures can facilitate a sense of belonging, connection, and relationship with a diaspora. Attitudes of community leaders that encourage dialogue, cultural exchange, and genuine interest are likely to be effective in demonstrating respect and communicating value.

A critical aid in the implementation of protective factors is the ability to identify an area of risk or a population at risk for self-radicalization, extremist exploitation, or terrorist activity. Post and Sheffer (2007) recommended five considerations in evaluating a community's risk: (1) the degree of diaspora community organization, (2) the level of tolerance provided to the diaspora by the host society, (3) the speed at which the diasporic group assimilates into the host culture, (4) the level of connectedness between the diaspora and its homeland communities, and (5) the local religious leader's degree of radicalization. These authors went further to highlight the risks associated with lack of integration among ethnonational diasporic communities. They identified a tendency for these individuals to choose either the communalist or autonomist approach to integration into their host cultures. In doing so, the members of these diaspora fail to adequately acculturate, and as a result, they often experience a sense of rejection by the host culture (which naturally expects them to integrate). They are left with a longing for belonging, connection, and identity. These preconditions, when combined with radicalized ideology (found in the local area or on the Internet), can lead some members of the diaspora down a dark path of radicalization, extremism, and potentially terrorist acts against their host nation or others.

The Committee on the Psychological Roots of Terrorism recommended that "Western governments actively integrate refugees and diaspora youth into the political culture of Western liberal democracies, while accepting immigrants' cultural and social beliefs and views" (Post & Sheffer, 2007, p. 104). The tradition of open society and embracing of diversity in the United States has been identified as a potential protective factor that has discouraged self-radicalization from within our own nation.

CONCLUSION

In this chapter we've explored culture and its influence on individuals engaged in terrorist activities, including those willing to use weapons of mass psychological destruction. Although much of the discussion has centered on contemporary issues of Islamic terrorism and risks to self-radicalization, it is important to note that terrorists come from all walks of life and across ethnic lines and cultural groups. Furthermore, it is important not to focus on one cultural group or ideological position related to militant extremism over another.

Research examining the culture-related preconditions for terrorism and extremist behavior has identified a number of factors associated with greater risk. Cultures that incorporate a strong sense of fatalism, those that are socially or normatively tight, and those that have high male dominance and low gender egalitarianism represent cultures that may be ripe for extremist ideology and growing radicalized actors who seek to perpetrate terrorist acts. Research has also identified connections between terrorist involvement and collective cultures. These risk factors include distinctions between in-group and out-group morality, intolerance for violations of in-group moral truths, and a sense of moral superiority as perceived by the in-group culture. Lastly, the ability of ethnonational diasporic communities to integrate into their host culture may be predictive of their level of risk for radicalization and extremism.

Conditions can be set in a way that preventatively protects societies against terrorism and the rise of extremist ideology. Respect for cultural differences, facilitating cultural integration between diasporas and their host cultures, and implementing community based interventions that target at-risk populations are critical in defending against the rise of ideological precursors and their resulting acts of terror.

REFERENCES

Al-Banna, H. (1978). *Five Tracts of Hasan Al Banna, 1906–1949*. Santa Barbara, CA: University of California Press.

Ali, M. M. (2001). *A Manual of Hadith*. Chelsea, MI: Sheridan.

Al-Krenawi, A., & Graham, J. R. (2000). Culturally Sensitive Social Work Practice with Arab Clients in Mental Health Settings. *Health & Social Work, 25*, 9–23.

American Psychological Association. (2014). *Guidelines on Multicultural Education, Training, Research, Practice, and Organizational Change for Psychologists* (2002). http://www.apa.org/pi/oema/resources/policy/multicultural-guidelines.aspx (Accessed November 4, 2014).

Atran, S. (2003). Genesis of Suicide Terrorism. *Science, 299*, 1534–1539.

Atran, S., Axelrod, R., & Davis, R. (2007). Sacred Barriers to Conflict Resolution. *Science, 317*, 1039–1040.

Atran, S. & Ginges, J. (2012). Religious and Sacred Imperatives in Human Conflict. *Science, 336*, 855–857.

Bandura, A. (1986). *Social Foundations of Thought and Action: A Social Cognitive Theory*. Englewood Cliffs, NJ: Prentice-Hall.

BBC. (July 1, 2014). *European Court Upholds French Full Veil Ban*. Retrieved from http://www.bbc.com/news/world-europe-28106900

Bierbrauer, G. (1992). Reactions to Violation of Normative Standards: A Cross-Cultural Analysis of Shame and Guilt. *International Journal of Psychology, 27*, 181–194.

Bloom, M. (2005). *Dying to Kill: The Allure of Suicide Terror*. New York: Columbia.

Bonner, M. (2006). *Jihad in Islamic History*. Princeton, NJ: Princeton University Press.

Caner, E. M. & Caner, E. F. (2002). *Unveiling Islam*. Grand Rapids, MI: Kregel.

Castano, E., Yzerbyt, V., & Bourguignon, D. (2003). We are One and I Like It: The Impact of in Group Entitativity on Ingroup Identification. *European Journal of Social Psychology, 33*, 735–754.

Christopher, J. C., Wendt, D. C., Marecek, J., & Goodman, D. M. (2014). Critical Cultural Awareness: Contributions to a Globalizing Psychology. *American Psychologist, 69*(7), 645–655.

Clark, M. (2003). *Islam for Dummies*. Indianapolis: Wiley.

Dwairy, M. & Van Sickle, T. D. (1996). Western Psychotherapy in Traditional Arabic Societies. *Clinical Psychology Review, 16*, 231–249.

El Fadl, K. A. (2005). *The Great Theft: Wrestling Islam from the Extremists*. New York: Harper.

Fiske, A., Kitayama, S., Markus, H. R., & Nisbett, R. E. (1998). The Cultural Matrix of Social Psychology. In D. Gilbert, S. Fiske, & G. Lindzey (Eds.), *The Handbook of Social Psychology, Vol. 2* (4th ed., pp. 915–981). San Francisco: McGraw-Hill.

Ganor, B. (2002). Suicide Attacks in Israel. In J. Haslam (Ed.), *Countering Suicide Terrorism* (pp. 140–152). Herzilya, Israel. The International Policy Institute for Counter-Terrorism.

Gelfand, M., LaFree, G., Fahey, S., & Feinberg, E. (2013). Culture and Extremism. *Journal of Social Issues, 69*(3), 495–517.

Gelfand, M. J., Raver, J. L., Nishii, L., Leslie, L. M., Lun, J., Lim, B. L., & Yamaguchi, S. (2011). Differences between Tight and Loose Cultures: A 33-Nation Study. *Science, 332*, 1100–1104.

Ginges, J., & Atran, S. (2009). What Motivates Participation in Violent Political Action. *Annals of the New York Academy of Sciences, 1167*(1), 115–123.

Haboush, K. L. (2007). Working with Arab American Families: Culturally Competent Practice for School Psychologists. *Psychology in the Schools, 44*, 183–198.

Harari, H. (2005). *A View from the Eye of the Storm: Terror and Reason in the Middle East*. New York: Harper Collins.

Hardin, E. E., Robitschek, C., Flores, L. Y., Navarro, R. O., & Ashton, M. W. (2014). The Cultural Lens Approach to Evaluating Cultural Validity of Psychological Theory. *American Psychologist, 69*(7), 656–668.

Hoffman, B. (1998). Old Madness New Methods. *Rand Review*, 12–17.

Hogg, M. A. (2000). Subjective Uncertainty Reduction through Self-Categorization: A Motivational Theory of Social Identity Processes. *European Review of Social Psychology, 11*, 223–255.

House, R. J., Hanges, P. J., Javidan, M., Dorfman, P. W., & Gupta, V. (2004). *Leadership, Culture, and Organizations: The GLOBE Study of 62 Societies*. Thousand Oaks, CA: Sage Publications.

Huntington, S. (1996). *Clash of Civilizations and the Remaking of World Order*. New York: Simon and Schuster.

Khan, Q. (1973). *The Political Thought of Ibn Taymiyah*. Islamabad, Pakistan: Islamic Research Institute.

Khomeini, A. R. (1979). *Islamic Government*. Arlington, VA: Manor.

Knapp, M. G. (2002). Distortion of Islam by Muslim extremists. *Military Intelligence Professional Bulletin, 28*, 37.

Kruglanski, A. W., Chen, X., Dechesne, M., Fishman, S., & Orehek, E. (2009). Fully committed: Suicide Bombers' Motivation and the Quest for Personal Significance. *Political Psychology, 30*(3), 331–357.

Lawrence, T. E. (1926). *Seven Pillars of Wisdom*. New York: Doubleday.

Lawrence, T. E. (1927). *Revolt in the Desert*. London: Jonathan Cape.

Leung, K., & Bond, M. H. (2004). Social Axioms: A Model for Social Beliefs in Multicultural Perspective. *Advances in Experimental Social Psychology, 36*, 119–97.

Lewis, B. (2002). *The Arabs in History*. New York: Oxford University.

Mamdani, M. (2002). Good Muslim, Bad Muslim: A Political Perspective on Culture and Terrorism. *American Anthropologist, 104*(3), 766–775.

Maududi, A. A. A. (1940). *Economic System of Islam.* Lahore, Pakistan: Islamic Publications Ltd.

Maududi, A. A. (1947). *The Process of Islamic Revolution.* Lahore, Pakistan: Islamic Publications Limited.

Maududi, A. A. (1960). *Towards Understanding Islam.* Lahore, Pakistan: Islamic Publications Limited.

Maududi, A. A. (1975). *Fundamentals of Islam.* Lahore, Pakistan: Islamic Publications Limited.

Maududi, A. A. (1976). *Human Rights in Islam.* Leicester, UK: The Islamic Foundation.

Maududi, A. A. (1995). *Jihad in Islam.* Birmingham, UK: UK Islamic Mission Dawah Centre.

Maxwell, G. (1994). *A Reed Shaken by the Wind: Travels Among the Marsh Arabs of Iraq.* London: Eland.

Nydell, M. K. (2002). *Understanding Arabs: A Guide for Westerners* (3rd ed.). Yarmouth, ME: Intercultural.

Obeid, N., Chang, D., & Ginges, J. (2010). Beliefs of Wife Beating: A Lebanese Case. *Violence Against Women, 16*, 691–712.

Oyserman, D. (1993). The Lens of Personhood: Viewing the Self and Others in a Multicultural Society. *Journal of Personality and Social Psychology, 65*, 993–1009.

Patai, R. (1973). *The Arab Mind.* New York: Macmillan.

Peters, R. (1996). *Jihad in Classical and Modern Islam.* Princeton, NJ: Markus Weiner.

Pickthall, M. M. (2002). *The Meaning of the Glorious Qur'an.* Beltsville, MD: Amana.

Post, J. M., & Sheffer, G. (2007). The Risk of Radicalization and Terrorism in U.S. Muslim Communities. *The Brown Journal of World Affairs, 13*(2), 101–112.

Qutb, S. (1964). *Milestones.* Damascus, Syria: Dar al-Lim.

Rossiter, C. (1999). *The Federalist Papers.* New York: Penguin.

Rynning, S. (2003). The European Union: Towards a Strategic Culture? *Security Dialogue, 34*(4), 479–496.

Sageman, M. (2004). *Understanding Terror Networks.* Philadelphia: University of Pennsylvania Press.

Saucier, G., Akers, L. G., Shen-Miller, S., Knezevic, G., & Stankov, L. (2009). Patterns of Thinking in Militant Extremism. *Perspectives on Psychological Science, 4*, 256–271.

Shiqaqi, K. (2002). The Views of Palestinian Society on Suicide Terrorism. In J. Haslam (Ed.), *Countering Suicide Terrorism* (pp. 155–164). Herzilya, Israel: The International Policy Institute for Counter-Terrorism.

Staal, M. A. (2012). Assessing Iraqi Arab Personality Using the Nonverbal Personality Questionnaire. *Military Medicine, 177*(6), 732–739.

Taymiyah, A. I. (2001). *The Religious and Moral Doctrine of Jihad.* Birmingham, UK: Maktabah Al Ansar Publications.

Thesiger, W. (1964). *The Marsh Arabs.* England: Penguin.

Triandis, H. (1989). The Self and Social Behavior in Differing Social Contexts. *Psychological Review, 96*, 506–520.

Victor, B. (2003). *Army of Roses: Inside the World of Palestinian Women Suicide Bombers.* Emmaus, PA: Rodale.

Wenzlaff, K. (2004). *Terrorism: Game Theory and Other Explanations.* Universitat Bayreuth Student Paper.

6

Economic Factors for Weapons of Mass Psychological Destruction

Vikram Sethi with the assistance of Sandip Chakraborty

Economic factors as precedents, process variables, and consequences of material and psychological destruction are often neglected in the study and consideration of terrorism. Yet, economic considerations are an envelope for such traumatic events and their immediate long-term effects. David Gold notes that much of the discussion related to economics deals with issues of poverty, inequality, and limits of opportunity shapes and ignites terrorism responses, and if/how an alleviation of such conditions may lead to a reduction of such actions (Gold, 2004).

In 2011, a very different and intriguing concept for most authors was a statement by Gregg Carlson, which referred to the 9/11 attack on the United States as follows, "The attacks, which cost perhaps $400,000 to execute, will cost the United States more than $5 trillion!" We often wonder if the astronomical costs (i.e., $5 trillion) are unique to that specific instance or if such costs accompany similar attacks. Is it then accurate to term such costs as "costs of fear" and to question if these economic consequences are the real outcomes of weapons of mass psychological destruction?

In this chapter, we explore the above ideas by following differing and sometimes disparate lines of thought. The chapter establishes a framework in which instruments of mass psychological destruction are interpreted generally as "instruments of fear," which create disproportionate consequences in the economy, thereby explaining one of the greatest weapons of mass psychological destruction—fear—which causes society to take extraordinary measures and endure extraordinary costs to protect itself from that fear reaction.

It might be correct to assume that such endured costs will vary with the fear acceptance thresholds of society; that is, acceptance of fear in Syrian society is different from acceptance of fear in the American context. In the end, we hope to explain some of the behavioral reactions of individuals and societies to terrorist attacks, and events that engender fear from deviant actions by members of one's own society or from external forces. In all cases, the economic consequences of such events are higher.

We also provide references to alternate areas of work related to the economics of terror attacks. In particular, a vast literature on terrorism and crime will be drawn from various incidents documented in the Global Terrorism Database (GTD) at the National Consortium for the Study of Terrorism and Responses to Terrorism, University of Maryland.

FOCI OF DISCOURSE

Research in modern-day terrorism and war follows a vastly different tone and process than has been in the past. In fact, as we ponder the phrase "weapons of mass psychological destruction," we realize that the term favors plausible destruction of life and property, and not real destruction. It is not destruction as represented by traditional war between organized armies. Instead, the term is rather more nebulous in its interpretation today than it has ever been.

Part of this change is due to the difference in what are and what creates "weapons of mass psychological destruction"—certainly not bombs and missiles that represented the wars of the past. In fact, the definition of "war" today has undergone a rather substantive change in its meaning and interpretation.

Consider, for example, what Robert Smith (2007) writes as the beginning paragraph of his treatise:

> War no longer exists. Confrontation, conflict and combat undoubtedly exist all around the world—most noticeably, but not only, in Iraq, Afghanistan, the Democratic Republic of Congo and the Palestinian Territories—and states still have armed forces which they use as a symbol of power. Nonetheless, war as cognitively known to most non-combatants, war as a battle in a field between men and machinery, war as a massive deciding event in a dispute in international affairs; such war no longer exists. (p. 3)

Yet, events that create fear and psychological impact on society are numerous and more than what most of us expect. Consider, for example, a database created by the National Consortium for the Study of Terrorism and Responses to Terrorism at the University of Maryland. Called the Global Terrorism Database (GTD), it lists 2,381 incidents in the United States alone since 1970. Many of these incidents would not fall with the generally accepted notion of "terrorist attack" but are certainly events that create fear in society, which is exactly the purpose of such event after all.

In general, there have been three themes in the examination of the economics of terror incidents:

1. Economic precursors
2. Financing channels
3. Direct economic impact

It should be noted that most of the literature focuses on state-sponsored terrorism and organized terrorist events that cause mass hysteria and fear, and use psychological destruction and impact as outcomes of such attacks. There is relatively little written and known of ad hoc events (such as school shooting), which arouse similar anxiety and stress in individuals.

Theme 1: Economic Precursors

There is a generally accepted hypothesis that poverty and lack of economic wellness correlate with terror activity. The argument is, of course, that engaging in such activities allays the economic situation of individuals engaging in such activity. However, there is a weakness in most such studies or rather a dichotomy in their application.

Krueger and Maleckova's (2003) survey data revealed that terrorist perpetrators from the West Bank and Gaza Strip do not necessarily possess a low socioeconomic background. Piazza's (2003) cross-national analysis, likewise, shows no evidence to support the crux of the "rooted-in-poverty" thesis, and Abadie's (2006) empirical research found little or no evidence that income inequality is related to terrorism. Lai's (2007) work did find a substantial correlation between economic inequality and higher levels of terrorism, and this supports the general (while unsubstantiated) sentiment that the poor turn to violence simply because they are poor.

In trying to understand how to resolve the discrepancy between a generally accepted principle and a lack of empirical evidence, one must recognize that that basis of the argument that poverty leads to terrorism lies in the extension of the principle of "poverty leads to crime" (Levitt & Venkatesh, 2000).

We rely on recent work by Paul-Philippe Pare and Richard Felson (2014) to address this discrepancy. Their review of prior literature does show that poverty and criminal behavior are correlated and they find evidence in Cusson (2005) to support this relationship. As they note, such correlations are based directly or indirectly on the frustration hypothesis, a theory that proposes a biological link between attainment of goals and reactive or angry aggression. Yet they build a reasonable argument that the poor attack the rich or those in power to seek relief of frustration is not correct. In fact, the reverse is perhaps more accurate—crime and violence tend to be contained mostly in one's own referent group; that is, the poor attack those of similar economic status. This, in fact, explains the fact that lower-status people have much higher rates of victimization.

The same logic is extended to economic status and terror activities. Choi and Luo (2013) demonstrate that poverty by itself does not drive actions that cause destructive harm or terror activities. Rather, actions such as economic sanctions cause disproportionate harm to the weakest members of society, which creates hatred for those who instigate such actions and thereby support a movement of the affected. This causes material or psychological harm to the perpetrator.

Rather than a cause of poverty (due to regime policies) leading to outward terroristic activities, the relationship becomes more complex and does not support the general sentiment that nations that have economic inequality or are generally poor are home to those who would create or orchestrate the events of a destructive nature in societies/nations outside of their own.

Theme 2: Financing Channels and Funding of Events of Mass Psychological Destruction

A lot of research and work went into identifying the channels used by terror groups to fund and use the monies to encourage activities disruptive to societies perceived as targets by them. One such work is particularly noteworthy—Steve Kiser in his dissertation entitled "Financing Terror" (2004) completed perhaps the most detailed articulation of sources and channels used by terror organizations.

Based on work by Kiser and later by Freeman and Ruehsen (2013), six methods are generally employed by terrorists to fund their efforts. These are described below.

Cash Couriers

This is one of the simplest and oldest method of moving liquid assets and was actively employed prior to 9/11 attacks. The 9/11 Commission monographs document a transfer of $1 million from the United Arab Emirates (UAE) to Pakistan and then onward to Afghanistan. The report describes how Khalid Sheik Mohammed delivered $120,000 in cash to Abdul Aziz Ali in Dubai, who then used the cash to wire funds to the hijackers in the United States. Khalid Sheikh Mohammed also gave 13 of the hijackers $10,000 each as they left Pakistan, and when they entered the United States, this money was deposited at banks such as Bank of America, SunTrust, and other smaller banks. Similarly Zacarious Moussaoui brought in $35,000, which he declared to customs upon entering the country.

Informal Cash Transfer

Generally known as the *hawala* system in Asia and the Middle East, this process used informal channels to transfer funds across international borders.

For example, to transfer money from Dubai to India, the transferor of funds contacts a *hawaldar* in Dubai and hands him UAE dirhams. The *hawaldar* contacts his/her counterpart in India and hands over equivalent Indian rupees to the recipient. A settlement of accounts among *hawaldars* occurs periodically.

Freeman and Ruehsen (2013) detail how besides Al Qaeda, Lashkar-e-Toiba used the hawala network to move funds before its 2000 Red Fort attack in Delhi. Similarly, it is noted that funds were transferred to the Times Square bomber, Faisal Shahzad, first, of $4,900 and then $7,000.

Money Service Businesses

Money service businesses (MSBs) are registered currency dealers or exchanges and there are over 33,000 in the United States alone. Unlike banks, MSBs do not require detailed information from their customers to transfer funds from them—hence, these channels can be used to fund terrorist organizations or directly their leaders. As described by Freeman and Ruehsen (2013), in February 2013, a federal jury in San Diego convicted four Somali immigrants of conspiring to fund al-Shabaab, a militant terrorist group in Somalia.

The 9/11 Commission reported that Al Qaeda made extensive use of MSBs in its financing of the 9/11 attack and used to the Wall Street Exchange Center and the UAE Exchange Center in Dubai to transfer funds to the hijackers via Royal Bank of Canada and Citibank.

Formal Banking

While the formal banking sector is highly regulated and watched, it has been used liberally for terrorist financing. As highlighted by Freeman and Ruehsen (2013), the Al-Madina Bank in Lebanon was such a case. The bank under the control of a woman named Rana Qolieilat knowingly facilitated the laundering of funds by Saddam Hussein, diamond dealers, Russian Mafia groups, and an arms dealer for Hezbollah. She is also alleged to have embezzled funds from the bank to enrich powerful Syrian generals and politicians during the Syrian occupation of Lebanon.

The 9/11 Commission report noted that the formal banking system was used to deposit $300,000 in U.S. banks. This amount was deposited in accounts in Union Bank of California and Sun Trust Bank in Florida, among others. All the hijackers opened accounts with their real identities and accessed money via ATMs and debit cards.

False Trade Invoicing

In this mechanism, the over/underinvoicing is used to hide the value of the assets and redirect excess monies to terrorist operations. Consider a shipment of goods from the United States to Dubai. The shipment, as an example, is overinvoiced by $100,000. When the payment is received by the shipper in the United States, part of the money is used to compensate the producer of goods and the excess invoice amount of $100,000 is redirected to terrorist operators.

Following 9/11 investigation, it was discovered that there was an extraordinary shipment of honey from the United States to Yemen and later the Yemen-based Al Nur Honey Center, Al Nur Honey Shop, and Al-Shifa Honey Press for Industry and Commerce were placed on the list of terrorism-related entities.

High-Value Commodities

High-value commodities such as gold and diamonds are a perpetual method of transmitting value assets across borders. Both are easy to hide and offer a lack of traceability, especially in the case of gold. The prevalence of large gold markets (called gold souks) in the Middle East has provided an easy method of asset conversion for illegal purposes.

The above are just some of the methods used to fund operations and operatives who are willing to design events to create fear in society. The list does go on and speak remarkably to the ease with which these methods can be combined, changed, and hidden along with thousands of legitimate transactions, which makes them much harder to detect.

It is also worth considering that each local terror incident is uniquely funded, and mixes terror and crime. One of the most deadly illustrations is the Spanish cell responsible for bombing the Madrid train system on March 11, 2004. The group, recruited from local mosques, largely funded the operation through the sale of drugs. The 440 pounds of explosives were obtained from a Spanish mine, obtained by bribing the mine's guard with drugs and cash.

Theme 3: Direct Economic Impact

The direct cost of terrorism includes damage to property and tangible assets such as housing, factories, inventories, and other goods and material. However, it also includes disruption of economic activity, lost wages, and other charges as insurance payments. It is reported that private property destruction (including the value of the four downed planes) was $14 billion and government entities lost $2.2 billion. Wages and salaries lost accounted for $3.3 billion. Clean-up costs were estimated to be $10 billion.

Various authors estimate total costs differently, but in the end the magnitude is large. The Bureau of Labor Statistics (2003) reported 145,000 workers were laid off as a direct result of the attacks. Navarro and Spencer (2001) calculate a total output loss of $47 billion.

Table 6.1
Examining costs of terrorist attacks: The case of 9/11 attacks

Cost area	Cost
Combatting terrorism	$53 billion by the United States
Insurance	a. 5% increase in premiums on property in the United States b. Higher increases overseas
9/11	a. $34 billion+ uninsured losses b. $576 million for the Pentagon c. 2,973 deaths
Travel and tourism	a. 279,000 jobs lost in the United States
Macroeconomic effects	a. Approx. $300 billion in lower growth in 2001 and 2002
Afghanistan	a. $50 billion+ for Department of Defense b. $3.3 billion for reconstruction c. $4.5 billion pledged for other countries
Iraq	a. $125 billion+ for Department of Defense b. $21 billion for reconstruction c. $13 billion pledged for other countries d. 1,058+ Americans killed
Shipping	a. 1–3% of shipment value increases for security costs

Source: Nanto, D. (2004). *9/11 Terrorism: Global Economic Costs*. CRS Report for Congress.

A detailed analysis was prepared by a CRS report. This report, entitled "9/11 Terrorism: Global Economic Costs," is a detailed account of the direct costs as a consequence of the 9/11 attacks (Table 6.1).

Over and beyond the direct costs, events such as 9/11 do have a ripple effect upon the world economy. Prior to 9/11, the world economy was expected to grow at 2.8 percent in 2001 and 3.1 percent in 2002. After 9/11, world GDP grew by 1.4 percent in 2001 and 1.9 percent in 2002. A 1 percent reduction in expected growth amounted to $300 billion loss in world production and income in 2002.

These numbers are staggering, but are supported by results of similar nature. In 2002, Bali bombings reduced Indonesia's growth rate by an estimated one percentage point.

However, the period immediately following events such as 9/11 and others, which inject mass psychological fear in society, provides important lessons related to economic consequences and recovery.

Lesson 1: The Immediate Consequences Are Significant

As shown above, direct and immediate costs of 9/11 stand in billions of dollars. The economic impact of the Oklahoma City bombing was significant.

The estimated insured damage was $300 million (Library, 2014). Approximately 77 buildings and 500 cars were damaged and more than 500 businesses were interrupted.

Lesson 2: Economies Are Resilient and Recover

The OECD (Organization of Economic Co-operation and Development) Economic Outlook 71 (2002) noted that after a terrorist attack the initial reaction of financial markets was dramatic and equity prices tumbled. Spreads between corporate and government bond yields, as well as spreads between emerging market and U.S. bond index yields widened. Implied volatility as derived from traded options on equity indices, government bond prices, short-term interest rates, exchange rates, and commodities spiked upward.

However, the recovery period from such events is short. The OECD report prepared the following table (Table 6.2) of stock price recoveries from a few major events:

Thus, the recovery from incidents is swift.

Lesson 3: But the Recovery Has Costs Too

Economic recovery from events of mass psychological destruction has costs that should not be ignored. The 9/11 attack disabled whole portion of the New York financial infrastructure. However, only by quick and aggressive action of

Table 6.2

Economic recovery from global terror incidents

	S&P 500, percent changes		
	Reaction period	Reaction	One year later*
Pearl Harbor	December 7 to 29, 1941	−10.2	15.3
Korean War	June 23 to July 17, 1950	−12.9	31.4
Cuban missile crisis	August 23 to October 26, 1961	−8.8	36.6
Tet offensive, Vietnam War	January 31 to March 5, 1968	−5.6	13.7
Iraqi invasion of Kuwait	August 2, 1990, to January 16, 1991	−11.1	32.3
September 11, 2001	September 11 to 19, 2001	−7.0	15.0

Six months later in the case of the September 11 attacks.
The reaction period is defined as ending when the U.S. military buildup starts.

Sources: Bank of England, *Financial Stability Review*, December 2001; and OECD Economic Outlook 71.

the Federal Reserve was an economic disaster avoided. The Federal Reserve instantly indicated that it stood ready to inject virtually unlimited amounts of liquidity to avoid payment failures and cascading defaults. The fund rate plunged to levels last seen in the early 1960s—1.2 percent on September 19, 2001. The Federal Reserve established or expanded 30-day swap lines with European Central Bank, the Bank of England, and the Bank of Canada, which totaled a record $90 billion, so as to enable them to provide dollars to their financial institutions. These are extraordinary measures, but only through this, is it possible to restore normalcy and improve consumer confidence.

AN ORGANIZING FRAMEWORK FOR LONG-TERM ECONOMIC EFFECTS: THE LONG TRAIL OF FEAR HYSTERESIS

In consideration of an organizing framework for the economics of terrorism, we are guided by several observations:

1. Economic consequences of a terrorist event mostly follow unpredictable outcomes.
2. There are short-term economic consequences such as loss and damage to property.
3. Midterm effects appear as loss in the stock markets and a flight of capital.
4. Long-term effects are apparent after some incidents and appear to be moderated by a complex set of interactions between:
   a. The perception of threat from a terror event
   b. The visibility of the event

SHORT- AND MIDTERM EFFECTS

Consider, once again, Table 6.1 that describes the cost from the 9/11 attacks. Now, in Table 6.3, we have classified each cost as short term, midterm, and long term.

From this event, we note various cost categories as:

1. Short term and midterm: $34 billion
2. Long term: $1,721 billion

The long-term cost was estimated in 2004 and has certainly grown since then. These long-term costs are the costs of providing security responses, building an infrastructure of protection, and establishing agencies such as Department of Homeland Security and others as preventive measures. Other costs such as the cost of insurance cover against terror attacks are so large that they are hard to estimate.

One of the immediate consequences of terror events is the loss of stock markets—after all, this is the one piece of news that flood radio waves immediately after any such event. It has also been noted that the recovery of the stock market

Table 6.3

Short and long term impacts of global terror events

Cost area	Cost	Cost horizon
Combatting terrorism	$53 billion by the United States	Long term
Insurance	a. 5% increase in premiums on property in the United States b. Higher increases overseas	Midterm
9/11	a. $34 billion+ uninsured losses b. $576 million for the Pentagon c. 2,973 deaths	Short term Long term
Travel and tourism	a. 279,000 jobs lost in the United States	Short term
Macroeconomic effects	a. Approx. $300 billion in lower growth in 2001 and 2002	Long term
Afghanistan	a. $50 billion+ for Department of Defense b. $3.3 billion for reconstruction c. $4.5 billion pledged for other countries	Long term
Iraq	a. $125 billion+ for Department of Defense b. $21 billion for reconstruction c. $13 billion pledged for other countries d. 1,058+ Americans killed	Long term
Shipping	a. 1–3% of shipment value increases for security costs	Long term

is rapid in some cases. In other cases, recovery can take longer, and in the case of 9/11, it takes extraordinary measures to stop the ripple effect of the capital market losses to not plunge the world economy into recession.

Does each event cause an effect on the stock market? The answer is yes. We show this by taking data from the GTD. The figures presented here show a series of events selectively chosen over a period 1984–2013. Please note that is a nonrepresentative sample, selected to simply explore if the stock market (S&P 500) reacts to events and the time period of recovery.

Now, to focus attention on specific time period, we created a panel of graphs for specific event dates. As an example, the first event we examine is September 9, 1984, which from Figure 6.1 was an unarmed assault in the state of Oregon. The bottom panel shows the reaction of the S&P 500 on the date of the event and the postevent recovery.

Similarly, now we show other events in Figures 6.2–6.10. The interpretation is the same—the top panel shows the pre-event window and the bottom panel shows the postevent changes in the S&P 500.

Figure 6.1
Cumulative return, 20 days preceding (top) and following (bottom) September 9, 1984,
unarmed assault

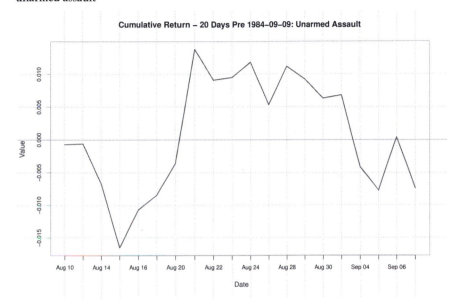

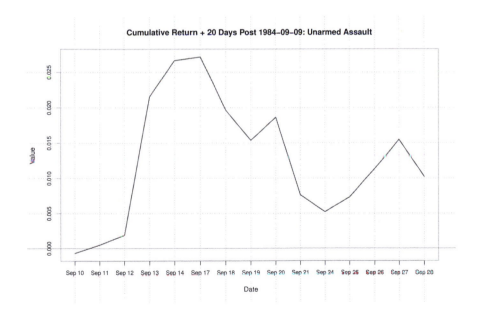

Figure 6.2
Cumulative return, 20 days preceding (top) and following (bottom) September 20, 1984, unarmed assault

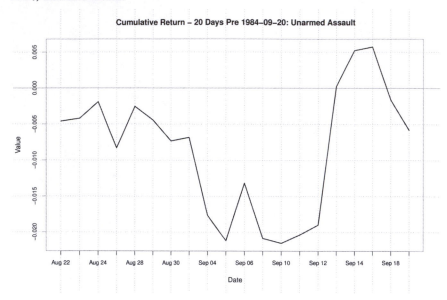

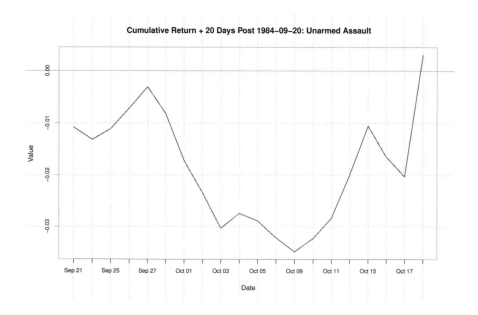

Figure 6.3
Cumulative return, 20 days preceding (top) and following (bottom) April 19, 1995, bombing/explosion

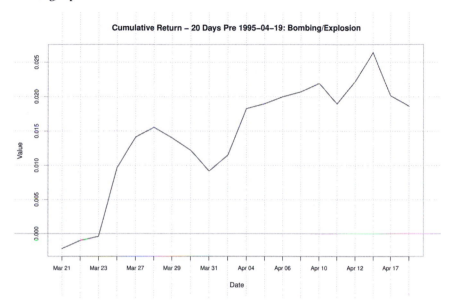

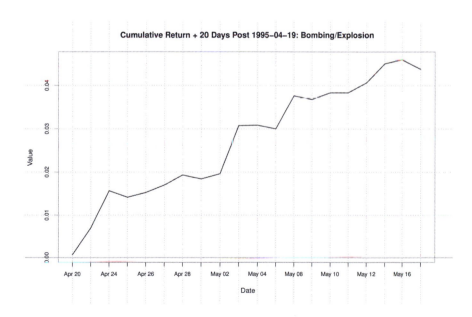

Figure 6.4
Cumulative return, 20 days preceding (top) and following (bottom) October 9, 1995, facility/infrastructure attack

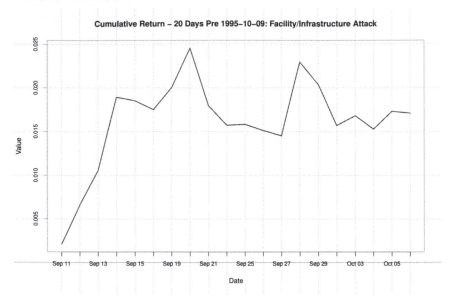

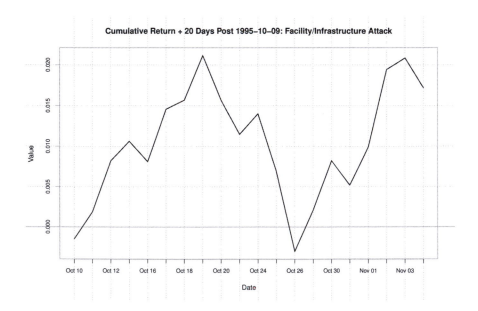

Figure 6.5
Cumulative return, 20 days preceding (top) and following (bottom) July 27, 1996,
bombing/explosion

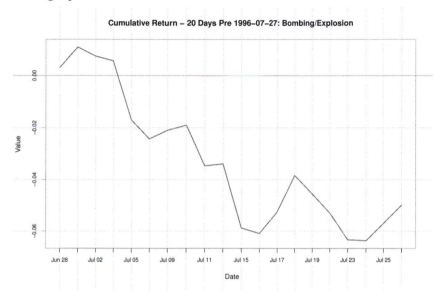

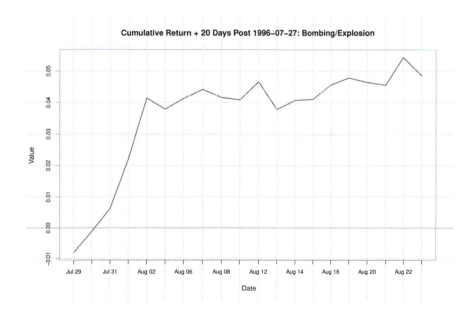

Figure 6.6
Cumulative return, 20 days preceding (top) and following (bottom) April 20, 1999, armed assault

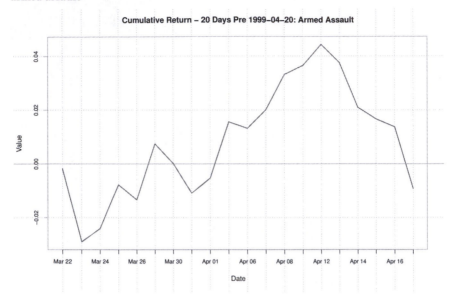

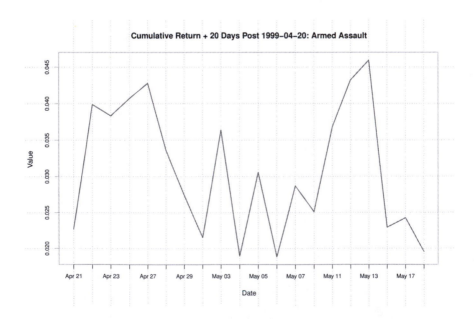

Figure 6.7

Cumulative return, 20 days preceding (top) and following (bottom) September 11, 2001, hijacking

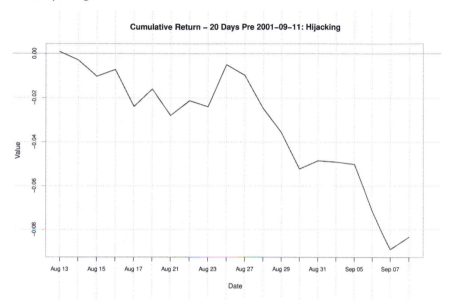

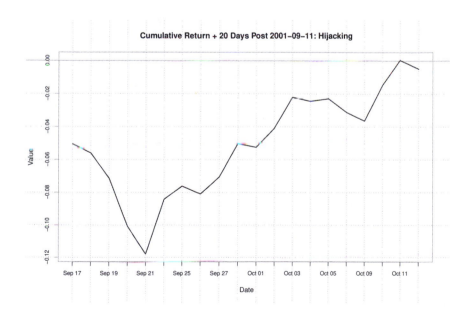

Figure 6.8
Cumulative return, 20 days preceding (top) and following (bottom) February 18, 2010, facility/infrastructure attack

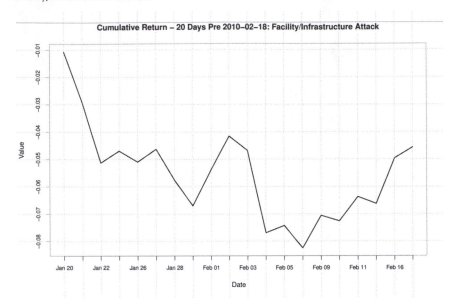

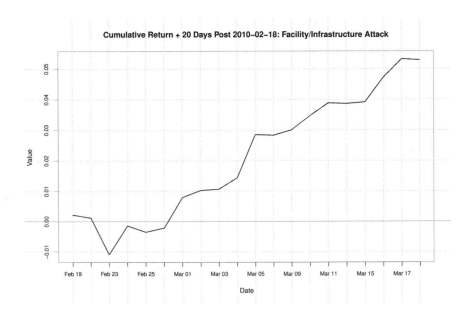

Figure 6.9
Cumulative return, 20 days preceding (top) and following (bottom) August 5, 2012, armed assault

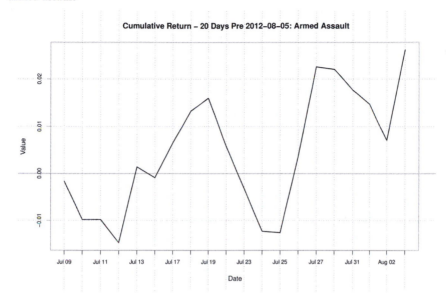

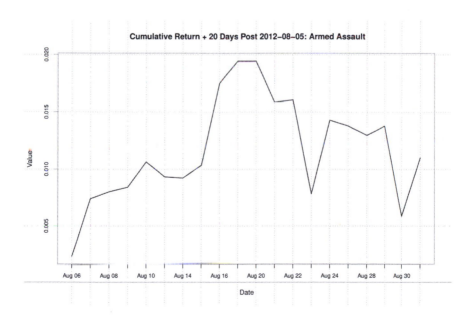

Figure 6.10

Cumulative return, 20 days preceding (top) and following (bottom) April 15, 2013, bombing/explosion

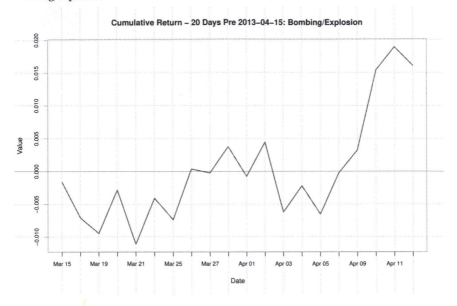

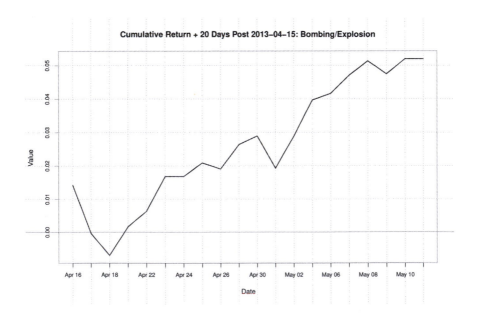

The reaction of the markets is swift and the loss is significant. But also, the recovery of the market is within the 20-day window. However, the loss should not be ignored—these are real losses and affect the economy of the nation. It is critical to note that these events are only those that occurred in the United States. We do not imply any extension of these results to other countries.

LONG-LASTING EFFECTS

Another topic we now discuss is the long-term impacts. One of the most noticeable items from what was described before is that some incidents like 9/11 have a very long-term effect on security investments such as airport security, domestic security, and investment in the fight against terror. Yet, not every incident has such associated costs. We ask ourselves, what distinguishes events that lead to a long-lasting economic impact from those that generally do not? It is not the immediate cost of the loss—the Oklahoma City bombing led to a lot of immediate losses, but did not have an associated long-term cost implication. The attack of 9/11 did. It could be that one was an event caused by a U.S. citizen and the others were masterminded by foreign nationals.

We encourage a thought process wherein each event can be modeled as controlled by two factors:

1. Threat perception
2. Visibility of the event

The threat perception in the case of 9/11 attacks was extremely high and so was visibility. In the case of the Oklahoma City bombing, the event could be classified as a high-visibility, but low-threat perception—a one-off incident that ended with the capture of the perpetrator.

In general, we conclude that the above phenomena observed in occurrence of terror events, including behavioral responses such as fear and the desire to invest in security measures, are not smooth and continuous changes nor are they step functions. They do not follow any path of continuous change, and do not meet the assumptions of simple step functions such as stationary and independence of path.

We ask if causes and consequences (in economic terms) can be modeled as a nonlinear process. In a nonlinear model, a sudden change in a behavior or criterion variable is not accompanied by abrupt or large changes in presumed causes. Such events are readily observable in society. For example, "a jury's perception of the evidence, the productivity of a manufacturing organization, an industrial accident or disease, urban renewal, fatigue, and overwork" are some examples of nonlinear change (Guastello, 1995).

One classical example of nonlinear behavior was presented by Zeeman (1976). According to Zeeman, two variables—anger and fear—cause an animal to fight or flee. Anger alone causes it to attack, and fear alone causes it to flee. However, when the influence of both anger and fear increases simultaneously, unpredictable behavior may result. A slight preponderance of one influence over the other may cause discontinuous behavior. Thus, no abrupt or large change is needed in either one of these causal variables or control factors for an abrupt change to occur in the dependent variable. When a threshold level of causal variables is reached, behavior readily changes from one state to another.

Similar examples of nonlinearity have been proposed in areas such as the behavior of large groups, economic theory, inflation and expectations, and politics.

We propose that terror process outcome as an economic response "to a variety of factors related to the delivery of a terror event" is also amenable to nonlinear modeling. This model construction suggests that the perception of threat from an event, the visibility of the event, and the economic outcome of the event show a nonlinear relationship.

We find evidence of a nonlinear model in our understanding of terror tactics and investment, and outcomes that make this process amenable to catastrophic modeling. According to Flay (1978), there are five properties common to all nonlinear phenomena:

1. The behavior of the phenomenon is bimodal for some values of the control factors.
2. Abrupt, catastrophic changes are observed between one state and another.
3. There is hysteresis; that is, the abrupt change from one mode to another takes place at different values of the control factors depending on the direction of change.
4. There is an inaccessible zone for some values of the control factors. The possibility of divergent behavior is implied.
5. When these properties are found in a phenomenon, a condition known as the singularity is present and a cusp catastrophe is implied.

We propose that global terror process exhibit the above five properties. Economic outcomes do not show a linear relationship with the visibility of the attack. The relationship, instead, is controlled by the degree of threat perception. At lower levels of threat perception, economic outcomes change linearly with visibility of the attack. However, at higher levels of threat perception, small changes in visibility can translate into catastrophic changes in economic outcomes.

The above relationship looks like Figure 6.11.

The cusp catastrophe occurs in systems whose behavior is dependent on two control factors. Its graph is three-dimensional with every point on the surface representing an equilibrium state. All points on the underside of the pleat are unstable, points along the fold line are semistable, and all other points are stable. For certain conditions of the two control factors, there are two possible stable states: one on the upper surface of the pleat and one on the lower.

Figure 6.11
Short and long term impacts of global terror events

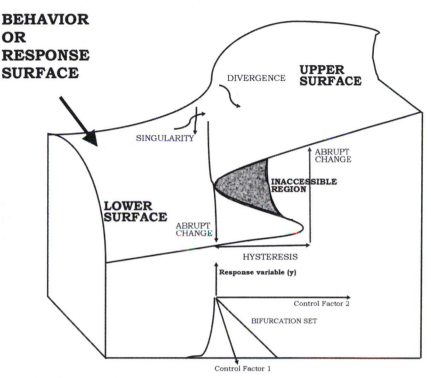

Source: Sethi, V., & King, R., "An Application of the Cusp Catastrophe Model to User Information Satisfaction," *Information & Management,* 34, (1998), pp. 41–53.

Consider two points at the far edge of the surface (near the axis of control factor 2). They represent systems with the same value of control factor 1, but slightly different values of control factor 2. If the value of control factor 1 increases, the points move forward toward the front of the surface, tracing parallel paths. If both paths are on one side of the pleat, the behavior of both systems is the same. If, however, one travels to the upper surface and the other to the bottom surface, the behavior of the two systems is *divergent.* Thus, two points start together, undergo the same transition, but at the end of the change are at very different stable states.

The figure also shows *discontinuous* change when a point moves from the left to the right of the surface. At the far edge of the surface a point can pass smoothly from left to right or vice versa. But if the point is at the front of the surface (high factor 1), a discontinuous jump will occur at the pleat. This is called *hysteresis* and is found to occur in many dynamic systems, from electrical circuits to manic-depressive psychoses.

Figure 6.12
Behavioral threat perception response

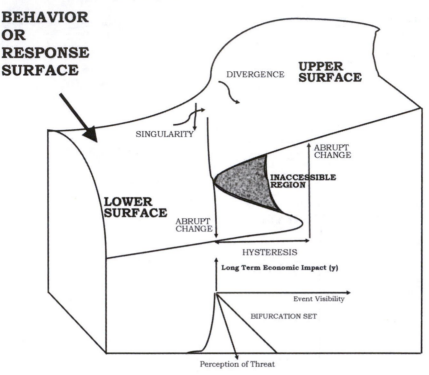

In the application of the model to the process and events of mass destruction, factor 1 is threat perception and factor 2 is incident visibility. Consider the Oklahoma City bombing—it had high visibility, but low threat perception. On the other hand, 9/11 attack had high visibility and high threat perception.

The model can then be shown as in Figure 6.12.

The model suggests that when as threat perception increases, visibility triggers a volatile, uncontrolled, and an abrupt change that can last for years. The extraordinary investments in security measures, agencies, and government efforts at surveillance speak to the incredible measures supported by society to defend itself from future attacks.

In addition, over time, threat perception falls, but the changes to conditions prior to the event never fall to prior levels. That is why, even after more than 10 years of the 9/11 attacks, investments in security measures are at an all-time high.

We term this as *terror hysteresis*—the unidimensional stress on economic conditions as an aftermath of incidents designed to create mass psychological destruction in society.

REFERENCES

Abadie, A., (2006). Poverty, Political Freedom, and the Roots of Terrorism. *The American Economic Review, 96*(2), 50–56.

Bureau of Labor Statistics. (2003). Reported in GAO Report, Recent Estimates of Fiscal Impact of 2001 Terrorist Attack on New York, March 2005, GAO-05-269.

Choi, S.-W., & Luo, S. (2013). Economic Sanctions, Poverty, and International Terrorism: An Empirical Analysis. *International Interactions, 39*(2), 217–245.

Cusson, M. (2005). *La delinquance: Une vie choisie.* Montreal: Hurtubise HMH.

Flay, B. R. (1978). Catastrophe Theory in Social Psychology: Some Applications to Attitudes and Social Behavior. *Behavioral Science, 23*, 335–350.

Freeman, M., & Ruehsen, M. (2013). Terrorism Financing Methods: An Overview. *Terrorism Research Initiative, 7*(4), 2–26.

Gold, D. (2004). *Economics of Terrorism.* New York: Columbia University Press.

Guastello, Chaos, Catastrophe & Human Affairs (1995). New Jersey: Lawrence Erlbaum Associates.

Krueger, A. B., & Malečková, J. (2003). Education, Poverty and Terrorism: Is There a Causal Connection? *The Journal of Economic Perspectives, 17*(4), 119–144.

Kiser, S. (2004). *Financing Terror: An Analysis and Simulation for Affecting Al Qaeda's Financial Infrastructure.* Santa Monica, CA: Pardee Rand Graduate School.

Lai, B. (2007). "Draining the Swamp": An Empirical Examination of the Production of International Terrorism, 1968–1998. *Conflict Management & Peace Science (Routledge), 24*(4), 297–310.

Levitt, S., & Venkatesh, S. (2000). An Economic Analysis of a Drug-Selling Gang's Finances. *Quarterly Journal of Economics, 115*, 755–789.

Library, T. F. (2014). *Oklahom Disaster: The Economic Impact.* Washington, D.C.: The Free Library.

Pare, P., & Felson, R. (2014). Income Inequality, Poverty and Crime Across Nations. *The British Journal of Sociology, 65*(3), 434–458.

Piazza, J. A. (2003). *Rooted in Poverty?: Terrorism, Poor Economic Development and Social Change.* Mimeo, Raleigh, North Carolina: Meredith College.

Smith, R. (2007). *The Utility of Force: The Art of War in the Modern World.* Deckle Edge.

Zeeman, E. C. (1976). A Catastrophe Theory. *Scientific American, 234*(4), 65–83.

7

Political and Religious Factors for Weapons of Mass Psychological Destruction

R. William Ayres

Although widely depicted in the media and public discourse as "crazy," "barbaric," and "incomprehensible," terrorism is in fact a rational strategy chosen by groups in conflict to achieve strategic and tactical ends. Because the ends which terrorist groups seek are often radical or far beyond the mainstream, we tend to paint terrorists with a broad and inaccurate brush as wide-eyed maniacs bent on the destruction of everything. In fact, the strategic goals and objectives of terrorist groups vary widely and tend to fall into recognizable categories. Terrorism is a set of tactics adopted by groups in conflict where those groups are at a substantial material disadvantage and seek to use the asymmetric advantages of terrorism to advance their cause. Because the goals and objectives of terrorist organizations are recognizable as a means toward their chosen ends, their behavior becomes analyzable. While we deplore the methods they choose (and often the ends that they seek) and therefore often do not want to "understand" terrorists, we can develop an understanding of the choices they make. One of the most important of these choices is the subject of this book: the decision to pursue the capacity to develop, acquire, and use weapons of mass psychological destruction (WMPDs). When we characterize all terrorists as being alike, we assume that every terrorist wants to get his hands on weapons of mass destruction (WMDs). But this turns out not to be the case—some groups choose to spend their limited resources attempting to acquire WMDs while others do not. Predicting the difference flows from an understanding of the political, psychological, and (sometimes) religious motivations of terrorist organizations themselves. This chapter lays out a typology of political goals and motives, examines which ones are well-suited for WMPDs, and examines the evidence we have about what factors drive terrorists' decisions to pursue WMDs. Lessons are drawn both for counterterrorism efforts and future research.

This chapter will provide the reader with an overview of the factors that provide motivation for terrorist groups to pursue, plan for, and potentially use

WMDs. As is detailed elsewhere in this volume, these weapons (chemical, bio-logical, radiological, nuclear, and explosive) can have significant effects far beyond the physical damage they cause. This section provides an overview of the political and religious motivations that drive terrorist organizations to pursue these particular capabilities, and examines what evidence is available to support hypotheses regarding various motivational factors among terrorist groups.

TERRORISM AS ASYMMETRIC WARFARE

Terrorism has many definitions in the literature, but most focus on the use of specific kinds of force against specific kinds of targets to gain leverage far in excess of the resources expended. For example, Hoffman (2012) constructs the following definition after an extensive overview of the literature on terrorism:

> Terrorism is "the deliberate creation and exploitation of fear through violence or the threat of violence in the pursuit of political change. All terrorist acts involve violence or the threat of violence. Terrorism is specifically designed to have far-reaching psychological effects beyond the immediate victim(s) or object of the terrorist attack. It is meant to instill fear within, and thereby intimidate, a wider 'target audience' that might include a rival ethnic or religious group, an entire country, a national government or political party, or public opinion in general. Terrorism is designed to create power where there is none or to consolidate power where there is very little. Through the publicity generated by their violence, terro-rists seek to obtain the leverage, influence, and power they otherwise lack to effect political change on either a local or an international scale." (Hoffman, 2012, p. 33)

Terrorism, in the view of most scholars, is a tool of *asymmetric warfare*—that is, it is a tool used by groups to achieve ends in conflict when those groups lack the means to win in more conventional ways (Crenshaw, 1998). In this way it is sometimes referred to as the "weapon of the weak," although this is something if a misnomer given that terrorism can have extremely powerful effects and is sometimes effective at achieving the goals of the groups that employ it. This is perhaps best illustrated by a quote from a 1957 novel, used as prologue for Richard Betts's 2002 article "The Soft Underbelly of American Primacy":

> In given conditions, action and reaction can be ridiculously out of proportion. . . . One can obtain results monstrously in excess of the effort. . . . Let's consider this auto smash-up. . . . The driver lost control at high speed while swiping at a wasp which had flown in through a window and was buzzing around his face. . . . The weight of the wasp is under half an ounce. Compared with a human being, the wasp's size is minute, its strength negligible. Its sole armament is a tiny syringe holding a drop of irritant, formic acid. . . . Nevertheless, that wasp killed four big men and converted a large, powerful car into a heap of scrap. (Russell, 1957)

The strategic advantage of terrorism is therefore precisely in the overreaction it causes—an overreaction driven by fear. The effectiveness of terrorism in general lies not in the level of destruction terrorists can cause, but in the response of their target audience. Terrorism is ultimately about *psychology*—getting the opponents to change their behavior by changing the way they think, rather than by physical force. What matters is not so much *how much* damage is caused but *how, under what circumstances*, and *to whom*.

WMDs—chemicals, bioweapons, radiological weapons, and the like—are potentially effective terrorist tools precisely because of this "fear factor." They combine two elements ideal for generating fear in a target population or audience: lethality (often of a particularly horrible kind) coupled with the threat of undetectability, such that lethal and fearsome agents can strike anyone at any time, in any place. Two of the most notable attacks of the last 20 years, the Anthrax mailings of 2001 and the sarin gas attack on the Tokyo subway in 1995, both fit this profile—lethal agents deployed in ordinary, everyday places.

The question, then, is this: why do organizations seeking (often radical) political change turn to WMDs as their tools? What leads some groups to do so, while others stick to more conventional methods? This chapter will explore these questions through a variety of channels. The next section will examine the logic of terrorism as a rational goal-seeking strategy, and discuss which kinds of goals can be fruitfully pursued with WMD capabilities and which cannot. The following section will then examine existing empirical evidence about terrorist organizations and their pursuit and use of WMDs to see what is currently known about the factors that drive this behavior. The chapter will then conclude with the policy implications of these findings as well as pointing to important directions for needed additional research.

TERRORISM AS A RATIONAL STRATEGY

Terrorists are often seen, especially in the more developed countries of the West, as "crazy," "sociopathic," or "irrational." And while it may be true that individual terrorists suffer from diagnosable mental illnesses, such observations are largely irrelevant when discussing terrorist *organizations*. The tendency to label terrorism as "crazy," and indeed the stigma attached to the term itself, stems largely from our psychological need to distance ourselves from those with whom we have strong disagreements, or whom we are afraid of (e.g., Heider, 1958; Stein, 1996). There is also an element of cognitive distance; since we do not understand the goals, motives, and worldviews of those driven to what seem to us horrific acts of violence, we can turn to emotional explanations as a means of trying to understand what otherwise appears unexplainable (e.g., Fanon, 1963).

In fact, terrorist organizations—like nearly all organizations—are founded and driven by the pursuit of goals. As one of the seminal articles in the field put it over three decades ago, "Campaigns of terrorism depend on rational political choice. As a purposeful activity, terrorism is the result of an organization's decision that it is a politically useful means to oppose a government. . . . Terrorism is seen collectively as a logical means to advance desired ends" (Crenshaw, 1981). As goal-directed behavior, therefore, terrorism is indeed rational in that terrorists will choose means that they think (correctly or otherwise) are likely to help them achieve their goals. Because terrorism relies for its effectiveness on the reactions engendered in the target population or government, it tends to be adopted only in particular kinds of conflicts—those in which the organization seeking change has much less structural power than the government or society it is trying to influence (Habeeb, 1988; Hoffman, 2012). Change-seeking organizations that possess the power to create the change they seek, or to win by more conventional means, usually choose to do so. The Chechen independence movement, for example, fought an almost entirely conventional war in its first phase from 1991 through 1996, largely because they were winning. It was only after Russian power returned in much greater force in 1999 and afterward that terrorism became a staple tactic in that campaign (Ayres, 2001).

Given that terrorism is a rational strategy, what goals do terrorist organizations seek? The particulars of these goals are as varied as the groups themselves, and need not concern us here—there is a broad variety of political outcomes that these organizations seek. Whatever the desired end state, however, there are a limited number of tactical objectives that groups seek when they choose to adopt methods of terrorist violence. These objectives fall into definable categories:

Forcing Change

This is "classic warfare" thinking—von Clauswitz's famous "politics by other means." To use terrorism to alter behavior, groups focus their attacks on tactical targets—the Marine base in Lebanon in 1983, for example. In that case, the goal was to force a U.S. withdrawal by doing damage to that government's resources and causing it to rethink its willingness to be involved in the Lebanese war. In the United States, Terry Nichols and Timothy McVeigh attacked a government target because they hoped, in a broad general sense, to alter the direction of the government and change its behavior. In Latin America, drug cartels often use terrorist attacks against law enforcement and judicial targets to encourage other police and law officials to rethink their choices and change their behavior. In all of these cases, the audience for the attack is not the general population, but the key decision makers within the government who control the choices the terrorists seek to affect.

Getting Attention or Getting to the Table

Terrorists may attack a variety of targets to get noticed, to prove they have power that cannot be ignored. If an organization feels that it has been excluded from a political process which it would like access to, or that its point of view is being ignored, it may decide that terrorist violence provides a cost-effective way of getting the desired attention and respect. Its aim may be to get included in the political process or to get a seat at the negotiating table if there is an ongoing dialogue about how to end a conflict. This is a variation of "forcing change"—groups are trying to, in essence, "muscle in" on an arena where they have been ignored. Their ultimate goal is to use that political process to bring about the change they seek; terrorism is simply a way to gain access to that process. Much of the history of the Palestine Liberation Organization and related groups, especially during the 1970s, falls into this category, including the Munich Olympics attack in 1972 and various Popular Front for the Liberation of Palestine hijackings in the 1970s.

Playing Spoiler

Sometimes terrorists do not want to join the political process; they want to put a stop to it. This is especially true if there are peace negotiations ongoing that some factions do not like. Terrorist organizations can become convinced that the ongoing peace process is going to yield a bad outcome, that those negotiating on their side's behalf are "sellouts," or that a negotiated peace with their enemies is not possible. Terrorist violence, particularly of an emotionally symbolic nature, can be seen a way of inflaming passions and getting one or both sides to back away from the negotiating table by making further negotiation politically untenable (Stedman, 1997). Examples are the formation of the Real IRA in 1997 and Baruch Goldstein's Cave of the Patriarchs massacre in 1994.

Mobilizing a Domestic Political Audience

Sometimes the terrorism is not aimed so much at the other side of the conflict as it is at the terrorists' own constituents. This is most likely where there are multiple factions vying for power and influence over a population in conflict (Cunningham, Bakke, & Seymour, 2012), which is particularly likely in cases where the underlying conflict is ethnic in nature (Byman, 1998). In this case, factions can seek to "outbid" each other by being the one that can cause the most damage to the enemy. This dynamic permeated the competition among groups for leadership of the Palestinian liberation movement in the 1970s, with some groups trying to outflank others by carrying out progressively more extreme attacks. This approach is mostly likely in cases where the population is actively supportive of violence against the enemy; in some cases (Northern Ireland in

the 1990s being one example), this can backfire if the population is not supportive of attacks that may injure or kill civilians and noncombatants.

Provoking Overreaction

As was discussed above, the most effective means for a terrorist organization
to create change is by using asymmetric terrorist violence against civilians to
provoke a costly overreaction by the other side. Terrorists are, by definition,
weaker than their opponents; one path to victory lies in getting the enemy to
expend far more of its resources than the terrorist does, thereby wearing the
enemy down and sapping his will (and potential ability) to fight. This can also
take place where the conflict is being watched by outsiders and the "moral high
ground" is a strategic place to hold. The Provisional IRA's "long war" strategy
in the 1970s and 1980s fits this profile; in it the organization sought to engage
in a war of attrition with the British and to make the six northern counties
"ungovernable" except by direct military rule—an extremely costly enterprise
for the British government. Irgun's campaign of terrorist violence directed
against the British in mandate Palestine in the 1940s was another example
(Hoffman, 2015). A variant of this can include "false flag" attacks to discredit
the other side or to provoke intervention by outside parties, as happened during
the Yugoslav wars in the early 1990s.

Retribution

Sometimes terrorist acts are undertaken as a retributive response to perceived
wrongs committed by others. We think of this kind of "eye for an eye" logic as
irrational, emotional, or even barbaric. But there are a number of cultures in
which answering violence with violence is an obligation, such that these attacks
are seen as necessary. There is also a strategic component to such thinking: in
the face of an ongoing conflict, a response to a successful strike by the enemy
may be seen as essential lest inaction lead to a perception of weakness, either
by the enemy or among one's own constituency. Many attacks by Hezbollah or
Hamas against Israel have had this as their claimed justification. Unlike the
goals listed above, this category appears less "rational" in that the violence and
damage caused is itself the desired outcome, rather than the means to a political
end. As such, retribution tends to be the only goal of individual incidents, rather
than the motivation behind extended campaigns of terrorist violence. Such
attacks also tend to have shorter planning time frames, in that they are often
responsive to specific antecedent events.

While this list is not exhaustive, it covers in broad strokes the kinds of tactical
and strategic logic behind the adoption of terrorist violence. Given that terrorism is goal-directed behavior, any attempt to acquire or use WMDs should fit

into that mold. A decision to seek and deploy WMD capability is a tactical decision for a terrorist organization, one likely undertaken at some significant cost relative to other more conventional alternatives. Such weapons are not well suited to all ends, but may be particularly well suited to some. It therefore makes sense to examine the possible logic under which a terrorist group would want to acquire and possibly use such technologies in light of the goals outlined above.

WMDS AND THEIR STRATEGIC USES

Nuclear, chemical, biological, radiological, and high explosive weapons are more suited to some of the strategic objectives listed above than others. The defining characteristics of these weapons are two: first, their tendency to cause widespread casualties among innocent civilian populations, and second (and derivative), their tendency to instill fear and terror in those same populations. That fear may indirectly affect political elites and decision makers, who can often insulate themselves personally from such attacks, but who may be subject to intense political pressures by frightened populations. Matching these general characteristics to the goals discussed in the previous section yields both matches and mismatches.

WMDs are not especially useful for terrorist groups trying to directly *force or influence a change in behavior*. Forcing change through terrorism usually relies on attacks directed at or near the elites themselves. The indiscriminate nature of WMDs makes them difficult to use in targeting the right audience, while the tendency to cause "collateral damage" can often have unintended effects. The Oklahoma City bombing of 1995 was ostensibly directed at a government target, but it ended up killing a large number of children in the area—an effect that strengthened the government rather than weakening it. The caveat to this is that terrorist groups that are seeking *massive and radical* political change may see large-scale destruction as the only way to accomplish their goal. The lure of WMDs in this case may lie on their psychological effects on their would-be users: those that seek to "remake the world" may be drawn in by the taboo and "unthinkable" nature of these weapons into thinking that they are the ideal tools for effecting drastic changes to the political and social order. This logic underlies the widespread suspicion that organizations with fanatical and apocalyptic ideologies—for example, Japan's Aum Shinrikyo movement—may be more likely to seek such capabilities.

Likewise, WMD attacks are not very useful for *getting to the table* of a political process. The use of such weapons is widely seen as politically and morally anathema, such that any group that engages in such use essentially cuts itself off from any kind of future political dialogue. Participation in political processes relies on a sense of *legitimacy*—participants must see each other as legitimate players representing real interests that should be listened to. Actually deploying a WMD device largely destroys that legitimacy, rendering this goal out of reach. An exception here might occur for a group seeking to *acquire*, but not *use* a WMD capability—in that case, possession of the capacity might be seen as a sign of power that would get the group notice and respect. While this logic applies well to nation-states (this motive may apply in part to WMD programs in Iran, Israel, South Africa, North Korea, and others), it may not work as well for nonstate terrorist organizations, as the prevailing assumption is that a terrorist organization would only seek such a capability if it intends to use it.

WMDs could be very effective weapons for groups seeking to put a stop to political negotiations by *playing spoiler*. Since negotiations are often derailed by violence directed at highly sensitive and symbolic targets, successful deployment of a WMD device could convince one side in a peace process that "the other side cannot be trusted" to follow through with any deal. Although he did not use a WMD, this may have been Baruch Goldstein's goal in opening fire on Muslim worshippers in early 1994—an act that did spur widespread unrest and temporarily halted the ongoing process of implementing the Oslo Accords. An attack with a chemical, biological, or radiological agent, particularly one with large numbers of casualties, would make further peace negotiations extremely difficult if committed in the name of one side of a conflict against the other because of the taboo nature of such weapons.

WMDs are useful for *mobilizing a domestic political audience* only under certain circumstances. The constituency that the terrorist group is trying to win favor from must value violence and the widespread killing of civilians on the other side of the conflict—a condition that is rarer than it might seem. While "outbidding" is a common political dynamic, terrorist organizations do not often find themselves in a situation in which such outbidding works because, at some point, the level of violence is too horrific to garner much support. Moreover, outbidding usually takes place in the context of competition among rival factions for power—competition that is likely to occupy some of the group's resources, which makes it more difficult to develop WMD capabilities in the first place, especially in secret from other factions. By this logic, terrorist organizations engaged in political struggles for dominance and leadership within a broader movement are unlikely to see WMD development as a key priority.

WMD deployment and use are an unparalleled way of *provoking an overreaction* on the part of a targeted population or government. In this case, the moral and cultural taboos against WMD use and the killing of large numbers of innocent civilians work in the terrorists' strategic favor by ensuring that responses are likely to be massive and swift, rather than measured and carefully thought out. However, unlike the PIRA and Irgun strategies of making territories "ungovernable" and ensuring that opposing powers spent massive resources trying to pacify a large area (with predictable consequences in terms of further alienating the local population), WMD deployment is likely to provide a counterstrike and/or search-and-destroy response as targeted governments attempt to hunt down and destroy the group in question as quickly as possible. While this might well lead to a lot of collateral damage along the way if the organization is embedded within a civilian population, the near-term effect may be more loss than gain. Certainly the U.S. response to 9/11—a wholesale invasion of Afghanistan—did not help the Al Qaeda cause very much despite its success in getting the United States to expend vastly more resources than Al Qaeda had. In essence, WMD deployment is a very good way to pick a fight with someone. If that fight is what a terrorist organization is looking for, then WMDs become a very rational strategic option (as might be true, for example, of the Daesh/ISIS movement in Iraq and Syria—see Wood, 2015).

Finally, WMD use would seem to be an excellent option for motives of *retribution*. After all, if the objective of an attack is to "strike back" against a foe as "payback" for some previous injury or injustice, what better way than to cause as much damage as possible? However, while this logic makes sense in terms of motive, it leaves out the operational challenges of developing and deploying WMDs. It takes organizations years to develop and carefully stockpile these kinds of capabilities, and operations for deploying them are much more complex and more difficult than many conventional terrorist plans that can be developed and executed much more quickly (Asal, Ackerman, & Rethemeyer, 2012). Because most retribution-oriented attacks are reactionary in nature, it is unlikely that an organization would take the time and effort to develop and deploy these capabilities in pursue of this goal—the lag time is simply too long to send an effective message in response to a perceived wrong or an attack by one's enemy. Only under very special circumstances, therefore—in which the organization had already developed and stockpiled a WMD capability *and* had plans for using that capability already "on the shelf"—could a terrorist group engage in a retaliatory attack with WMDs. As this confluence of circumstances is rare, it is unlikely that these kinds of attacks will occur, although a prolonged sense of grievance may lead organizations to seek WMD capabilities for the future.

The punch line here is that knowing what kinds of goals and strategies a given terrorist organization is pursuing can tell us a lot about the likelihood of an organization pursuing and deploying WMD capabilities. It is unreasonable to assume that all terrorists will pursue WMDs simply because they are terrorists—such a broad-brush approach obscures important differences among organizations that can give us clues to where and when to expect attempts at WMD development and use. Important in any threat analysis, therefore, is a careful political and strategic analysis of the conflict in question and the goals and strategies of the groups involved. Such an analysis, while not 100 percent definitive, can yield important insights into how likely attempts at WMD development and deployment are by any given organization.

ENEMIES AND DEMONS—THE POLITICAL AND RELIGIOUS PSYCHOLOGY OF CONFLICT

As discussed above, terrorism involves the creation and exploitation of fear through the threat and deployment of violence. While this violence is sometimes targeted at specific individuals who are not "innocent bystanders" in a conflict (e.g., the targeting of police officials in Mexico by drug cartels, or of organizational and local leaders in Northern Ireland by offshoots of the IRA), frequently the victims of terrorism are noncombatants who do not have a direct role in the conflict. Violence directed against civilians is an effective means of threatening a much wider population of civilians—a task for which WMDs, which tend to be widespread and indiscriminate in their effects, are almost uniquely suited.

To direct violence and terror against a civilian population, however, requires a particular kind of psychological justification. Nearly every culture in the history of human civilization has included a social norm against the indiscriminate use of violence against innocents, even if this norm is widely violated in practice. In the twentieth century, the rise of a global discourse about universal human rights raised the visibility of these kinds of norms and took them around the world. To deliberately violate social rules of this kind requires a countervailing psychological justification of greater strength than the rule. As Fritz Heider pointed out decades ago, good people do not do bad things without reasons for thinking that they are not really bad things—we cannot live with ourselves otherwise (Heider, 1958). Consequently, terrorists who plan and execute widespread attacks on civilian populations need to have significant justifications (in their own minds) for doing so.

Of course, conflict tends to create grounds for such justifications. Political conflict generates stereotyped images of one's enemies as a matter of course, as the motivations of fear and greed strengthen our tendencies to bias our judgments about people outside our own social groups (Ayres, 1997; Herrmann & Fischerkeller, 1995; Stein, 1996). These images vary in intensity and therefore in the kinds of behaviors which they can serve to justify (Cottam, 1977; McCauley & Moskalenko, 2008). Given both the global taboos against WMD use in general and the deeply ingrained social norms against the slaughter of innocents, such images would need to be particularly intense to justify the deployment of CBRN weapons.

This has led scholars in the field of terrorism studies to posit that certain kinds of ideologies or worldviews make it more likely that a terrorist organization will seek to acquire and use CBRN weapons. Jonathan Tucker (2000), for example, engaged in a comparative analysis of a dozen cases of terrorist organizations seeking WMD capabilities to arrive at a list of attributes that made such behavior more likely. These included an apocalyptic ideology, paranoia with a concomitant sense of grandiosity, and a belief that the group has "nothing left to lose" (see also Campbell, 2000). Among scholars of conflict, these sorts of beliefs are most often attributed to organizations seeking radical social and political change, and to groups motivated by a religious or theological set of ideas. This latter hypothesis stems from the belief that divinely ordained goals are more likely to override other human social norms (Hoffman, 1993; Ranstorp, 1996; Snowden, 2003) as well as research that indicates that religiously motivated terrorist organizations are more likely to commit extravagant forms of violence (Asal & Rethemeyer, 2008) and are associated with higher fatality rates in their attacks (Cameron & Bajema, 2012). It has also been suggested that terrorist groups based on religion may be drawn to WMDs because of perceived parallels to apocalyptic stories about plagues and other sorts of divine punishments (Stern, 2000). Given this, it seems likely that the underlying ideology and motivational makeup of a terrorist organization should play a role in its likelihood of seeking to acquire and deploy CBRN weapons.

Subsequent empirical research, however, has so far failed to find evidence that religiously motivated terrorist organizations are more likely to pursue WMD capability than nonreligious ones. In one of the few rigorous large-N studies to date, Asal et al. (2012) examined a database of nearly 400 terrorist organizations that conducted at least one attack between 1998 and 2005. Data included information about whether the organizations had sought or deployed CBRN capabilities during that time period, as well as a host of other motivational, ideological, and situational factors. Many of their results confirm commonsense expectations: larger organizations are more likely to pursue CBRN weapons, as are those with more experience in conducting terrorist operations. Interestingly, state support is *not* a predictor of whether groups will chase WMDs, suggesting that the logic of deterrence among sovereign governments holds: states, being fixed targets that have a permanent presence on the world stage, are "leery of assisting or encouraging their terrorist proxies in any CBRN endeavors, viewing such a proposition as far too risky and destabilizing" (Asal et al., 2012, p. 243).

The most significant findings of the study, however, were twofold. First, the authors found that terrorist organizations that are more densely networked with other like-minded terrorist groups are more likely to pursue WMDs. This confirms what many scholars of terrorism have long suggested: networks among terrorist organizations matter as a primary means for them to get information, equipment, and materials for various kinds of operations. Isolated groups are therefore less likely to pursue WMDs. Even more surprising, however, the authors found no correlation at all between religious ideology and the tendency to pursue or not pursue WMDs. This is true whether the analysis was conducted on groups that simply have a "religious component" to their ideology or more narrowly focused on those that are exclusively religious in their orientation.

Why this lack of a correlation between religious motivation and WMD pursuit? The authors suggest that other factors in their model (like being embedded in networks of terrorist organizations) may be better explainers. It is also the case that religiously motivated groups tend to cluster geographically in places that have good access to the global economy—another important enabling factor for groups that are trying to pursue high-technology capabilities. But perhaps most importantly, the authors acknowledge that the data they use do not include "the specific nature of the religious beliefs" and "the extent to which broader political concerns enter an organization's calculus" (Asal et al., 2012, p. 246). In other words the fact that the group is based on a religious ideology itself tells you relatively little about its real-world goals, which can range from the mundane and political (the Muslim Brotherhood's long-running campaign to capture control of the government of Egypt) to the apocalyptic (Aum Shinrikyo's visions of the end of the world). Interpretations of religion are as varied as the political goals that terrorist groups pursue, such that "religious" is no more helpful of a label than "nationalist" in telling us what a given group wants (Saideman & Ayres, 2008). Other empirical research has demonstrated that there is variation in the lethality of terrorist attacks committed by Islamist terrorist groups that can be explained with reference to their strategic aims rather than their theological orientation (Piazza, 2009). This leads back to the conclusion of the first section of this chapter: understanding *what* a terrorist organization is trying to accomplish is at least as important as understanding *why*.

This, of course, is difficult and tricky work that must be done on a case-by-case basis. The usefulness of large-N statistical studies is to demonstrate where there might be patterns in the world—to show where certain outcomes (like the pursuit of WMDs) are more or less likely. But the importance of psychological justifications does not lend itself well to these kinds of broad-brush approaches. The psychology of a given conflict and the goals and justifying worldviews that a given organization adopts are critical to understanding its likelihood of adopting or pursuing CBRN weapons but do not fit well into large-N datasets. Moreover, ideas, ideologies, and theological interpretations can change over time, sometimes fairly quickly, which can lead to shifts in behavior (Blaydes & Rubin, 2008). Measuring and analyzing worldviews and goals is challenging and painstaking but necessary work if we want to be able to pinpoint where CBRN use by terrorists is more likely in the world.

LESSONS FOR COUNTERTERRORISM AND IMPLICATIONS FOR TERRORISM RESEARCH

Efforts to combat terrorism take place at a range of different levels, from the tactical and reactive to the strategic and preventative. All of these efforts are important, particularly in the face of possible CBRN terrorism that has the potential to cause widespread destruction and panic. Tactical counterterrorism seeks to prevent or blunt attacks by groups already committed to carrying them out. Such efforts are largely a function of intelligence—the more that is known about terrorist organizations, the more effective tactical countermeasures can be. Indeed, such intelligence is critical precisely because terrorism leverages on the asymmetry of resources to its advantage: by remaining small and difficult to detect, terrorist organizations can cause governments to expend vast amounts of time and money in an effort simply to locate or get information on them.

At the other end of the spectrum, strategic terrorism prevention efforts often focus on "draining the swamp"—that is, taking away the underlying conditions that breed terrorist organizations and/or that enable these organizations to recruit new people into their ranks. These kinds of efforts are focused more on resolving underlying conflicts or addressing the deeper issues that lead to disaffection and radicalization. Such efforts require a careful analysis of the underlying causes of conflict that lead to radicalization, and often lead to long-term efforts that take time to bear fruit.

Efforts at both of these levels are informed by a deep understanding of the political goals and justifying worldviews of terrorist organizations. There are hundreds, if not thousands, of terrorist organizations worldwide capable of conducting some level of violence. Being able to focus tactical counterterrorism resources on those most likely to seek to acquire and use CBRN weapons is critical to blunting the threat of terrorist-deployed WMDs. Doing so, however, requires a careful, detailed analysis of the organizations' goals and worldviews as well as their networked connections to each other (Asal et al., 2012). Likewise, any effort at "draining the swamp" to take away the conditions that breed certain kinds of terrorists requires an in-depth understanding of what those conditions are. Such efforts are unlikely to succeed across the board, because radicalization can and does occur across the political spectrum. A recent study by the Canadian Service Intelligence Service revealed that "lone wolf" terrorist attacks by individuals were slightly more likely to come from far-right white supremacists than from Islamic extremists (Boutilier, 2015).

This work is of course hampered by the difficulty of gathering reliable information about terrorist attacks and the organizations that carry them out. Most databases of terrorist events have large categories of attacks coded as "no clear motivation" or "unclaimed" (Asal et al., 2012; Boutilier, 2015). Terrorists often do not claim credit for their actions, either to avoid reprisal or because the message is intended only for a specific audience and not for the wider world. Governments with extensive intelligence apparatuses have difficulty sorting out the information because of the asymmetries involved—too many potential sources of information and too many possible "suspects," but not enough resources to track them all down.

This makes academic research into terrorism even more challenging but no less important. Scholars have access to even less reliable information than governments do. On the other hand, because academic organizations are not hampered by the need to focus on day-to-day tactical counterterrorism, they have the freedom to gather data carefully, as the Memorial Institute for the Prevention of Terrorism, the National Consortium for the Study of Terrorism and Responses to Terrorism, and the Monterey Institute for International Studies have done. These data can be mined for patterns, and individual cases can be followed up for more in-depth analyses into organizations' motivations, justifications, and goals.

Ultimately a given terrorist organization's decision to pursue and deploy CBRN weapons is a rational one, taken in pursuit of that group's goals and objectives. Knowing those goals and the justifications underlying them are key to understanding when terrorists are likely to make that decision. WMD terrorism represents perhaps the greatest danger in merging politics, psychology, and technology. In our efforts to combat this threat, we must make sure we have a thorough understanding of all of these.

REFERENCES

Asal, V., Ackerman, G., & Rethemeyer, R. K. (2012). Connections Can Be Toxic: Terrorist Organizational Factors and the Pursuit of CBRN Weapons. *Studies in Conflict & Terrorism*, 35(3), 229–254.

Asal, V., & Rethemeyer, R. K. (2008). The Nature of the Beast: Organizational Structures and the Lethality of Terrorist Attacks. *Journal of Politics*, 70(2), 437–449.

Ayres, R. W. (1997). Mediating International Conflicts: Is Image Change Necessary? *Journal of Peace Research*, 34(4), 431–447.

Ayres, R. W. (2001). Chechnya and Russia: A War of Secession. In M. O'Meara (Ed.), *History Behind the Headlines: The Origin of Conflicts Worldwide*. Farmington Hills, MI: Gale Group.

Betts, R. (2002). The Soft Underbelly of American Primacy: Tactical Advantages of Terror. *Political Science Quarterly*, 117(1), 19–36.

Blaydes, L., & Rubin, L. (2008). Ideological Reorientation and Counterterrorism: Confronting Militant Islam in Egypt. *Terrorism and Political Violence*, 20(4), 461–479.

Boutilier, A. (2015). CSIS Highlights White Supremacist Threat Ahead of Radical Islam. *Toronto Star*. March 15. http://www.thestar.com/news/canada/2015/03/15/csis -highlights-white-supremacist-threat-ahead-of-radical-islam.html

Byman, D. (1998). The Logic of Ethnic Terrorism. *Studies in Conflict & Terrorism*, 21(2), 149–169.

Cameron, G., & Bajema, M. (2012). Assessing the Post-9/11 Threat of CBRN Terrorism: A Threat of Mass Destruction or Mass Disruption? In R. Howard, & B. Hoffman (Eds.), *Terrorism and Counterterrorism: Understanding the New Security Environment*. New York: McGraw-Hill, pp. 266–87.

Campbell, J. (2000). On Not Understanding the Problem. In B. Roberts (Ed.), *Hype or Reality? The "New Terrorism" and Mass Casualty Attacks*. Alexandria, VA: Chemical and Biological Arms Control Institute, pp. 17–45.

Cottam, R. (1977). *Foreign Policy Motivation: A General Theory and a Case Study*. Pittsburgh, PA: University of Pittsburgh Press.

Crenshaw, M. (1981). The Causes of Terrorism. *Comparative Politics*, *13*(4), 379–399.

Crenshaw, M. (1998). The Logic of Terrorism: Terrorist Behavior as a Product of Strategic Choice. In W. Reich (Ed.), *Origins of Terrorism: Psychologies, Ideologies, Theologies, States of Mind*. Washington, DC: Woodrow Wilson Center Press, pp. 54–64.

Cunningham, K., Bakke, K., & Seymour, L. (2012). Shirts Today, Skins Tomorrow: Dual Contests and the Effects of Fragmentation in Self-Determination Disputes. *Journal of Conflict Resolution*, *56*(1), 67–93.

Fanon, F. (1963). *The Wretched of the Earth*. New York: Grove Press.

Habeeb, W. M. (1988). *Power and Tactics in International Negotiation: How Weak Nations Bargain with Strong Nations*. Baltimore, MD: Johns Hopkins University Press.

Heider, F. (1958). *The Psychology of Interpersonal Relations*. New York: Wiley.

Herrmann, R., & Fischerkeller, M. (1995). Beyond the Enemy Image and the Spiral Model: Cognitive-Strategic Research after the Cold War. *International Organization*, *39*(3), 415–450.

Hoffman, B. (1993). Holy Terror: The Implications of Terrorism Motivated by a Religious Perspective. *RAND Paper*. Santa Monica, CA: RAND.

Hoffman, B. (2012). Defining Terrorism: Means, Ends, and Motives. Chapter 1in R. Howard, & B. Hoffman (Eds.), *Terrorism and Counterterrorism: Understanding the New Security Environment* (4th ed.). New York: McGraw-Hill.

Hoffman, B. (2015). Why Terrorism Works. *The Chronicle of Higher Education*. March 2.

McCauley, C., & Moskalenko, S. (2008). Mechanisms of Political Radicalization: Pathways toward Terrorism. *Terrorism and Political Violence*, *20*(3), 415–433.

Piazza, J. (2009). Is Islamist Terrorist More Dangerous? An Empirical Study of Group Ideology, Organization, and Goal Structure. *Terrorism and Political Violence*, *21*(1), 62–88.

Ranstorp, M. (1996). Terrorism in the Name of Religion. *Journal of International Affairs*, *50*(1), 41–63.

Russell, E. F. (1957). *Wasp*. London: Gollancz.

Saideman, S., & Ayres, R. W. (2008). *For Kin or Country: Xenophobia, Nationalism, and War*. New York, NY: Columbia University Press.

Snowden, L. (2003). How Likely Are Terrorists to Use a Nuclear Strategy? *American Behavioral Scientist*, *46*(6), 699–713.

Stedman, S. J. (1997). Spoiler Problems in Peace Processes. *International Security*, *22*(2), 5–53.

Stein, J. G. (1996). Image, Identity, and Conflict Resolution. Chapter 6in C. Crocker, F. O. Hampson, & P. Aall (Eds.), *Managing Global Chaos: Sources of and Responses to International Conflict*. Washington, DC: United States Institute of Peace Press.

Stern, J. (2000). *The Ultimate Terrorists*. Cambridge, MA: Harvard University Press.

Tucker, J. (2000). Lessons from the Case Studies. In J. Tucker (Ed.), *Toxic Terror: Assessing Terrorist Uses of Chemical and Biological Weapons*. Cambridge, MA: MIT Press, 249–70.

Wood, G. (2015). What ISIS Really Wants. *The Atlantic*, March. http://www.theatlantic.com/features/archive/2015/02/what-isis-really-wants/384980/

8

The Suicide Bomber as a Weapon of Mass Psychological Destruction

Joseph Tomlins, Elvin Sheykhani, James Sottile, and Bruce Bongar

A terrorist organization may recruit a suicide bomber in order to elicit fear, create a sense of "mass panic" within the civilian population, or to achieve a politically motivated goal within a target audience. Terrorism by suicide hopes to gain supporters by bringing attention to a specific conflict or to coerce opponents to abandoning their positions. Suicide attacks and varying techniques have been used by military and insurgent forces throughout the history of warfare. There is no archetype of suicide bombers. Suicide bombers have been historically viewed as strongly nationalistic individuals, while typically male, 15 percent of all suicide bombers have been women. Recruitment is often performed by a family or acquaintance. Motivation to become a suicide bomber is often seen as a tool to seek revenge for the death of a loved one, to restore honor, religion, pressure, or exploitation. Suicide bombers seek to make their life personally significant. Suicide bombing may serve as a route out of impoverishment for the families of bombers. Research on the motivations and goals of suicide bombing is difficult to achieve when the bomber is dead, and the family refuses to talk. Suicide bombings spread fear, foster uncertainty, and undermine confidence in government and leadership. Suicide bombings are known to be a source of psychological trauma. Suicide bombings instill terror into the public and to undermine their sense of security. Suicide bombers can now carry out less costly, more restrained acts of terror that could have disproportionately enormous consequences, generating fear and alarm and thus serving the terrorists' purpose just as well as a larger weapon or more ambitious attack with massive casualties.

Salah Shaqqer, by many accounts, was a well to-do twenty-five-year-old nurse who worked in the Palestinian territories. Salah was from a middle-class family; he was seen as a devoted father and a kind husband. He was well known, and liked by those within his community. In January of 1995, Salah walked into a bus stop carrying an improvised explosive, denoted it, killing himself, 20 Israel Defense Forces (IDF) soldiers, and an unarmed civilian (Nolan, 1996). This sent shockwaves within his community; Salah was seen as a humanitarian, and was not known in jihadi circles. Salah, identified as a Muslim, did not fit the typical profile of a suicide terrorist. He was not known as a radical, he did not come from an impoverished background, and he was well educated (Hoffman, 2003; Nolan, 1996). Many times suicide terrorists fail to fall within the stereotype we come to believe, as impoverished, young, unmarried, military-aged men (Hutchinson, 2007). Upon examining historical context, Salah was a civilian injured during the Palestinian Intifada of the early 1990s; there were reports of detainment by the IDF, and unconfirmed reports of abuses during his internment (Hoffman, 2003). Although certain archetypes of suicide terrorists exist, suicide terrorists continue to be a heterogeneous group differing of gender, creed, nationality, political aim, and motivation. This chapter seeks to discuss suicide bombers, characteristics of perpetrators, and a historical context in the use of the technique.

WHAT IS SUICIDE TERRORISM?

The definition of "suicide terrorism" is often murky, marred by differing views of different organizations and governing bodies (Hutchinson, 2007; Pape, 2003). The most widely agreed-upon definition of "suicide terrorism" refers to instances where a terrorist organization will utilize suicide techniques (e.g., suicide bombing) against civilians and noncombatants as a means of eliciting fear within a target populace to achieve a politically motivated goal (Burke, 2004; Pape, 2003). Suicide techniques are also used against strategic targets of governmental and military importance (Hutchinson, 2007). These instances are typically referred to as suicide attacks because they do not target civilian populations specifically (Hutchinson, 2007; Kurz & Bartles, 2007; Pape, 2003). Although this remains a point of semantics and contention, the UN General Assembly defines "suicide terrorism" as, "Actions intended to cause death or serious bodily harm to civilians and non-combatants for the purposes of intimidation" (United Nations, 2010). This distinction is important as suicide terrorism is often used as a political tool, as demonstrated by the conflicts within Iraq, Afghanistan, Chechnya, Sri Lanka, and the Palestinian Territories (Bloom, 2002; Hutchinson, 2007; Kurz & Bartles, 2007; Pape, 2003).

Terrorism has two main purposes: (1) to gain supporters by bringing attention to a specific conflict and (2) to coerce opponents to abandoning their positions (Bloom, 2002; Pape, 2003). Suicide terrorism is often used as a means of coercing governments to change their policies through the threat of violence. These are not lone instances of strife. Suicide terrorism is a concerted effort by an organization in which a campaign of violence is waged against an intended target (Bloom, 2002). These organizations time these attacks as part of a broader campaign toward obtaining a nationalistic goal. For instance, a terrorist organization might perceive acts of violence as an effort to expel an invading force from its homeland (Clutterbuck, 1975). These terrorist organizations meticulously plan their intended targets, be they strategic assassinations of high-value targets, or targeting of densely populated urban environment, designed to maximize casualties and strife within a community (Crenshaw, 1981). Suicide terrorism is considered the most aggressive form of terrorism, as it often alienates supporters who may have been otherwise sympathetic toward the cause (Hutchinson, 2007). As suicide terrorism is designed to maximize the number of casualties, it attracts more radical elements of a cause while ostracizing more moderate voices within the same group (Clutterbuck, 1975; Crenshaw, 1981; Pape, 2003).

HISTORICAL USE OF SUICIDE TECHNIQUES DURING WARFARE

Suicide attacks and varying techniques have been used by military and insurgent forces throughout the history of warfare. Suicide attacks have been reported as far back as the 1500s, during the Spanish-Moro Conflict (Gowing, 1988; Roces, 1978). Moro Muslims would attack large groups of Spanish occupying forces in the Philippines with a blade, knowing well they would die in the process (Gowing, 1988). The Moro knew well there was little chance for survival, but continued to use the technique up until the 1800s (Powell & Royce, 1978). There are incidental reports of Moro Muslims using similar techniques against American occupying forces during the Moro Rebellion, and against the Japanese during WWII (Gowing, 1988).

In the early twentieth century, "Suicide Squads" were formed in China, used originally by warlords in fighting the central government. These suicide squads dubbed "the Dare to Die Corps" would attach explosives on their bodies and attack government forces or loyalists of the central government (Harmsen, 2013; Olsen, 2012). This tactic continued during the Second Sino-Japanese War and during WW II (Olsen, 2012). The Dare to Die Corps was eventually incorporated within the Chinese military, and was made up of mainly young, college-aged students, of both genders. These students were often revolutionaries, strongly nationalistic, and held allegiances to Mao Zedong (Harmsen, 2013). The Japanese were also known to utilize suicide attack tactics in the form of Kamikaze attacks utilizing planes, boats, and piloted torpedoes against mainly military targets (Olsen, 2012).

HISTORICAL USE OF SUICIDE BOMBINGS

Suicide bombing has been utilized throughout much of the late twentieth century and into the twenty-first century as a popular instrument of destruction in conflicts ranging from the Sri Lankan Civil War to the First and Second Chechen Wars (Burke, 2004; Hoffman, 2005; Hutchinson, 2007; Pape, 2003).

Contemporary examples of suicide bombings include the 1983 attack on a Marine Barracks in Beirut, Lebanon, which resulted in the deaths of over 150 U.S. military personnel (Hutchinson, 2007). Suicide bombing tactics includes contemporary utilization by opposing forces against coalition forces during Operation Iraqi Freedom and Operation Enduring Freedom (Hutchinson, 2007). These opposing forces have utilized suicide vests (an improvised explosive that an individual wears), vehicle-borne explosive devices (cars and trucks that are filled with various explosives), and jetliners that are hijacked and crashed into populated civilian areas (e.g., the September 11 attacks). Although these tactics may vary among the different groups, the aim remains the same—to cause widespread destruction and coerce a government to abandon its current position (Pape, 2003, 2005). In an analysis of the use of suicide bombing tactics, it was found that between 2003 and 2011, there were over 1,000 reported suicide attacks in Iraq. Moreover, during the 10-year period between 2001 and 2011, Afghanistan and Pakistan each reported over 300 suicide attacks within their borders (Amir, 2011). Suicide attacks were reported against civilian targets such as various ethnic minorities (especially within Iraq during the sectarian violence between Shia and Sunni Muslims from 2007 to 2009), NGOs such as the Red Cross, and individuals thought to be aiding coalition forces (Amir, 2011; Hutchinson, 2007; Pape, 2005). Suicide terrorism remains a largely utilized tactic by insurgent forces against both civilian and military forces.

WHO ARE SUICIDE BOMBERS?

Suicide bombers have been historically seen as strongly nationalistic individuals, who are mainly unmarried men and have been indoctrinated by a larger terrorist group (Hoffman, 2003; Hutchinson, 2007; Pape, 2005). A recent analysis of suicide attacks found that 15 percent of all suicide bombings are conducted by women (Rajan, 2011). Although males make up a large majority of suicide terrorists (85 percent of all complete attacks), groups such as Al Qaeda in Iraq and Hamas have actively recruited women in the last decade (Jacques & Taylor, 2013; Rajan, 2011). It is clear then that although men make a significant portion of perpetrators, women are also driven to commit acts of self-destruction in an effort to attain their goals.

RECRUITMENT

Recent studies have found that three-fourths of all individuals within terrorist organizations have been recruited by an acquaintance or family member (Hoffman, 2003; Pape, 2005; Rajan, 2011). These individuals report motivations such as seeking revenge for the death of a confidant or family member (Pape, 2005), to save face or restore honor due to a perceived humiliation (Hutchinson,

2007), religious or communal pressure (Jacques & Taylor, 2013), or exploitation due to being part of a vulnerable group (Hoffman, 2003; Hutchinson, 2007; Jacques & Taylor, 2013; Pape, 2003, 2005).

Suicide bombers are often conceptualized as being characterized by a mix of altruism and suicidal tendencies (Riemer, 1998). As these individuals become more integrated within a given group, they see themselves as having a duty to commit suicide for the good of the group. The act of suicide is perceived as an act of altruism, displaying loyalty to their cause (Riemer, 1998; Taylor, 1982). Durkheim noted this phenomenon as acute altruistic suicide, and referred to the suicide of martyrs (Riemer, 1998). Individuals recruited for suicide attacks are also characterized as fatalistic, in that they are politically and economically oppressed, and view their situation as obdurate (Taylor, 1982). As the individual becomes hopeless, he or she is attracted to more evocative displays to escape the normative situation that he or she holds no esteem for (Taylor, 1982). Thus, the suicide bomber may likely be an oppressed individual, driven to violent and suicidal extremes, who believes he or she is committing an act for a virtuous greater good.

DEMOGRAPHICS

There is no archetype of suicide bombers. Suicide bombers vary based on their age, gender, creed, political affiliation, and religious status, as well as their socioeconomic status and relational histories (Clutterbuck; 1975; Hoffman, 2003; Pape, 2005). Although there is no literature on what specifically makes up a suicide bomber, there has been some research on suicide terrorism as a whole. It was originally postulated that suicide terrorists were mainly unmarried college-aged men, with strong nationalistic ties and few social supports (Merari, 1990; Post, 1990). In a study conducted by Sprinzak, it was found that suicide terrorists are a heterogeneous group varying in gender and age (2000). Sprinzak found that the age ranged from 13 years to 47. The individuals also varied in their levels of education, with 20 percent holding an elementary education, 28 percent holding a postsecondary school education, and 31 percent having some college education (2000). Suicide terrorists are largely younger adults; the median age is 26.2 years (Jacques & Taylor, 2013).

TRAINING

Training of suicide bombers is as heterogeneous as the individuals themselves. Multiple factors such as social status, economic status of the terrorist group, and the area in which the acts are committed lead to varying degrees of training (Hoffman, 2003). In intelligence reports by the U.S. Army, it is noted that often the terrorist is fitted with an explosive vest and walks into a populated area and sets off the device (Khimi & Even, 2004).

Although limited information is available regarding the differing training, individuals are indoctrinated via religious or nationalistic rhetoric, which reifies the individual's resolve to commit the act (Khimi & Even, 2004). Current reports state that often the individuals committing the act have limited expertise in terms of explosives; instead, they are the vessel in which the form of asymmetric warfare is delivered (Pape, 2005). This is done so that the individual cannot disable the device, and in many instances, a second detonator is available to the group members observing the act, as they may be able to initiate the attack (Hoffman, 2003; Khimi & Even, 2004; Pape, 2003, 2005).

WHAT DO SUICIDE BOMBERS WANT?

Suicide bombers are driven to commit acts of sacrificial violence for a variety of social, political, and religious reasons, which are difficult to ascertain. Research on the motivations and goals of suicide bombing is challenging for two primary reasons. Most suicide bombers are dead and cannot be interviewed. The family members of suicide bombers may still be alive; however, the accuracy of family members' perceptions of suicide bombers' goals and motivations may be biased (Araj, 2012). Would be suicide bombers who failed in their missions are usually in prison. For instance, although Israel imprisons many failed suicide bombers, the state is reluctant to allow researchers to interview prisoners for varying political reasons (Araj, 2012). These factors make it difficult to accurately assess the goals of suicide bombers as individual actors as well as agents of larger institutional forces.

RELIGIOUS GOALS

Research suggests martyrdom may be the primary religious motivation for suicide bombers (Post, 2009). Martyrdom is a difficult concept to define because the religious significance of a person's death ultimately lies in the eyes of the beholder. In response to the increase in suicide bombing attacks since 9/11, many Christian scholars have attempted to argue that the martyrdom claimed by suicide bombers is a false ideology used to justify their actions (Middleton, 2014). However, Middleton (2014) investigated the history of martyrdom in Christianity, Judaism, and Islam and found numerous examples of controversial deaths used to support religious causes. In fact, most martyrs die for church politics and ideological divides within their religion (Middleton, 2014). Numerous protestant martyrs died to justify their separation from the oppression of the Catholic Church, which viewed their deaths as supportive of a false ideology (Middleton, 2014). Martyrdom is often about the story constructed after a person's death rather than the action of the death itself (Middleton, 2014).

These stories are often created to legitimize religious separatism and extremism (Post, 2009).

Martyrdom is particularly relevant for many extant, would-be suicide bombers. Modern Islamic extremists rely on an interpretation of the Koran, the holy text of Islam, which forbids suicide except as a path to martyrdom (Dadoo, 2010). Suicide has many negative moral connotations within the Koran; however, Prophet Muhammad claimed that people may only look forward to death in seeking rewards in the afterlife through martyrdom (Dadoo, 2010; Post, 2009).

Martyrdom is typically considered a somewhat passive act in that one is killed in the course of serving religious goals (Dadoo, 2010). Prophet Muhammad's famous decree regarding martyrdom promised that martyrs would ascend to their place in paradise after death, would be presented with 72 virgins for marriage, and would have the opportunity to help 72 of his relatives in the afterlife (Araj, 2012; Dadoo, 2010). While there have been several precedents of sacrifice in the name of Islam, most of these deaths were not suicides in the traditional sense. Islamic martyrs typically sacrifice their lives in the course of retaliating with violence as part of a war or religious conflict (Dadoo, 2010). This is quite distinct from suicide bombers. For instance, although suicide bombers operate within the context of religious and political conflicts, their acts are premeditated and seek to cause violence in order to elicit terror (Dadoo, 2012).

Osama bin Laden and Al Qaeda helped proliferate interpretations of the Koran to justify the use of suicide bombers in its conflicts with Western military forces (Dadoo, 2012). Bin Laden argued that the disparity in resources between Muslim freedom fighters and the American military justified the use of guerilla warfare tactics including suicide bombing in the course of liberating the Holy Land (Dadoo, 2012). Therefore, if a suicide bomber truly believed he or she was sacrificing his or her life in the service of Allah, they could consider themselves a martyr, which would grant him or her divine pleasures in the afterlife, provide prosperity for relatives, and aid their nation (Dadoo, 2012). In sum, from the perspective of the suicide bomber, his or her death would not be perceived as in vain.

Suicide bombing within the context of Islam is considered to be an action in the service of jihad (Post, 2009). Post (2009) separates the construct of jihad into two parts: the greater jihad, which is a determination to lead a morally sound life free of evil, and the lesser jihad of the sword, which is a duty to defend Islam when under attack. Osama bin Laden and Al Qaeda have construed the lesser jihad to be of utmost importance in response to extremist Islam's perceived American threat to the Muslim people (Dadoo, 2012). However, many of these suicide bombings that are justified through the rationale of jihad are not retaliatory defensive actions, but premeditated assaults on Americans intended to elicit terror. The presence of long-standing ongoing religious conflicts has created a climate where every attack from both sides can be construed as a defensive action.

POLITICAL GOALS

Suicide bombers are often motivated by state repression as seen in Palestine's response to Israeli aggression. Araj (2012) found that many of the suicide bombers' families he interviewed claimed that state repression was the primary reason for their actions. While this motivation appears to be politically driven, many of the bombers' families reported that this motivation arose from personal experiences of loss as a result of state repression (Araj, 2012). Palestinian bombers were seeking recourse after Israeli killings of friends and family members (Araj, 2012). Based on interviews with family members, most of these attacks appear to be more personally motivated to avenge loved ones killed by the rival state, rather than to achieve political goals (Araj, 2012). There are also examples of Palestinian bombers motivated by a sense of injustice at Israel's killing of Palestinians in general and report themes of redemption in their final messages to loved ones (Post, 2009).

Retaliation is a recurring theme used to justify the bombings on a political level as well. The Palestinian bombers describe experiencing harsh treatment by the Israeli authorities and attacks on friends and family members (Araj, 2012; Post, 2009). Bombers are able to legitimize their actions as defensive due to the ongoing political conflict (Post, 2009). However, the nature of long-standing, ongoing conflicts makes it possible to construe every violent action as retaliation for some past transgression.

De Figueiredo and Weingast (1998) proposed that terrorism and state repression are locked in a vicious cycle, which can be explained by game theory. Terrorist organizations plan attacks in order to provoke the occupying state to suppress them. Suppression is effective for a time; however, the state's retaliatory violence draws moderates away from the state and toward the insurgent group. The repressed group then retaliates for the suppressed violence, which perpetuates the cycle. This cycle will only work if the dominant group is motivated to suppress the insurgent group. If suppression will have no effect on the level of violence, the state has no motivation to play the game (De Figueiredo & Weingast, 1998).

The cycle of terrorist violence and state repression in Israel and Palestine has been going on for so long that many acts of violence are retaliations for suppressive actions committed by the state years before (De Figueiredo & Weingast, 1998). At an institutional level, state repression and terrorist violence are struggles for popular support and positive perception (Bloom, 2005; De Figueiredo & Weingast, 1998). However, at the individual level, personal revenge against oppressive actions committed by rival states such as Israel underlies many political goals (Araj, 2012).

Political conflicts based on state repression are fueled and maintained by both larger institutions and the individual actors that make up those institutions. While an individual bomber's goal may be to avenge the death of a loved one, that micro goal feeds into the larger institutional goal of liberating one's people from a repressive occupying state (Araj, 2012). Bloom (2005) contends that suicide bombing is a bargaining chip used by terrorist organizations to barter for popular support. The hearts and minds of the people are the ultimate resource in political struggles. If an organization can engage the emotions of their people in a struggle, it becomes easier to justify and legitimize violence as a pathway to liberation. Thus, a culture of retaliatory violence is created and perpetuated by the human experience of loss and oppression.

OTHER MOTIVATIONS

While many suicide bombers claim to act in accordance with larger religious or political goals, personal significance may underlie many of the overt motivations for their actions. Victoroff (2009) stakes the claim that suicide bombers seek self-actualization and are on a quest to make their life personally significant. Suicide bombing can be seen as an altruistic suicide in that bombers make a personal sacrifice to improve their reputation, which leads others in the group to ensure the well-being of their families (Victoroff, 2009). Victoroff (2009) further argues that altruistic suicide is evolutionarily rewarding for suicide bombers because their actions lead to the proliferation of their genes (offspring have better lives) even if this adaptive drive comes at a high personal cost. This explanation suggests that although suicide bombings are often carried out for religious or political reasons, it is this evolutionary drive for personal significance and prosocial goal of proliferating one's family that separates bombers from other political or religious activists (Victoroff, 2009).

Researchers have speculated that suicide bombing may serve as a path out of poverty for the families of bombers. This argument is based on the fact that many terrorist organizations provide financial support to suicide bombers' families in exchange for their commitment (Araj, 2012). However, this argument does not hold up for two primary reasons. Suicide bombers appear to be more educated and come from families with higher socioeconomic status (Krueger & Maleckova, 2003). In addition, the amount of money provided for bombers' families is typically not enough to justify the loss of a primary breadwinner (Araj, 2012). Saddam Hussein provided suicide bombers' families with a single payment ranging from $10,000 to $25,000 (Araj, 2012). While this is not an insignificant amount of money, it would not cover a family's expenses for very long.

As a result, poverty or deprivation does not seem to be a primary goal of suicide bombers' actions.

Strategic motivations aimed at liberating Palestine or other occupied territories appear to be the impetus for many suicide bomber attacks (Araj, 2012). Araj (2012) interviewed several bombers' families who reported that liberating the homeland was one of the bombers' goals. However, none of the bombers' family members claimed that strategic motivations were the primary goal. Religious motivations or personal vengeance was more commonly reported as the most important reason suicide bombers' chose to act (Araj, 2012). The bombers' family members who did report strategic motivations as one of their goals claimed that suicide attacks were intended to compel other Palestinians to realize that negotiations with Israel would never be successful and to switch tactics to the jihad of the sword (Araj, 2012; Post, 2009).

Taken together, this body of research suggests that suicide bombers are motivated by a variety of religious, political, and social goals. Suicide bombers can be viewed as individual actors with personal motives, as well as parts of larger institutions. Personal narratives of loss and struggle compel bombers' to act according to the larger goals of state and religious organizations. The cycle of violence present in these political and religious conflicts perpetuates due to the struggle to win the hearts and minds of individuals. Suicide bombers demonstrate the power individual lives possess to affect peoples' perception of nations and have the potential to alter the course of long-standing conflicts.

HOW DO SUICIDE BOMBERS AFFECT US?

Suicide bombings constitute a political and strategic problem that manifests a pernicious, yet palpable, psychological effect on both micro and macro levels. They spread fear, foster uncertainty, and undermine confidence in government and leadership. This observation appears evident after the 9/11 attacks in the United States. Yet even prior to the attacks in New York and Washington, suicide attacks had—on some occasions—far-reaching political consequences. For instance, in 1983, attacks against U.S. and French forces and diplomatic missions in Lebanon resulted in the evacuation of the multinational force from that country (Merari, 2007). This step, in turn, enabled the Syrian de facto takeover of the country and, in the following years, had a vast influence on Lebanese domestic and international politics. In another arena, Palestinian suicidal terrorist attacks in Israel in 1996 resulted in a change of government and had a major deleterious impact on the Middle Eastern peace process (Merari, 2007).

In addition to the large-scale impact of suicide bombings, they also have a profound effect on the individual. For instance, many individuals have posttraumatic reactions to witnessing and/or hearing about suicide bombings (Cohen Silver, Holman, McIntosh, Poulin, & Gil-Rivas, 2002; Galea et al., 2002;

Gidron, 2002). As a result of the deleterious effects on the psyche, suicide bomb-ings also attract significant public interest and concern. The phenomenon of vol-untarily blowing oneself up in an effort to take the lives of others has always been surrounded by mystery and fear; unlike ordinary suicidal actions, suicide bombings are murderous and often directed against random public locations (Hoffman, 1998; Israeli, 1997; Taylor, 1988). This sense of insecurity naturally fosters a sense of impending danger and a need to understand the perpetrator. This section will unpack the suicide bomber as a weapon of mass psychological destruction against the individual and against groups.

PSYCHOLOGICAL EFFECT ON THE INDIVIDUAL

Suicide bombings are known to be a source of psychological trauma. Potential individual psychological reactions to suicide bombings include numbness; anxi-ety, and fear; horror and disgust; anger and scapegoating; paranoia; loss of trust; demoralization, hopelessness, and helplessness; and survivor guilt (Holloway, Norwood, Fullerton, Engel, & Ursano, 1997). In addition to acute stress disorder, which appears immediately following such an event, a long-term posttraumatic stress disorder (PTSD) emerges in some of those exposed to the traumatic event. In a review of several studies of PTSD among people in various countries who witnessed a suicide bombing, Gidron (2002) found an average PTSD rate of 28.2 percent. Symptoms of PTSD may appear not only among those present at the site of an attack, but also among some of those who consider themselves as potential victims or who are exposed to the event through the mass media or per-sonal accounts by relatives and friends. For instance, studies conducted after the 9/11 attacks in New York found PTSD symptoms among people who had not personally witnessed the attack (Cohen Silver et al., 2002; Galea et al., 2002).

Despite these findings, it should be noted that many individuals who might previously have met criteria for PTSD after learning about the attack through the media are no longer meeting the PTSD criteria. The criteria for PTSD have shifted within the *Diagnostic and Statistical Manual of Mental Disorders'* (DSM) fourth to the fifth edition. The DSM 5 now states that the individual must experience the trauma directly (i.e., witness the suicide bombing firsthand) (American Psychiatric Association, 2013). Nevertheless, people often experi-ence profound psychological stress after hearing about a suicide bombing. Furthermore, posttraumatic symptoms are often higher among people who lived in proximity to the site of the attack and therefore felt a greater direct danger. Therefore, learning about a suicide bombing close to home likely has a stronger impact on the individual.

Suicide bombings are unique in how they affect the individual psyche. Survi-vors of suicide bombings are more likely to suffer subsequent psychiatric illness than are survivors of natural or technological disasters (Norris et al., 2002).

One reason for this is that intentional attacks "might happen again at any moment," whereas there are expected times of peace and respite following a natural disaster. Furthermore, some might argue that suicide bombings "are more frightening than other forms of terrorism" not only because they generate a larger number of victims, but also because these incomprehensible acts of suicide seem unstoppable (Merari, 2007, p. 111). They create a sense of insecurity and lack of control. Suddenly, an innocuous pedestrian could potentially transform into a terrorist. Merari (2007) argues that this type of thinking leads people to avoid public places, such as shopping centers, coffee shops, and buses because these are the targets of suicide attacks.

It should be noted that the exposure to a suicide bombing and/or the worry of a suicide bombing does not necessarily constitute a stress disorder. In Israel, since the 2000 start of the al-Aqsa Intifada, suicide bombers have killed more than 300 people and injured more than 3,900 others. In 2002, a nationally representative sample of about 500 Israelis queried by a telephone survey after 19 months of attacks that had occurred with increasing frequency showed that about 10 percent exhibited symptom criteria for PTSD, 77 percent reported at least one traumatic stress-related symptom, and 59 percent reported feeling depressed (Bleich, Gelkopf, & Solomon, 2003). A significant portion of the respondents in this survey had experienced earlier traumatic attacks such as previous wars, terrorist attacks, or the Holocaust.

Despite these histories and the fact that almost half of the participants in the sample had been exposed to civilian violence either personally or through a friend or family member (with 60 percent reporting that they felt their lives were in danger), the emotional impact appeared to be moderate. The rate of PTSD found among Israelis after 19 months of repeated attacks was lower than the rates reported for people in the immediate vicinity of the World Trade Center towers two months after 9/11. For instance, various surveys conducted following 9/11 found that 10–20 percent of participants suffered from several PTSD symptoms (Cohen Silver et al., 2002; Schlenger et al., 2002).

PSYCHOLOGICAL EFFECT ON THE PUBLIC

The effect of a suicide bombing transcends the individual level. Suicide bombings instill terror into the public and undermine their sense of security on a macro level. Suicide bombings disrupt everyday life and sway public opinion by "creating an unremitting, paralyzing sensation of fear" (Ganor, 2004).

Pastel (2001) posits that the aim of suicide bombings is to create a sense of "mass panic" within the civilian population. Mass panic was originally defined as an "acute fear reaction marked by loss of self-control which is followed by nonsocial and nonrational flight" (Quarantelli, 1954, p. 265). It is important to note that although fear is often widespread in the aftermath of suicide bombings, mass panic is rare (Breckenridge & Zimbardo, 2007). Panic is highly situation specific. Studies of natural and technological disasters indicate that only on some occasions, when there is a perception of immediate, severe danger coupled with the appearance of narrowing opportunities for escape, has mass panic been observed (Perry & Lindell, 2003). Even in such circumstances, panic is not inevitable.

Although the public is not overcome by mass hysteria and panic, there are serious and insidious effects caused by suicide bombings on the macro level. A pervasive feeling of threat comes to assume priority over major social, political, and economic concerns. Breckenridge and Zimbardo (2007) posit that because terrorists lack the military prowess, political power, and material resources of their adversary, their strategy is critically dependent upon "the strategic benefits of inciting a perception of vulnerability that far exceeds realistic dangers, an aim that depends heavily upon mass-media publicity" (p. 117). What is clear is that acts of terror, such as suicide bombings, have a profound effect on the public, which in turn affects social, economic, and political movements.

It is not surprising that fear and apprehension can have a considerable impact politics. The role of emotions in most matters of political interest is powerful and pervasive because emotions bias judgments, frame perceptions, prime memories, and influence agenda setting (Marcus, 2000, 2003). Affective influences on attention, memory, and judgment contribute to widespread experience of disproportionate vulnerability and looming threat appraisal that make terrorism a more psychologically complex phenomenon than mere "scare tactics" (Breckenridge & Zimbardo, 2007).

Mass-mediated acts of terror can also strengthen popular support for a more militant counterterrorism policy and for bold restrictions on civil liberty, as well as encourage public acceptance of potentially misplaced priorities. For instance, a U.S. survey conducted soon after 9/11 found that the greater the public's sense of threat, the greater the willingness to place restrictions on civil liberties to increase safety and security (Davis & Silver, 2004). Another post-9/11 *New York Times* poll found widespread support for military action against terrorism, even if "many thousands of innocent people" were killed (Berke & Elder, 2001). A longitudinal review of national polling data found that public support for restricting civil liberties to combat terrorism peaked in the early days following 9/11, and although support diminished over the next year, a majority of Americans continued to support restrictions on their civil liberties if personal costs were relatively low (Kuzma, 2004).

Breckenridge and Zimbardo (2007) suggest that the public perceives that these risks pose a much greater threat than is actually present. This perceived threat has had enormous consequences to U.S. society. One tangible example includes the economic costs of avoiding airline travel in the aftermath of 9/11. The volume of U.S. commercial airline traffic did not return to pre-9/11 levels until February 2005. Moreover, the economic damage to the national and international airline industry and to tourism was massive—more than $57 billion was lost in the U.S. travel industry alone (Frey, Luechinger, & Stutzer, 2004).

THE ROLE OF THE MEDIA

A common thread in both the macro and micro effects of suicide bombings is the media. The primary strategic goal of terrorism is to communicate its message via violent acts such as suicide bombings (Hoffman, 2002). Dettmer (2004) even refers to the mass media as the essential "oxygen" of terrorism. The terrorists' aim to maximize their audience and commercial journalism's competition for readers and viewers have spawned a symbiotic terrorist-media relationship on the macro level, which sustains itself on the fear experienced by the individual.

Although the majority of reputable media outlets exercise disciplined restraint with respect to obvious terrorist propaganda, unfortunately, the terrorists can readily circumvent journalistic censorship. Recorded instructions and coded communications, as well as videos of executions, beheadings, hostage pleadings, and "documentaries" of suicide bombings, are now easily distributed over the Internet and nonmainstream sources (Cho et al., 2003).

Negativity bias is a fundamental factor in the media's selection and framing of news and events and the public's trust in media analysis and reporting, and studies reveal a powerful bias toward coverage of negative events and outcomes (Niven, 2001). In their recent comprehensive review of the intersection of media, communication, and psychology, Reeves and Nass (2003) conclude that people relate to mediated events in ways that reflect fundamental psychological processes that underlie human information processing. In particular, they note that human attention and memory assign priority to negatively valenced, high-arousal stimuli. The underlying processes occur automatically and without conscious awareness and are probably the result of evolutionary adaptation advantages accrued from increased vigilance to potential threats.

In sum, the psychology of risk perception plays a significant role in the interplay between terrorism and the media. Vivid, repetitive coverage of acts and threats of terror prime the cognitive and emotional processes that help create a disproportionate sense of risk and vulnerability (Breckenridge and Zimbardo, 2007). Images of terror become more readily available and underscore the sense of emotional dread.

THE SUICIDE BOMBER AS A WEAPON OF MASS PSYCHOLOGICAL DESTRUCTION

Despite the enormity of September 11, subsequent dramatic bombings in Madrid and Bali and the increase in terrorist attacks internationally following

U.S. wars in Iraq and Afghanistan may yet prove to be a new and, somewhat, "conservative" approach to high-technology weapons of mass destruction (Crenshaw, 2000; Hoffman, 2001; Lesser et al., 1999; Tucker, 2001). Suicide bombers can now carry out less costly, more restrained acts of terror that nevertheless "could have disproportionately enormous consequences, generating fear and alarm and thus serving the terrorists' purpose just as well as a larger weapon or more ambitious attack with massive casualties" (Hoffman, 2001, p. 8). These smaller, isolated, yet substantial attacks generate fear and terror on both the micro and macro levels, which in turn is deftly manipulated by terrorists through the media as a weapon of mass psychological destruction. Interestingly, although newspaper, magazine, and television accounts have often focused on the potential use of chemical, biological, radiological, or nuclear weapons to inflict mass casualties or severe damage to critical infrastructure, experts have long questioned whether such extremes are essential, or perhaps even counterproductive to the strategy of terrorism. In place of weapons of mass destruction, terrorists have skillfully adapted into weapons of mass psychological destruction, the suicide bomber.

REFERENCES

American Psychiatric Association. (2013). *Diagnostic and Statistical Manual of Mental Disorders: DSM-5.* Washington, DC: American Psychiatric Association.

Araj, B. (2012). The Motivations of Palestinian Suicide Bombers in the Second Intifada (2000 to 2005). *Canadian Review of Sociology, 49*(3), 211–232. doi:10.1111/j.1755 -618X.2012.01292.x

Amir, M. (2011). Pakistan: The Suicide Bomb Capital of the World. *Asia Times Online.*

Berke, R., & Elder, J. (2001, September 16). Poll Finds Strong Support for U.S. Use of Military Force. *New York Times*, p. 6.

Bleich, A., Gelkopf, M., & Solomon, Z. (2003). Exposure to Terrorism, Stress-related Mental Health Symptoms, and Coping Behaviors among a Nationally Representative Sample in Israel. *Journal of the American Medical Association, 290*(5), 612–620.

Bloom, M. (2002). Rational Interpretations of Palestinian Suicide Bombing. Paper presented at the Program on International Security Policy, University of Chicago.

Bloom, M. (2005). *Dying to Kill: The Allure of Suicide Terror.* New York: Columbia University Press.

Breckenridge, J. N., & Zimbardo, P. G. (2007). The Strategy of Terrorism and the Psychology of Mass-Mediated Fear. *Psychology of Terrorism* (116–133). New York: Oxford University Press.

Burke, J. (2004). *Al-Qaeda: The True Story of Radical Islam.* I.B.Tauris. pp. 1–24.

Cho, J., Boyle, M. P., Keum, H., Shevy, M. D., McLeod, D. M., Shah, D. V., et al. (2003). Media, Terrorism, and Emotionality: Emotional Differences in Media Content and Public Reactions to September 11 Terrorist Attacks. *Journal of Broadcasting and Electronic Media, 47*(3), 309–327.

Cohen Silver, R., Holman, E. A., McIntosh, D. N., Poulin, M., & Gil-Rivas, V. (2002). Nationwide Longitudinal Study of Psychological Responses to September 11. *Journal of the American Medical Association, 288*, 1235–1244.

Crenshaw, M. (1981). The Causes of Terrorism. *Comparative Politics, 13*(1), 397–399.

Crenshaw, M. (2000). The Psychology of Terrorism: An Agenda for the 21st Century. *Political Psychology, 21*(2), 405–420.

Clutterbuck, R. (1975). *Living with Terrorism*. London: Faber & Faber.

Galea, S., Ahern, J., Resnick, H., Kilpatrick, D., Bucuvalas, M., Gold, J., et al. (2002). Psychological Sequelae of the September 11 Terrorist Attacks in New York City. *New England Journal of Medicine, 346*(13), 982–987.

Ganor, B. (2004). Terror as a Strategy of Psychological Warfare. In T. J. Badey (Ed.), *Annual Editions: Violence and Terrorism, 2004–2205* (pp. 5–8). Guilford, CT: McGraw-Hill/Dushkin.

Gidron, Y. (2002). Posttraumatic Stress Disorder after Terrorist Attacks: A Review. *Journal of Nervous and Mental Disease, 190*, 118–121.

Gowing, P. (1988). *Understanding Islam and Muslims in the Philippines* (illustrated ed.) (p. 56). Quezon City, Republic of Philippines: New Day Publishers.

Dadoo, Y. (2010). Suicide Bombers or Martyrdom Operatives? Their Status among Muslim Thinkers, Jurists and Activists. *Religion & Theology, 17*(1/2), 104–132. doi:10.1163/157430110X517942

Davis, D. W., & Silver, B. D. (2004, January). Civil Liberties vs. Security: Public Opinion in the Context of the Terrorist Attacks on America. *American Journal of Political Science, 48*(1), 28–46.

de Figueiredo, R. J. P., & Weingast, B. R. (1998). *Vicious Cycles: Endogenous Political Extremism and Political Violence* (Working Paper No. 2001-9). Berkeley: University of California. Retrieved from http://faculty.haas.berkeley.edu/rui/m13.04.pdf

Dettmer, J. (2004). Supplying Terrorists the "Oxygen of Publicity." In T. J. Badey (Ed.), *Annual Editions: Violence and Terrorism, 2004/2005* (pp. 136–137). Guilford, CT: McGraw-Hill/ Dushkin.

Frey, B. S., Luechinger, S., & Stutzer, A. (2004). Calculating Tragedy: Assessing the Costs of Terrorism. Unpublished manuscript.

Harmsen, P. (2013). *Shanghai 1937: Stalingrad on the Yangtze* (illustrated ed.) (p. 112.) Havertown, PA: Casemate.

Hoffman, B. (1998). *Inside Terrorism*. London: Victor Gollancz.

Hoffman, B. (2001). Change and Continuity in Terrorism. *Studies in Conflict and Terrorism, 24*, 417–428.

Hoffman, B. (2002). The Mind of the Terrorist: Perspectives from Social Psychology. In H. W. Kushner (Ed.), *Essential Readings on Political Terrorism: Analyses of Problems and Prospects for the 21st Century* (pp. 62–69). Lincoln: University of Nebraska Press/Gordon Knot Books.

Hoffman, B. (2003). *The Logic of Suicide Terrorism*. New York, NY: The Atlantic.

Holloway, H. C., Norwood, A. E., Fullerton, C. S., Engel, C. C., & Ursano, R. J. (1997). The Threat of Biological Weapons: Prophylaxis and Mitigation of Psychological and Social Consequences. *Journal of the American Medical Association, 278*(5), 425–427.

Hutchinson, W. (2007). The Systematic Roots of Suicide Bombing. *Systems Research and Behavioral Science, 24*(2), 191–200.

Israeli, R. (1997). Islamikaze and their Significance. *Terrorism and Political Violence, 9*, 96–121.

Jacques, K., & Taylor, P. J. (2013). Myths and Realities of Female-perpetrated Terrorism. *Law and Human Behavior, 37*(1), 35.

Khimi, S., & Even, S. (2004). Who are Palestinian Suicide Bombers? *Terrorism and Political Violence, 16*(4), 815–840.

Krueger, A., Maleckova, J. (2003). Education, Poverty and Terrorism: Is There a Causal Connection? *Journal of Economic Perspectives, 17*(14), 119–144. doi:10.1257/089533003772034925

Kurz, R. W., & Bartles, C. K. (2007). Chechen Suicide Bombers. *Journal of Slavic Military Studies, 20,* 529–547.

Kuzma, L. M. (2004). Security versus Liberty: 9/11 and the American Public. In W. Crotty (Ed.), *The Politics of Terror: The U.S. Response to 9/11* (pp. 160–190). Boston: Northeastern University Press.

Lesser, I. O., Hoffman, B., Arquilla, J., Ronfeldt, D. F., Zanini, M., & Jenkins, B. M. (1999). *Countering the New Terrorism.* Santa Monica: RAND.

Marcus, G. E. (2000). Emotions in Politics. *Annual Review of Political Science, 3,* 221–250.

Marcus, G. E. (2003). The Psychology of Emotion and Politics. In D. O. Sears, L. Huddy, & R. Jervis (Eds.), *Oxford Handbook of Political Psychology* (pp. 182–221). New York: Oxford University Press.

Merari, A. (1990). The Readiness to Kill and Die: Suicidal Terrorism in the Middle East. In W. Reich (Ed.), (pp. 192–206). *Origins of Terrorism.* New York: Cambridge University Press.

Merari, A. (2007). Suicide Attacks As a Terrorist Tactic: Characteristics and Countermeasures. *Strategic Review for Southern Africa, 29*(2), 23.

Middleton, P. (2014). What is Martyrdom? *Mortality, 19*(2), 117–133. doi:10.1080/13576275.2014.894013

Niven, D. (2001). Bias in the News: Partisanship and Negativity in Media Coverage of Presidents George Bush and Bill Clinton. *Harvard International Journal of Press/Politics, 6,* 31–46.

Nolan, B. (1996). Portrait of a Suicide Bomber. *The Independent.* London: United Kingdom.

Norris, F. H., Friedman, M. J., Watson, P. J., Byrne, C. M., Diaz, E., & Kaniasty, K. (2002). 60,000 Disaster Victims Speak: Part 1: An Empirical Review of the Empirical Literature, 1981–2001. *Psychiatry, 65*(3), 207–239.

Olsen, L. (2012). *Taierzhuang 1938 – Stalingrad 1942. Numistamp.* Washington DC: Clear Mind Publishing.

Pape, R. A. (2003). The Strategic Logic of Suicide Terrorism. *American Political Science Review, 97*(3), 12–37.

Pape, R. A. (2005). *Dying to Win: The Strategic Logic of Suicide Terrorism.* New York: Random House.

Pastel, R. (2001). Collective Behaviors: Mass Panic and Outbreaks of Multiple Unexplained Symptoms. *Military Medicine, 166*(12), 44–46.

Perry, R. W., & Lindell, M. K. (2003). Understanding Citizen Response to Disasters with Implications for Terrorism. *Journal of Contingencies and Crisis Management, 11*(2), 49–60.

Post, J. M. (1990). Terrorist Psycho-logic: Terrorist Behavior as a Product of Psychological Forces. In W. Reich (Ed.), *Origins of Terrorism* (pp. 25–40). New York: Cambridge University Press.

Post, J. M. (2009). Reframing of Martyrdom and Jihad and the Socialization of Suicide Terrorists. *Political Psychology, 30*(3), 381–385. doi:10.1111/j.1467-9221.2009.00702.x

Powell, A., & Royce, J. R. (1978). Paths to Being, Life Style, and Individuality. *Psychological Reports, 42*(3), 987–1005.

Quarantelli, E. L. (1954). The Nature and Conditions of Panic. *American Journal of Sociology, 60*, 265–275.

Rajan, J. (2011). *Women Suicide Bombers: Narratives of Violence.* New York: Routledge, p. 79.

Reeves, B., & Nass, C. (2003). *The Media Equation: How People Treat Computers, Television, and New Media Like Real People and Places.* Palo Alto: CLSI Publications, Stanford University.

Riemer, J. W. (1998). Durkheim's "Heroic Suicide" in Military Combat. *Armed Forces & Society, 25*(1), 103–120.

Roces, A. R. (1978). *Filipino Heritage: The Spanish Colonial Period. Volume 7 of Filipino Heritage: The Making of a Nation.* Manila, Republic of Philippines: Lahing Pilipino Publishing.

Schlenger, W. E., Caddell, J. M., Ebert, L., Jordan, B. K., Rourke, K. M., Wilson, D., et al. (2002). Psychological Reactions to Terrorist Attacks: Findings from the National Study of Americans' Reactions to September 11. *Journal of the American Medical Association, 288*(5), 581–588.

Sprinzak, E. (2000). Rational Fanatics. *Foreign Policy, 120*, 66–73.

Taylor, S. (1982). *Durkheim and the Study of Suicide.* London: Macmillan.

Taylor, M. (1988). *The Terrorist.* London: Brassey's Defence Publishers.

Tucker, D. (2001, Autumn). What's New About the New Terrorism and How Dangerous Is It? *Terrorism and Political Violence, 13*, 1–14.

United Nations. (2010). Unifeed: Definitions Reform. United Nations Digital Feed. New York.

Victoroff, J. (2009). Suicide Terrorism and the Biology of Significance. *Political Psychology, 30*(3), 397–400. doi:10.1111/j.1467-9221.2009.00704.x

Part III

The Science of WMPDs and the Psychological Effects They Produce

Part Introduction

Kelley J. Williams

Weapons of mass destruction (WMDs) represent the most sinister aspects of human nature, brought into existence by some of man's greatest scientific and technological achievements. Under most definitions, WMDs are designed to inflict as many casualties as possible, but this does not deny their use in point attacks or assassinations. In many situations, nations developed WMD programs to deter similar aggression when classical deterrence was expected to fail.

Chemical, biological, radiological, nuclear, and high-yield explosive threats (CBRNE) represent the specific threat categories that fall under the broader definition of WMDs. In terms of this text, the two acronyms may be used interchangeably. Some may argue, perhaps semantically, that CBRNE are employed as WMDs. While all threat classes in the CBRNE spectrum are often categorized as WMD, one would be more accurate to classify chemical and biological as "weapons of mass casualty" and radiological, nuclear, and high-yield explosive as "weapons of mass destruction." Regardless of which position is taken, all WMDs carry a deeply negative psychological connotation when used to attack or threaten a population. A group or individual who is willing to use WMD is known as a WMD proliferator. Their selection of a particular CBRNE weapon likely lies in the proliferator's experience, resources, and desired effects. More often than not, one would need access to special equipment and materials required to engage in WMD proliferation.

Each class of WMD threat inflicts unique physical and psychological damage. Chemical and biological weapons have limited tactical (short-term) battlefield use due to environmental requirements, delayed onset of symptoms, or the risk of affecting friendly populations. For these reasons and the societal aversion to such weapons, most nations have rejected chemical and biological weapons. However, chemical and biological weapons have history as ideal weapons of terrorism. According to many media outlets and government officials, the use of WMDs is expected to cause mass panic and hysteria. Although the general public may also feel this way, several historic lessons often support the alternative hypothesis (Wessely, Hyams, & Barthelolomew, 2001).

In WWI, the first use of chlorine gas produced panic not observed with further use of this deadly agent. In fact, only four instances of panic related to gassing were recorded from WWI and two involved inadequate training with protective equipment (Pastel, 2002). During WWII, massive German bombing campaigns against London were expected to break the English will to fight. Those who survived the bombing seemed to develop an unexpected resilience to further attacks (Gladwell, 2013).

Several nationwide surveys indicate an alarming trend regarding terrorist attacks and the use of CBRNE weapons (Becker, 2012; *Personal Preparedness in America*, 2009). Common conclusions of these studies indicate the public is generally confused about how to prepare for terrorist attacks, the effects of CBRNE weapons, and how to protect themselves during an attack. In one survey, only 14 percent of individuals felt that a terrorist act would ever occur in their community. However, 59 percent of these individuals felt that if an act of terrorism occurred in their community it would be serious (*Personal Preparedness in America*, 2009). In their responses, the respondents displayed an attitude of fatalism; that if something were to occur that there is nothing they, or any responding entity, could do to protect them.

According to a 2008 survey of 3,300 respondents (Kano, Wood, Mileti, & Bourque, 2008), there is a general lack of knowledge of how to provide protection to CBRNE events. Interestingly, this study did not identify statistically significant differences in perceived knowledge of CBRNE events between high-risk areas (Los Angeles, District of Columbia, New York) and low-risk areas (remaining United States). In this study, while 29 percent of the respondents claim they were affected by terrorism in some way, only 5 percent of respondents claim they have changed their daily behavior or routines due to the threat of terrorism. The 29 percent of individuals (947 of the 3,300) affected by terrorism events in some way reported 1,047 combined events. Not surprisingly, 87 percent of this population reported that the 9/11 attack on the World Trade Center affected them. Although not stated in the report, it can be assumed that most of these people were not physically present for this attack and were therefore psychologically affected through indirect mechanisms, perhaps by graphic media footage, the loss of friends or family, or the feeling of vulnerability and anger. These results suggest that terrorism is often viewed as a high-consequence, low-probability event whose threat does not compel a long-term change in public behavior. The public's perception of threat and preparedness can strongly influence the psychological impact of CBRNE events in their lives. Through education, preparation, and confidence in support elements (e.g., government leaders, emergency responders), the psychological impact of terrorism can be minimized (Lasker, 2004).

REFERENCES

Becker, S. M. (2012). Psychological Issues in a Radiological or Nuclear Attack. In A. B. Mickelson (Ed.), *Medical Consequences of Radiological and Nuclear Weapons* (pp. 171–94). Fort Detrick: Office of The Surgeon General Department of the Army, United States of America. Retrieved from http://www.cs.amedd.army.mil/borden/FileDownloadpublic.aspx?docid=97c4ef32-c8c3-44cf-bf3b-ec325372b4f2

Kano, M., Wood, M. M., Mileti, D.S., & Bourque, L.B. (2008). Public Response to Terrorism. Retrieved from http://www.ph.ucla.edu/sciprc/pdf/NC+START+Descriptive+Report.pdf

Lasker, R. D. (2004). *Redefining Readiness: Terrorism Planning Through the Eyes of the Public.* New York. Retrieved from http://tap.gallaudet.edu/emergency/nov05conference/EmergencyReports/RedefiningReadinessStudy.pdf

Pastel, R. H. (2002). Collective Behaviors: Mass Panic and Outbreaks of Multiple Unexplained Symptoms. *Military Medicine, 298*(0704), 0–3.

Personal Preparedness in America: Findings from the 2009 Citizen Corps National Survey August 2009. (2009). Retrieved from http://www.fema.gov/media-library-data/20130726-1859-25045-2081/2009_citizen_corps_national_survey_findings_full_report.pdf

Wessely, S., Hyams, K.C., & Barthelolomew, R. (2001). Psychological Implications of Chemical and Biological Weapons. *BMJ 323 (October)*, 878–879.

RECOMMENDED READINGS

Alibek, K. & Handelman, S. (1999). *Biohazard.* New York: Random House.

Dembek, Z. F. & Lenhart, M. K. (Eds.). (2007). *Medical Aspects of Biological Warfare.* Washington, DC: Office of the Surgeon General.

Mickelson, A. B. (2012). *Medical Consequences of Radiological and Nuclear Weapons* (M. K. Lenhart, Ed.). Fort Detrick: Office of The Surgeon General Department of the Army, United States of America. Retrieved from http://www.cs.amedd.army.mil/borden/Portlet.aspx?id=b3cb37ed-08e7-4617-a40c-f148ee3d2303

Romano, J. A., Lukey, B. J., & Salem, H. (2007). *Chemical Warfare Agents: Chemistry, Pharmacology, Toxicology, and Therapeutics* (2nd ed.). Boca Raton: CRC Press.

Sidell, F. R., Takafuji, E. T., & Franz, D. R. (Eds.). (1997). *Medical Aspects of Chemical and Biological Warfare.* Washington, DC: Office of the Surgeon General Department of the Army, United States of America.

Tucker, J. B. (2000). *Toxic Terror: Assessing Terrorist Use of Chemical and Biological Weapons* (J. B. Tucker, Ed.). Cambridge: MIT Press.

Tucker, J. B. (2006). *War of Nerves: Chemical Warfare from World War I to Al-Quaeda* (J. B. Tucker, Ed.). New York: Pantheon. ISBN: 0-375-42229-3.

Tuorinsky, S. D. (2008). *The Medical Aspects of Chemical Warfare* (M. K. Lenhart & S. D. Tuorinsky, Eds.) 2nd ed., Vol. 85. Washington, DC: Department of the Army. Retrieved from http://jama.jamanetwork.com/article.aspx?doi=10.1001/jama.1925.02670140069034

9

Chemical Agents

Kelley J. Williams

A chemical agent is toxic and man-made, and can generally be dispersed as a gas, vapor, aerosol, or liquid. Chemical agents vary widely in their physiological mechanisms but all interfere with the proper bodily functions. The effects of chemical agents vary based on concentration, time, and route of exposure. Acute effects of chemical agent exposure can range from short-term pain to rapid death.

Chemical weapons are ancient weapons of mass destruction (WMDs). In Thucydides's history of the Peloponnesian War, he recorded that a toxic inhalant resulted from the Spartans' use of burning pitch, naphtha, and sulfur against Athenian cities in 423 BCE (Beswick, 1983). This mixture created the toxic gas sulfur dioxide, which interferes with normal breathing patterns. Unfortunately, modern civilization is not sheltered from the threat of chemical agents.

> Although the events of September 11, 2001, did not involve chemical weapons, they did underscore terrorists' willingness to use unconventional weapons and shocked the United States into awareness of its own vulnerability to terrorist attacks. The use of chemical agents by terrorist groups is now a recognized threat to the American population and to US troops deployed abroad. We know terrorist groups have the knowledge and the financial support to design and disperse chemical weapons. Also, as our world becomes more highly industrialized, chemicals, some of which are highly toxic, are used in numerous manufacturing processes; the world's population is at risk of exposure to these lethal chemicals through their inadvertent release from manufacturing plants and accidents during their transportation or intentional release by terrorists. (Lieutenant General Eric B. Schoomaker, Surgeon General, U.S. Army)

Why would a terrorist or WMD-criminal choose chemical weapons? Chemical weapons are equally well suited to produce great psychological and physical damage. The typical pattern of injury from chemical weapons is grotesque and shocking to survivors, unexposed onlookers, and medical personnel.

This quality demonstrates that chemical weapons need not be lethal to produce lasting psychological damage. Chemical weapons are often toxic through dermal contact and inhalation, making them effectively dispersed as liquids or aerosols.

Chemical weapons are most effective as weapons of terror (Wessely et al., 2001). Mass media outlets enforce the association between chemical weapons and terrorism. This confirms that a key purpose of these weapons is to wreak destruction via psychological means—by inducing fear, confusion, and uncertainty in everyday life (Guillemin, 1999). Unique psychological hazards of chemical agents include the potential for long-term physical effects and their delayed onset. Since chemical agents are often harmful at concentrations below the detectable limits of human senses, someone may not know if they have or have not been exposed during an incident or attack. Such people may live in fear of horrible symptoms years into the future even though they were not exposed. On the other hand, actual exposure could cause physical symptoms that challenge a victim's psyche on a regular basis. Examples of these possibilities include the use of Agent Orange in the Vietnam War and the Gulf War Syndrome.

Chemical agents are often categorized by their route of entry and their effects on the human body. The U.S. Centers for Disease Control and Prevention (CDC) divides chemical threats into 13 categories. This text will only address a sample of nerve agents, vesicants, and pulmonary agents since they present the greatest risk for use as WMD (Table 9.1). Nerve agents inhibit the normal function of the nervous system, often leading to death by suffocation. Vesicants essentially cause chemical burns to eyes, skin, and the airway, causing incapacitation but rarely death. Pulmonary agents interfere with breathing or the utilization of oxygen and often cause death by suffocation. Toxins are often considered both biological and chemical threats since they are poisons of biological origin. This text will refer to toxins as biological agents while recognizing the duality of toxin categorization.

Historically, chemical weapons have been used between nations more than biological or nuclear weapons. The potential for chemical agents to be used as a weapon of terrorism by lone-wolf or nonstate actors is low to moderate. Most chemical agents can be produced with WWI–WWII era technology and a solid understanding of organic chemistry. The two greatest barriers to entry into the chemical weapon field is the acquisition of precursor chemicals and the highly specialized equipment required to produce chemical agents in appreciable quantities and efficiencies. Fortunately, the Chemical Weapons Convention in 1997 and international monitoring by the Organization for the Prohibition of Chemical Weapons placed significant challenges along one's path to a chemical weapons program.

According to a former employee of the Soviet chemical weapons complex, the resources of industrialized nations with modern chemical production facilities pose a chemical threat (Smithson, Mirzayanov, Lajoie, & Krepon, 1995).

Table 9.1
Chemical agent summary

Lethal Agents	
Nerve Agents	**Pulmonary Agents**
Tabun	Chlorine
Sarin	Phosgene
Soman	Ammonia
VX	**Blood Agents**
Cyclosarin	Hydrogen cyanide
Blister Agents	Cyanogen chloride
Mustard	**Toxins***
Lewisite	Botulinum toxin
Phosgene oxime	T-2 Mycotoxin
	Ricin
Incapacitating Agents	
Psychochemicals	**Toxins***
LSD	Staph. Enterotoxin
Agent BZ	
Harassing Agents	
CN	DM
CS	
Anticrop/antiplant	
Agent orange	Malathion

*Toxins are considered chemicals and biological agents: chemical weapons convention and biological weapons convention

A state-supported group could conceivably produce chemical agents of sufficient toxicity and quantity to represent a legitimate WMD threat using commercially available methods and unrestricted chemical precursors (Smithson et al., 1995).

NERVE AGENTS

Nerve agents are manmade chemicals that serve no peaceful purpose. Although there are numerous nerve agents known or suspected to exist, they all perform the same basic task—the inhibition of proper neuromuscular function. The purpose of a nerve agent is to kill the victims, not incapacitate them.

The first generation of nerve agents was discovered in 1936 by German chemist Dr. Gerhard Schrader while conducting industrial pesticide research. Throughout WWII, the Nazi regime amassed over 12,000 tons of nerve agents and conducted large open area testing of these weapons. Although nerve class of chemical weapons was many times more deadly than the mustard and chlorine weapons of WWI, Hitler never used these weapons. Common theories are that his top advisers, either erroneously or intentionally, convinced Hitler that the Allies had similar weapons and would use them against German population centers as retaliation-in-kind. Another, though less credible, theory is that Hitler was averse to the use of chemical weapons due to his personal injuries from mustard agent in 1918. The Allies did not know of German nerve agents until after the war, when they discovered technical documents and samples of tabun (GA), sarin (GB), and soman (GD), each more toxic than the last. This untimely discovery ranked among the top intelligence failures of WWII.

The chemical weapons arms race began in the post-WWII era between the United States (with British and Canadian involvement) and the Union of Soviet Socialist Republic (USSR) in the 1950s and 1960s. In true spirit of "victoribus spolia," scientists and engineers from the German chemical weapons complex were patriated into the United States and USSR in exchange for pardons. Although resistance would not likely have been met kindly, the chemists and engineers flourished in each post-war military establishment. The chemical arms race was no less significant than its nuclear brother. Entire industries were developed to produce the precursors and equipment required to develop nerve agents of such toxicity and quantity that it bordered on ridiculous.

Similarly to Gerhard Schrader's discovery of tabun in 1936, two British chemists discovered a new pesticide in 1952. After realizing its extreme lethality to humans it was transferred to military control and dubbed the V-series for "venomous." Along with sarin, VX became a central focus of the Allies' chemical weapons programs. Until the official denouncing of chemical weapons by President Nixon in 1969, chemical weapons were viewed by many as a means to avoid a nuclear exchange under the concept of "graduated deterrence" (Leghorn, 1956).

The manifestation of symptoms from nerve agent exposure is highly dependent on the dose and particular agent. Common symptoms include rhinorrhea (runny nose), chest tightness, pinpoint pupils, shortness of breath, excessive salivation and sweating, nausea, vomiting, abdominal cramps, involuntary defecation and urination, muscle twitching, confusion, seizures, flaccid paralysis, coma, respiratory failure, and death. Initial symptoms depend on the dose and route of exposure.

- Low to moderate vapor exposure causes pinpoint pupils (miosis), rhinorrhea, bronchoconstriction, excessive bronchial secretions, and slight to moderate dyspnea.

- Mild to moderate dermal exposure results in sweating and muscular twitching at the site of contact, nausea, vomiting, diarrhea, and weakness. The onset of these mild to moderate signs and symptoms following dermal exposure may be delayed for as long as 18 hours.
- Acute exposure (higher exposures; any route) causes loss of consciousness, seizures, muscle twitching, flaccid paralysis, copious secretions, apnea, and death.

Acute nerve agent exposures are typically focused at the site of an attack or release. The concentration of gaseous nerve agents declines quickly outside the immediate area but can be carried hundreds of meters by the wind or may remain a persistent threat if released indoors. Certain nerve agents were manipulated to remain a lethal threat under normal environmental conditions for several weeks. Low levels of exposure can also be experienced by emergency responders and health care workers when the clothing of patients serves as a secondary source of contamination prior to decontamination.

Nerve agents pose a significant psychological threat. To those who survive moderate acute doses of nerve agents, the symptoms of uncontrolled muscle movements, loss of bodily functions, and feeling of impending death will surely leave psychological wounds. Low to moderate exposures will likely leave victims feeling that worse symptoms or death are yet to come. For most people, the thought of an invisible cloud that can create these immediate or delayed symptoms is certainly disturbing. The credible threat of nerve agent use would be an effective weapon of mass psychological destruction. This threat can be extended to unaffected people through mass media coverage.

The popular nerve agent sarin was used against Syrian population centers near Damascus on August 21, 2013 (Charbonneau & Nichols, 2013). Although the casualty estimates range from 280 to 1,700 deaths and up to 3,600 total patients, these attacks were undoubtedly devastating to the Syrian people. Syrians near the attacks recorded video footage and images with cell phones and spread these through social media and global news networks. The videos showed groups of women, children, and elderly victims twitching, foaming at the mouth, or dead from apparent asphyxiation. The attacks sparked outrage from the local and international community. Since neither the Syrian government nor the opposition forces took credit for the attacks, the perpetrator of this psychological attack was left ambiguous, though each side blamed the other.

The 1995 Tokyo subway sarin attack is studied from a wide range of perspectives, which include the psychological impact of chemical weapons against a civilian target. This event signifies the first notable terrorist attack using WMD not involving high-yield explosives (Raevskiy, 2014). This terrorist attack was perpetrated by the Japanese apocalyptic cult Aum Shinrikyo, the "Supreme Truth." Japanese police reports indicate that five cult members punctured eight of eleven plastic bags of impure (30 percent) sarin in five subway cars (Tuorin-sky, 2008). The environmental diffusion dispersal was inefficient but still resulted in 13 deaths and 6,252 seeking medical treatment. The 6,252 casu-alties include a high percentage of "worried wounded" who were not actually exposed to the nerve agent but developed psychosomatic symptoms due to the stress and fear of an invisible threat or were seeking financial compensation on false claims. The number of victims clinically exposed to the sarin is more likely in the hundreds. Of this population, postexposure memory function and psychomotor impairment persisted for over seven years (Iyaki et al., 2005). Prior to the subway attack, Aum carried out attacks with chemical agents against 11 smaller targets with mixed success (Danzig, Sageman, Leighton, & Hough, n.d.).

The psychological destruction of the Tokyo sarin attack created a paradigm shift in the Japanese people. This attack was accompanied with international shock, outrage, and feelings of vulnerability. Until this attack, the Japanese soci-ety placed great confidence in the secure functioning of their social system. This attack shattered the confidence of the Japanese people who now did not feel safe in their own country (Raevskiy, 2014). Even though the specific threat of nerve agent attack by Aum Shinrikyo was removed, the feeling of vulnerability remained. The perception of vulnerability and psychological distress generated rethinking among international security groups about the potential for future attacks and the new era of radial religious terrorism (Francis, 2012).

During the normal course of mammalian life, nerve impulses travel from the brain to their target muscles. Along the way, these signals pass through synapses, where electrical signals are converted to chemical signals. In discussions on nerve agents, the focus of this process is the activity of the chemical signal acetylcholine (ACh) and its natural rapid degradation by the enzyme acetylcho-linesterase (AChE) into two basic molecules acetate and choline.

Muscles are either "on" or "off." You cannot flex an individual muscle 50 percent, but you could recruit only 50 percent of your available muscle fibers. To avoid a very long discussion on neuromuscular biochemistry, think of excess ACh levels as an "on switch" to muscular activity and properly functioning AChE as the "off switch." A normal molecule of AChE is able to break down about 25,000 molecules of ACh every second, essentially turning off a muscle's on switches at a very high rate. Nerve agents are a special class of chemicals known as organophosphates (OP) that keep AChE from breaking down ACh in the normal course of activity. The result of OP inhibition of AChE is a high level of ACh, meaning the "on switch" stays on and the muscle is continually activated. If you have ever reached true fatigue during strenuous exercise, you have experienced a small portion of the end result of OP poisoning. At lethal doses, nerve agents cause muscle stimulation to the point of complete failure, and the victim dies of respiratory failure.

Fortunately, several effective medical treatments inhibit the action of nerve agents and reverse some of the symptoms in certain cases. The U.S. military issues a dual antidote to service members who may be at risk of nerve agent exposure. This FDA-approved, DOD-issued antidote contains atropine and 2-pyridine aldoxime methyl chloride, known commonly as 2-PAM or 2-PAM chloride. Atropine reverses the effects of nerve agent exposure in certain tissues, which results in relaxed breathing effort (reduced bronchioconstriction), drying of mouth and airway secretions, and reduced involuntary action in the digestive tract (Tuorinsky, 2008). The purpose of 2-PAM (oxime treatment) is to break the bond between the nerve agent and the AChE enzyme, effectively fixing the "always on" nerve impulse problem caused by the agent. When 2-PAM breaks the bond, the AChE molecule is reactivated and is able to return to the task of "turning off switches" when required.

This process is complicated by a phenomenon called "aging." Aging occurs when the bond between nerve agent and AChE molecule becomes irreversible and is no longer affected by 2-PAM treatment. The rate of aging is highly dependent on the nerve agent. The nerve agent soman (GD) ages in about 2 minutes in humans whereas sarin takes about 5 hours and VX 50–60 hours. Unless a nerve agent exposure involves soman, the permanent effects of aging should occur long after medical treatment is received. On the other hand, this will only benefit victims who survive long enough to receive medical treatment.

VESICANTS (SULFUR MUSTARD, LEWISITE, PHOSGENE OXIME)

Vesicant is a medical term for chemicals that produce blisters or vesicles. In terms of WMD, vesicants refer to WWI-era chemicals, classified as mustards, arsenicals, and phosgene oxime. These are all man-made chemicals that can damage the skin, eyes, lungs, and internal organs.

The most militarily significant vesicants are variants of the mustard class. Lewisite and phosgene oxime were also weaponized for use under special circumstances but considered secondary in military relevance (Tuorinsky, 2008). These secondary vesicants are discussed briefly, but the focus of this vesicant review is sulfur mustard, referred to simply as mustard.

Vesicants present unique psychological burden on victims and health care providers. As will be described in more detail below, vesicants produce painful and visually appalling injuries. Within several days, dermal contact with mustard agent often produces large dome-shaped blisters surrounded by redness and swelling (erythema and edema). These blisters may rupture, leaving wounds that heal very slowly and are susceptible to secondary infection. Exposure to vesicants creates a high probability that the victims' eyes and airway will become involved. This can occur from direct contact with the agent or by secondary contact as the agent or its vapors are transferred from the victims' clothing into the eyes and airway. These two routes of exposure create more rapid symptoms.

The blindness and painful cough associated with eye and airway involvement are certainly a psychological weapon for those exposed to mustard agents. These conditions also produce fear, helplessness, and additional psychological trauma to responding health care personnel and those who witness the event. In 1991, a committee appointed by the National Academy of Sciences identified links between over 250 WWII subjects in vesicant tests to certain long-term health problems. Psychological disorders were linked to the trauma of mustard exposure, not the actual effects of the agent (Pechura & Rall, 1993).

Lewisite (b-chlorovinyldichloroarsine) is an arsenical vesicant that has not seen verified battlefield use but may exist in international chemical weapon stockpiles (Lewis & Stiegler, 1925). Lewisite was discovered by the U.S. military in 1918, as synthesized by Army Captain W. L. Lewis. The Germans claim to have discovered the same compound in 1917 but never developed it for military use (Prentiss & Fisher, 1937). Lewisite is similar in many ways to mustard but several properties were seen as disadvantages for military use. The physical properties of Lewisite allow it to be dispersed at colder temperature than mustard. This also causes Lewisite to undergo hydrolysis and decomposition more rapidly, making it a short-lived hazard on the battlefield. The inflammation and vesicles formed from Lewisite exposure form more rapidly but also heal faster than mustard injuries (Buscher, 1932). Secondary infection from Lewisite vesicles is not considered as common as it is with mustard. Lewisite causes rapid pain to all exposed areas. This is advantageous to a military force wanting to stop or delay an advancing attack, but disadvantageous because it allows soldiers to don chemical protective equipment before becoming grossly contaminated.

Unlike mustard, a specific antidote exists that can improve the course of Lewisite exposure. British anti-Lewisite (BAL, dimercaprol) was developed during WWII by Oxford biochemists. BAL is used in modern medicine to treat poisoning of arsenic and heavy metals by binding the metals in a way that permits excretion in the urine.

Phosgene oxime (dichloroformoxime) is not a true vesicant, but is instead an urticant that produces an intense stinging sensation like nettles followed by tissue damage and necrosis of skin, eyes, and airways. Phosgene oxime should not be confused with phosgene gas, a slow-acting pulmonary agent. In expected military-grade concentrations (>70 percent purity), phosgene oxime is a yellowish-brown liquid that rapidly permeates clothing and rubber to create immediate pain and tissue damage similar to an acid burn (McAdams & Joffe, 1955). In fact, no other chemical agent is known to cause such immediate pain and rapid necrotic effects (~30 minutes on exposed skin) as phosgene oxime (Tuorinsky, 2008). Phosgene oxime was considered for use by the U.S. military prior to WWII but rejected for apparent lack of physiological effects and environmental instability (Borak & Sidell, 1992). The lack of symptoms in these early tests was due to concentrations (1–2 percent) below the threshold required to produce the pain and tissue necrosis previously mentioned (McAdams & Joffe, 1955).

Mustard agent (bis-(2-chloroethyl)sulfide) allegedly received its name from its smell or taste (onion, garlic, mustard) or its color that varies from yellow, to light tan, to dark brown based largely on the level of impurities (Fries & West, 1921; Medema, 1986). Sulfur mustard was the first vesicant, manufactured in 1822, and utilized in the 1880s as a pesticide and to treat minor tumors. Sulfur mustard was introduced as a weapon in 1917 by the Germans against the British in Ypres, Belgium. Chemical weaponeers in numerous countries created variations of mustard agents to provide particular attributes beneficial for different battlefield conditions.

Mustard agents were used extensively in WWI. Although mustard was introduced in the last year of WWI, it caused 70 percent of chemical casualties and 20 percent of total casualties from the war. As demonstrated in WWI, the devastating impact of vesicants is the long convalescence time and burden on medical resources that a mustard injury requires. If a soldier is killed by conventional or chemical weapons, he is no longer a burden to medical resources. On average, a mustard casualty will spend 42 days under medical care and require attention from numerous medical personnel. Additionally, mustard casualties were typically not able to remove themselves from the battlefield to seek medical attention. This often meant that between one and three healthy soldiers were used to transport the casualty, effectively removing two to four soldiers instead of just one. When mustard casualties became too great, long trains of mustard casualties would march in single file with hand on shoulders as the blind lead the blind off the battlefield to the field hospitals.

Sulfur mustard was used in numerous conflicts since WWI, typically against an enemy that did not possess a chemical weapons capability. Most notably, in 1936 the Italian dictator, Benito Mussolini, ordered the heavy use of sulfur mustard against Ethiopians by aerial bombardment. In 1983 Sadaam Hussain used mustard against the Kurds in Northern Iraq, and against the Iranians during the Iraq–Iran war (Schonwald, 1992). The televised aftermath of mustard use against Iran brought international attention to the atrocities of chemical warfare.

Exposure to mustard commonly affects the skin, eyes, and airways since these organs come into direct contact with mustard as an oil or vapor. In WWI, over 27,700 soldiers from the United States suffered injuries from mustard alone. Of these casualties, 80–90 percent of U.S. mustard casualties had skin lesions, 86 percent had eye involvement, and 75 percent had airway damage (Tuorinsky, 2008). Sulfur mustard is commonly distilled to enhance toxicity and stability during storage and use on the battlefield.

VESICANT MECHANISM HYPOTHESES

Mustard is a carcinogen, but there are no documented cases of cancer from acute exposures, as would result from a military attack. The precise mechanisms of mustard toxicity are unknown, but two dominant hypotheses describe mustard as a bifunctional alkylating agent.

One hypothesis is that exposure to mustard alkylates DNA (deoxyribonucleic acid). The resulting breaks in DNA activate a chain of metabolic events that lead to cell death and acute tissue injury. DNA alkylation also inhibits the classically termed "central dogma" of molecular biology, which is that DNA is transcribed into RNA (ribonucleic acid), which is then translated into proteins that serve as the basis for cellular life. Interruption of protein synthesis would also lead to cell death and tissue injury.

The second leading hypothesis is that mustard reacts with glutathione. This creates high levels of calcium in the cells, leading to oxidative stress, damage to cellular membranes, and eventually cell death and tissue injury.

Mustard Treatment

There is no specific postexposure treatment or antidote for mustard. Clinical responses focus on treating the symptoms and controlling secondary infection with antibiotics. Local anesthetics are used to relieve pain related to vesicles and plastic surgery is often used to restore the aesthetics of dermal exposure. Patients with pulmonary exposure will require bronchiodilatory treatment and the aid of cough suppressants.

PULMONARY AND BLOOD AGENTS

This review will focus on chlorine, phosgene, ammonia, and cyanide. These agents are still accessible and widely used for industrial purposes and cover a wide range of injury mechanisms. These chemicals also present a public threat due to common knowledge of their hazards as lethal and incapacitating agents. Pulmonary and blood agents are specialized toxic industrial chemicals, which by design or natural properties create injury but interfering with the body's ability to breathe or perform cellular respiration. During WWI, at least 23 chemical agents were used from 1914 to 1916 by both Allied and Axis forces to produce over 71,000 casualties. These included the pulmonary agents phosgene, chlorine, and diphosgene (Tuorinsky, 2008).

Chlorine and phosgene are primary pulmonary agents that were widely used in WWI to create inhalational casualties. The use of poison gas was particularly advantageous to the aggressor when engaged in trench warfare since it could penetrate no-man's-land and access the enemy in their trenched emplacements without exposing friendly troops to hostile fire. Chlorine and phosgene were also

Table 9.2
Airway compartment hazard properties

Affected Respiratory System Compartment	Inhalational Hazard Properties
Nasopharynx	Quick onset of symptoms (sneezing, pain, erythema)
	Highly soluble and reactive compounds
Central airways	From mouth to 2 mm size airways
	Highly soluble and reactive compounds
	Symptoms quick onset (choking, coughing, painful swallow)
Peripheral airways	2 mm airways to alveoli
	Poorly soluble and less reactive compounds
	Symptoms have slow onset (dyspnea)

relatively easy to produce in the quantities required for military use, using common industrial processes. Two key disadvantages of using these agents were the ability for wind shift to carry the agent to friendly troop positions and the speed with which an enemy can don protective masks once the agent is detected.

Pulmonary agents draw on basal human fears of suffocation and drowning. The psychological impact of pulmonary agents is significant. The helplessness of "dryland drowning" as one's lungs fill with mucus is an unbearable thought. Witnessing the effects of such an incident would be almost as traumatic, especially if friends and family are involved.

Pulmonary agents are characterized and treated based on the location of greatest lung compartment damage: the nasopharynx, the central airway, or the peripheral airway. Agents that cause injury within the central airway are sometimes known as choking agents. The affected airway compartment is largely determined by the size of the particle, its solubility, and its reactivity (Table 9.2). Pulmonary agents that affect the central airway often form strong acids or bases when in contact with moisture and destroy tissue. These highly reactive compounds (e.g., chlorine and ammonia) typically produce immediately repulsive effects in a victim.

Pulmonary agents that are less soluble (e.g., phosgene) may reach the alveolar compartment of the peripheral airway where the exchange between carbon dioxide and oxygen occurs. Peripherally acting agents often have delayed onset of symptoms due to lower solubility and may not alert the victim with a choking response or immediate pain. Indication of such an exposure is often a characteristic smell, such as freshly cut hay or green corn, for phosgene. These agents tend to cause buildup of fluid (pulmonary edema) hours after exposure (Tuorinsky, 2008). Since medical providers and emergency response personnel may not know what chemical a victim was exposed to, medical responses focus on determining the affected respiratory system compartment, then applying treatments specific to that compartment (Tuorinsky, 2008).

Chlorine is widely used to purify water and is involved in many other industrial processes and consumer products. As a gas, it is yellow-green in color and is heavier than air. During an intentional or accidental chlorine release, the noxious gas flows with the contours of the ground, is dispersed with the wind, and settles in low-lying areas. These properties were utilized in WWI to attack entrenched enemies. Since WWI over 200 major incidents involving chorine are documented (Baxter, Davies, & Murray, 1989).

On January 6, 2005, 11,500 gallons of chlorine were released from a rail tank car when two trains collided (Board, 2005). The release occurred in a small residential area in Graniteville, South Carolina, and prompted the evacuation of 5,400 residents within a one-mile radius of the accident (CDC, 2005). Nine people died and over 250 people received treatment for chlorine exposure. If the wind had been stronger that day, the toxic cloud would have traveled much further and likely created many more deaths and casualties.

Insurgent forces in Iraq detonated at least six chlorine devices in 2007. On April 6, 2007, a car bomb loaded with chlorine tanks was detonated in Ramadi, killing up to 30 and injuring over 50 (Rubin, 2007). Although most deaths were due to the explosions, these attacks demonstrate the will of extremist forces to utilize chemicals as deadly and psychologically destructive weapons.

Chlorine attacks both the central and peripheral airway compartments due to its intermediate solubility in water. Chlorine is also known as a choking agent and exerts pulmonary injuries through the mechanism of oxidation, causing chemical burns and immediate pain. Chlorine gas reacts with the moisture in mammalian airways and creates hydrochloric acid (HCl), the same chemical that digests your food and is used to etch concrete driveways. This causes swelling in the airway (pulmonary edema), constriction of the airway (bronchioconstriction), and death of the cells lining the airway (epithelial cell necrosis) (Adelson & Kaufman, 1971; White & Martin, 2010).

Phosgene is man-made compound that creates injury in the peripheral airway. Phosgene is an industrial chemical used to make precursors to plastic (polyurethane) and some pharmaceuticals. It is created when chloroform is exposed to UV light in the presence of oxygen. This spontaneous reaction is why chloroform is commonly stored in dark glass bottles or in closed cabinets.

In WWI, phosgene was the chemical weapon of choice because it could produce the most casualties. Although not responsible for a large number of deaths, phosgene casualties resulted in over 311,000 days of convalescence, which greatly impacted war efforts (Jackson, 1933). The main reason for high phosgene casualty rates is the delayed onset of symptoms. Those exposed to phosgene are typically asymptomatic for 30 minutes to 72 hours. Symptoms may begin with irritation of the eyes, nose, and throat, and then progress to unproductive coughing and damage deep in the lungs. This hallmark clinical effect known as dyspnea (damage to the alveolar-capillary membrane) causes difficulty in breathing and tightness of the chest. If the damage is severe, coughing may produce clear-to-yellow frothy sputum. The extent of exposure and timeline of proper medical treatment are the main factors that determine survival rates after phosgene exposure.

Ammonia is a naturally occurring gas that has a pungent odor and causes severe airway obstruction (Walton, 1973). Ammonia is primarily used in agricultural applications to make fertilizer due to its high nitrogen content. Ammonia is also used in industrial cooling applications since the boiling of ammonia is an endothermic (absorbing heat) process. Indoor ice-skating rinks and ice cream factories are made possible through cooling properties of ammonia. Unfortunately, pure ammonia is also used in one process to make methamphetamine in the illegal drug market. This has led to frequent incidents involving the accidental release of ammonia, causing inhalational and skin injuries and numerous deaths.

Pure ammonia is used in many industries and is more accurately called anhydrous ammonia. The ammonia you likely have in your home is mixed with water (aqua ammonia). While aqua ammonia (also called ammonium hydroxide) is helpful around the house, it still presents a hazard if ingested or gets into the eyes. Household ammonia is associated with numerous deaths when mixed with household (chlorine) bleach, creating toxic chloramine gases (Mrvos, Dean, & Krenzelok, 1993; Pascuzzi & Storrow, 1998).

Anhydrous means lacking water, but ammonia will absorb water from any source it is exposed to. Each molecule of ammonia can absorb ten molecules of water (TRANSCAER®, 2011). If inhaled, ammonia seeks out moisture in the airway and causes great tissue damage due to its alkalinity (pH 11.6). Exposure to concentrated ammonia vapor will immediately cause chemical burns in moist skin, permanent eye damage, and severe swelling and damage throughout the airway. Exposure to liquid ammonia can cause frostbite injuries.

Ammonia is transported in a compressed state, as a liquid, in cargo tanks across highways and tank cars along railways. Highway-bound cargo tanks typically range from 8,000 to 12,000 gallons whereas railway tank cars typically carry up to 30,000 gallons. As a compressed gas, ammonia has a high volumetric expansion ratio (850:1), meaning a small release of liquid ammonia will expand to produce a very large vapor cloud (TRANSCAER®, 2011).

Emergency responders often train for the release of ammonia, whether accidental or intentional, as through an act of terrorism. A large release of ammonia has the potential to cause devastating injuries over a large area. Although ammonia vapor is lighter than air, certain conditions cause it to behave as a fog, creeping along the ground and into houses, cars, and places of business.

Cyanides are not true pulmonary agents but are among the most toxic gasses. The U.S. military refers to hydrogen cyanide and cyanogen chloride as blood agents because victims tend to have bright red (highly oxygenated) blood. Whereas typical pulmonary agents inhibit the normal process of gas exchange between oxygen and carbon dioxide, cyanides block oxygen utilization at the cellular level, acting as a metabolic poison.

We need oxygen to survive. While that is certainly no revelation, it is how our body uses oxygen that is a true wonder. Nearly every cell in all mammalian and aquatic life requires oxygen. In general, cells have areas (mitochondria) dedicated to producing energy (ATP, adenosine triphosphate) for use in regular life. Once inhaled, cyanide gas is absorbed like oxygen and travels throughout the body and enters cells freely. Once in the cell, cyanide (cyanide ions, CN−) inhibits the process of energy production (cellular respiration) by binding to and blocking a critical step in the process (cytochrome C oxidase). When enough cyanide is present, cells cannot make enough energy (ATP) to keep up with demand and the cell dies. In large acute doses, death occurs within about three minutes. Fortunately, cyanide antidotes (amyl nitrite and others) can free cyanide from the cells and permit the production of energy once more. The critical step in this treatment is receiving the treatment before cyanide has the opportunity to cause death.

Toxic industrial chemicals/materials are not formal chemical agents but are capable of producing large numbers of casualties. The largest chemical incident in the world occurred in Bhopal, India. Known commonly as the Bhopal Disaster, over 200,000 people were exposed to methyl isocyanate (MIC) and other industrial chemicals while they slept the night of December 2, 1984. Although MIC is not detailed in this text, this incident highlights the great potential for mass casualties resulting from toxic industrial chemicals. In fact, this incident caused more casualties than any single chemical attack in known history. MIC is another pulmonary threat and is used to make pesticides (Sevin, a.k.a carbaryl), rubber, and adhesives. Like chlorine, MIC is heavier than air. When the release occurred at the Union Carbide India Limited facility, 30 metric tons of MIC are estimated to have been released over a 45–60 minute period (Varma, 2005). Estimates of deaths from this accident range from 5,000 to 20,000 with an estimated 60,000 chronic casualties that required long-term care (Bucher, 1987; Varma, 2005).

REFERENCES

Adelson, L., & Kaufman, J. (1971). Fatal Chlorine Poisoning: Report of Two Cases with Clinicopathologic Correlation. *American Journal of Clinical Pathology*, 56(4), 430–442. Retrieved from http://www.ncbi.nlm.nih.gov/pubmed/5113398

Baxter, P. J., Davies, P. C., & Murray, V. (1989). Medical Planning for Toxic Releases into the Community: The Example of Chlorine Gas. *British Journal of Industrial Medicine*, *46*(4), 277–285. Retrieved from http://www.pubmedcentral.nih.gov/articlerender.fcgi?artid=1009767&tool=pmcentrez&rendertype=abstract

Beswick, F. W. (1983). Chemical Agents Used in Riot Control and Warfare. *Human Toxicology*, *2*(2), 247–256. Retrieved from http://www.ncbi.nlm.nih.gov/pubmed/6407978

Board, S. (2005). Collision of Norfolk Southern Freight Train 192 with Standing Norfolk Southern Local Train P22 With Subsequent Hazardous Materials Release at Graniteville, South Carolina.

Borak, J., & Sidell, F. R. (1992). Agents of Chemical Warfare: Sulfur Mustard. *Annals of Emergency Medicine*, *21*(3), 303–308. doi:10.1016/S0196-0644(05)80892-3

Bucher, J. R. (1987). Methyl Isocyanante: A Review of Health Effects Research Since Bhopal. *Toxicological Sciences*, *9*(3), 367–379. doi:10.1093/toxsci/9.3.367

Buscher, H. (1932). *Green and Yellow Cross* (Translated.). Hamburg, Germany: Himmel-heber: Kettering Laboratory of Applied Physiology, Cincinnati, OH.

CDC. (2005). Public Health Consequences from Hazardous Substances Acutely Released During Rail Transit – South Carolina, 2005; Selected States, 1999–2004. *MMWR Weekly*, *54*(3), 64–67. Retrieved from http://www.cdc.gov/mmwr/preview/mmwrhtml/mm5403a2.htm

Charbonneau, L., & Nichols, M. (2013). U.N. conforms sarin used in Syria attack. *Reuters*. Retrieved from http://www.reuters.com/article/2013/09/16/us-syria-crisis-un-idUSBRE98F0ED20130916.

Danzig, B. R., Sageman, M., Leighton, T., & Hough, L. (n.d.). (2012, December). *Aum Shinrikyo Insights Into How Terrorists Develop Biological and Chemical Weapons* (2nd ed.). Washington, D.C.: Center for a New American Security.

Francis, M. (2012). In the Aftermath of Aum Shinrikyo: Lessons Learned from the Japanese Response. Retrieved from http://www.radicalisationresearch.org/debate/reader-2012-aftermath-2/

Fries, A. A., & West, C. J. (1921). *Chemical Warfare* (1st ed.). New York: McGraw-Hill Book Company, Inc.

Guillemin, J. (1999). *Anthrax: The Investigation of a Deadly Outbreak*. Los Angeles, CA: University of California Press.

Iyaki, K. M., Ishiwaki, Y. N., Aekawa, K. M., Gawa, Y. O., Sukai, N. A., & Mae, K. O. (2005). Effects of Sarin on the Nervous System of Subway Workers Seven Years after the Tokyo Subway Sarin Attack, *Environmental Health Perspectives*, *47*, 299–304.

Medema, J. (1986). Mustard Gas: The Science of H. Nuclear, Biological, and Chemical Defense and Technology International, *Nuclear, Biological, and Chemical Defense and Technology*, *1*, 66–71.

Jackson, K. E. (1933). Phosgene. *Journal of Chemical Education*, *10*(10), 622. doi:10.1021/ed010p622

Leghorn, R. S. (1956). Controlling the Nuclear Threat in the Second Atomic Decade. *Bulletin of the Atominc Scientists*, *12*(6), 189–195.

Lewis, W., & Stiegler, H. (1925). The Beta-Chlorovinyl-Arsines and their Derivatives. *American Chemical Society*, *47*, 2546–2555.

Wessely, S., Hyams, K. C., Barthelolomew, R. (2001). Psychological Implications of Chemical and Biological Weapons. *BMJ 323* (October), 878–879.

McAdams, A. J., & Joffe, M. (1955). *A Toxico-pathologic Study of Phosgene Oxime*. Army Chemical Center. Medical Laboratories Research Report 381.

Mrvos, R., Dean, B. S., & Krenzelok, E. P. (1993). Home Exposures to Chlorine/Chloramine Gas: Review of 216 Cases. *Southern Medical Journal*, 86(6), 654–657. Retrieved from http://www.ncbi.nlm.nih.gov/pubmed/8506487

Pascuzzi, T. A., & Storrow, A. B. (1998). Mass Casualties from Acute Inhalation of Chloramine Gas. *Military Medicine*, 163(2), 102–104. Retrieved from http://www.ncbi.nlm.nih.gov/pubmed/9503902

Pechura, C. M., & Rall, D. P. (1993). *Veterans at Risk: The Health Effects of Mustard Gas and Lewisite* (1st ed.). Washington, DC: National Academy Press.

Prentiss, A. M., & Fisher, G. J. B. (1937). *Chemicals in War : A Treatise on Chemical Warfare* (1st ed.). New York: McGraw-Hill Book Company, Inc.

Raevskiy, A. E. (2014). Psychological Aspects of the Aum Shinrikyo Affair. *Psychology in Russia: State of the Art. 7*(1). doi: 10.11621/pir.2014.0104

Rubin, A. J. (April 7, 2007). Chlorine Gas Attack by Truck Bomber Kills Up to 30 in Iraq. *The New York Times*. Retrieved from http://www.nytimes.com/2007/04/07/world/middleeast/07iraq.html?_r=0

Schonwald, S. (1992). Mustard Gas. *The PSR Quarterly*, 2(2), 45–60.

Smithson, A. E., Mirzayanov, V. S., Lajoie, R., & Krepon, M. (1995). *Chemical Weapons Disarmament in Russia: Problems and Prospects*. Washington, DC: The Henry L. Stimson Center.

TRANSCAER®. (2011). *Anhydrous Ammonia Training*. Retrieved October 2014 from http://www.transcaer.com/aa-tour.

Tuorinsky, S. D. (2008). *The Medical Aspects of Chemical Warfare* (M. K. Lenhart & S. D. Tuorinsky, Eds.) (2nd ed., Vol. 85). Washington, DC: Department of the Army. Retrieved from http://jama.jamanetwork.com/article.aspx?doi=10.1001/jama.1925.02670140069034

Varma, R. (2005). The Bhopal Disaster of 1984. *Bulletin of Science, Technology & Society*, 25(1), 37–45. doi:10.1177/0270467604273822

Walton, M. (1973). Industrial Ammonia Gassing. *British Journal of Industrial Medicine*, 30(1), 78–86. Retrieved from http://www.pubmedcentral.nih.gov/articlerender.fcgi?artid=1009482&tool=pmcentrez&rendertype=abstract

White, C. W., & Martin, J. G. (2010). Chlorine Gas Inhalation: Human Clinical Evidence of Toxicity and Experience in Animal Models. *Proceedings of the American Thoracic Society*, 7(4), 257–263. doi:10.1513/pats.201001-008SM

10

Biological Agents

Kelley J. Williams

Biological weapons are born out of naturally occurring pathogens, primarily bacteria and viruses, and toxins of biological origin. Scientists isolate the disease-causing pathogens during outbreaks or from natural hosts. Specific means of growing bacteria and viruses enabled nations to amass large quantities and concentrations of these pathogens far beyond what is found in nature. Some biological agents were made more virulent or drug resistant through genetic manipulation.

The most menacing bioterrorist is Mother Nature herself. (Drexler, 2002)

The term "pathogen" comes from the Greek, meaning "producer of suffering." The term is applied to any item of natural source that can produce disease or disrupt the normal physiology of organisms in the biological kingdom. This review will focus on pathogens deemed biological agents—those with applications in biological warfare, terrorism, or crime that are targeted against humans, livestock, or food crops. These agents include bacteria, viruses, and toxins.

The psychological impact of biological agent incidents is unmatched in the WMD (weapon of mass destruction) spectrum of threats. *Will biological weapons create more paranoia in the general population than the use of chemical, radiological, nuclear, or explosive weapons? Absolutely*. Compared to other WMD threats, most people can relate to biological weapons at some level. Someone does not need to understand how a virus spreads to be afraid of an unseen contagion. There are only a handful of survivors left from Hiroshima and Nagasaki with first-hand knowledge of a nuclear attack; everyone has been sick, often without knowing the specific source. When the public perceives a biological threat, they may realize this sickness could have easily been a deadly pathogen. Perhaps biological agents carry additional anxiety since people feel they can take measures to prevent infection. Those feelings can prompt behavioral changes toward

communities and public officials. Most notably, such feelings can prompt paranoia toward medical readiness. Military publications openly recognize the negative impact of biological threats on relationships between service members and
the proper care of casualties (Zajtchuk, 1995).

During biological incidents and natural outbreaks, hospitals prepare for
greatly increased numbers of self-diagnosed "worried wounded." Medical facilities and personnel are ill-equipped to handle the large influx of patients that a
biological incident will likely provoke. Whether they are correct or not, people
often feel a biological attack/outbreak must be contagious and that it may spread
to them and their family.

Why would a terrorist or WMD-criminal choose biological weapons? The use
of biological weapons or agents is very dependent on the form of use, be it warfare, terrorism, or another crime.

BIOLOGICAL WARFARE

Biological agents are particularly ineffective as military weapons (Wessely,
Hyams, & Barthelolomew, 2001). The strict conditions of their production,
weaponization, and use on the battlefield, combined with the relative ease of
biological agent defense, make biological warfare between nations highly
improbable (Dembek & Lenhart, 2007).

BIOLOGICAL TERRORISM

No single definition of "terrorism" has received universal acceptance.
According to the U.S. Department of State, terrorism is "premeditated, politically motivated violence perpetrated against noncombatant targets by subna-
tional or clandestine agents, usually intended to influence an audience" (U.S.
Department of State, 2002). Biological weapons are quintessential weapons of
terror (Wessely et al., 2001). The now-routine journalistic association between
chemical and biological weapons and the word "terror" confirms that the purpose
of these weapons is to wreak psychological destruction by inducing fear, confusion, and uncertainty in everyday life (Guillemin, 1999). "Bioterrorism" refers
to the use of biological agents by a group not otherwise recognized as an extension of a government or state. Such "non-State" actors include groups motivated
by political, religious, or ideological objectives.

BIOLOGICAL CRIMES

A biocrime is the use of biological agents in an attack of a personal nature,
such as revenge. Perpetrators of biocrimes often have specialized knowledge
and access to the biological materials used in the crime (Dembek & Lenhart,

2007). Common biocrimes include the contamination of food or medications with pathogens or toxins. There are even four known murder attempts using injections of HIV-infected blood.

BIOLOGICAL AGENT FUNDAMENTALS

The biological threat, in many ways, is more precarious and complex than other WMD threats since it increases with positive uses of biotechnology (Nuclear Threat Initiative, n.d.). Biological agents are among a large group of substances known as antigen (antibody-generating). When a host's immune system recognizes an antigen as a foreign invader, a complex cascade of events takes place in an attempt to protect itself and clear the antigen from the body. Unfortunately, sometimes the immune response is so severe that it proves more destructive than the infection alone and may be fatal. Biological agents are either replicating (bacteria, viruses, fungi) or nonreplicating (toxin, prion). However, the ability to replicate does not necessarily mean an agent is "alive" in the typical sense.

The "Central Dogma" of molecular biology describes how functional elements of life (protein) come from DNA (deoxyribonucleic acid) (Figure 10.1). It states that DNA is transcribed into RNA (ribonucleic acid), which in turn is translated into protein. Proteins are modified within a cell into a specific form or shape. In biology, form is function. The functions of these modified proteins are involved in every aspect of life. Cells are generally known as eukaryotic (i.e., mammalian, plant, fungal) or prokaryotic (i.e., bacterial). Eukaryotic cells are incredibly complex structures that can be very simply described as a small sphere (nucleus) that is contained inside another sphere (cellular membrane).

There are, of course, many other organelles and processes in the cell as well. Bacterial cells do not contain nuclei, lack the ability to generate a supply of energy known as Adenotriphosphate (ATP), and are generally smaller than mammalian cells.

Cells are constantly passing nutrients and chemical signals in and out of their membranes. Pathogens can interact with cells by passing foreign genomic material (DNA or RNA proteins) (antigen) through cellular membranes to cause infection or clinical symptoms. In mammals, DNA is the genetic codebook that remains protected within the nucleus of all mitotic (dividing) cells. RNA is a "reverse copy" of specific DNA fragments that leave the nucleus. In the cytosol or other compartments, this RNA acts as a messenger. Special complex proteins called ribosomes attach to the messenger RNA and move across it, start to finish, like a train on its tracks. The ribosomes read the RNA code and translate this code into a protein by taking the required building blocks from within the cell. Bacteria accomplish this in a similar fashion but do not have a nucleus; bacterial DNA is circular and floats freely inside the cytoplasm of a bacterium.

Figure 10.1
Central dogma of microbiology. (Courtesy of Kelley Williams)

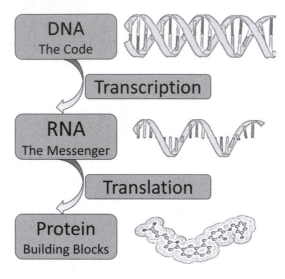

Are viruses alive? Since bacteria can exist outside of a host under certain conditions (with few exceptions), make their own protein, and are capable of self-replication, they are considered living organisms. Viruses do not have the genetic means to generate the energy necessary to drive all required biological processes and are absolutely dependent on host cells for meeting these requirements (Cann, 2012). For these reasons, one may not consider them living organisms. However, since viruses interact with host cellular functions to replicate and ensure a continued existence, some consider viruses subcellular living organisms. Fortunately for viruses, they can infect you without regard to your opinion of their existence.

This review of biological agents is intended to provide a broad overview of several threats and distinctions between biological agent categories. The agents selected to highlight these aspects represent a small fraction of potential threats. An abundance of references are available that present the details of biological agents that are known to have been weaponized, some of which are listed in the Recommended Readings section. This review will merely scratch the surface to facilitate the discussion on psychological effects of biological agents.

As previously mentioned, bacteria are single-celled organisms that do not contain a nucleus (prokaryotic cells). Although most bacteria are only several micrometers in size, bacteria constitute the greatest biomass on earth, beyond the combined mass of all plants and animals (Hogan, 2014). Bacteria are generally larger than viruses and can often be seen with common optical micro-scopes. Bacteria inhabit most corners of the earth, from hot springs and radioactive waste to deep ocean depths and the human mouth. Bacteria often serve beneficial purposes in the proper function of ecosystems but can cause widespread death and sickness if introduced to foreign and susceptible environments or hosts.

Bacteria can be transported by a great variety of physical means and some are known to possess an ability to adapt to new environmental conditions. Bacteria are equipped with the subcellular components (organelles) required to support self-replication. Bacteria only require suitable conditions for growth (e.g., tempera-ture, oxygen/nitrogen levels, nutrients, moisture) in which to thrive. Some bacteria are able to form spores when exposed to unsuitable conditions. These spores are essentially bacterial "seeds" that protect the bacterial genome for future genera-tions. If these spores encounter suitable conditions they will germinate and create new bacterial colonies. Unfortunately, some spore-forming bacteria are infamous as human pathogens. This review will briefly highlight *Bacillus anthracis* (Anthrax).

Anthrax is a disease caused by the bacteria *Bacillus anthracis*. According to a study by the World Health Organization (WHO), a 50 kg release of aerosolized *B. anthracis* spores in an urban city of 5 million people could spread 20 km down-wind and cause 100,000 deaths and over 250,000 serious casualties (WHO, 1970). Anthrax is a zoonotic disease because humans can be infected through interactions with animals, primarily cattle, sheep, goats, horse, and swine (Hugh-Jones & de Vos, 2002).

Anthrax manifests in three forms. Depending on the route of exposure, inha-lational, gastrointestinal, or cutaneous anthrax may occur. The symptoms can take between 1 day to 2 months to appear and all forms of anthrax have the potential to spread throughout the body and cause severe illness and death (CDC, 2013). The most deadly form is inhalational anthrax, which is the out-come of a weaponized release of spores in an aerosolized form. These spores ger-minate in the skin or airway, leading to bacterial proliferation and the production of two toxins (lethal and edema) (Dembek & Lenhart, 2007). These toxins interfere with the normal functions of cells, leading to cell death and leaky blood vessels (vascular permeability). Although the precise mechanisms these toxins use are not known, there is a high level of toxin in the blood in fatal cases (Dembek & Lenhart, 2007).

During inhalational anthrax, the toxins cause a bloody infection of the lymph nodes in the chest (hemorrhagic mediastinitis) and a buildup of fluid between the lungs and the chest cavity (pleural effusion). The hemorrhagic widening of the mediastinum is identified through a chest X-ray and is seen only in inhala-tional anthrax infections.

Cutaneous anthrax develops in open wounds and typically occurs in those with close contact with susceptible animal carcases and wool. Also known as "sheep shearers' disease," cutaneous anthrax can cause local infection in small knicks and cuts on the fingertips of those who process wool. Lesions are also commonly found on the arms, legs, and neck.

Gastrointestinal anthrax develops from the ingestion of meat that is contaminated with B. *anthracis* spores. The largest reported incident involving gastrointestinal anthrax occurred in 1979 in Sverdlovsk, Ukraine (formerly USSR). When this incident became public, Soviet leadership denied the claims that the incident was related to biological weapons. In its June 1980 statement, the official Soviet news agency declared that a "natural outbreak of anthrax among domestic animals" had caused "cases of skin and intestinal forms of anthrax" in the Sverdlovsk region (Alibek & Handelman, 1999). The medical records for these people were removed or altered to cover up that many injuries were from inhalational anthrax. The death toll from this release is estimated at 105 but altered medical records blur the truth. Secondary aerosols, settled particles that get kicked up by wind, people, or animals, caused casualties for a month and a half. In 1993 Russian president Boris Yeltsin admitted to a reporter that the accident was due to "our military developments" and when asked why he had been silent for so long, he replied "Nobody asked me" (Alibek & Handelman, 1999). As of 1998, the official Russian stance is again that the incident was due to contaminated meat.

The source facility in this incident was Compound 19 of the USSR Fifteenth Directorate (biological weapons production), which dried anthrax slurries for weaponization. The unofficial (but accepted) story is that between shift changes, a protective air filter was removed but not replaced. This permitted the release of spores, which were disseminated downwind to the local citizens. Dr. Ken Alibek was a leader in the Soviet biological weapons establishment (Biopreparat). On his defection to the United States in 1992, he revealed this information to U.S. officials and that strains of B. *anthracis* were modified for antibacterial resistance and increased virulence (Alibek & Handelman, 1999).

VIRUSES

Viruses are submicroscopic, obligate, intracellular parasites. This means they cannot replicate outside of a suitable host and are too small to be seen with optical microscopes (Cann, 2012). Viruses present unique challenges for biological defense and medical personnel. Viruses utilize host cellular mechanisms to replicate, so treatments against the virus may also be destructive to the host. Additionally, viruses are prone to genetic mutations, which cause the phenomena called antigenic drift and shift. Antigenic drift is the gradual accumulation of small changes, which decreases recognition by an immune system. This is one reason why last year's flu shot may be less effective in the current year. Antigenic shift is a sudden and dramatic change in the properties of a virus such that it may be able to evade the immune system and cause a severe infection

(Cann, 2012). Antigenic shift was observed in the 2009 H1N1 pandemic. This novel (new) virus strain presented a unique combination of genes from American pigs, Eurasian pigs, birds, and humans in a manner unknown to most immune systems (CDC, 2010).

This review will briefly highlight Ebola and the influenza viruses.

As of April 28, 2015, the 2014 Ebola epidemic has claimed 10,884 lives in West Africa from over 14,800 laboratory-confirmed cases since it began in Guinea in December 2013. This is the largest Ebola outbreak since the virus was discovered in 1976 and accounts for more fatalities than all previous outbreaks combined (BBC, 2014). Ebola is the dominant virus in the family known as Filoviruses. Named for their unusual filamentous (thread-like) structure, Filoviruses (Ebola and Marburg) are also known as hemorrhagic fever viruses. While there are many viral hemorrhagic fevers (VHFs), Ebola is particularly virulent and causes horrific symptoms. Ebola outbreaks typically produce 50–90 percent fatality rates (depending on the species) at an explosive rate. Filoviruses spread through contact with infected bodily fluids (saliva, blood, semen, breast milk, feces, and vomit).

The potential for transmission of Ebola through air (similar to influenza) was demonstrated during an outbreak of Ebola in Reston, Virginia. Although this particular strain did not cause disease in humans, it is possible that antigenic shift or drift could occur in the strains, which are fatal in people. The rapid spread of Ebola virus disease is often attributed to the virus properties but assisted by the cultural practices of West African peoples and lack of modern medical response capabilities in endemic areas.

The 2013 Ebola epidemic renewed concerns of VHFs as agents in biological warfare and terrorism. Aid workers from several countries acquired Ebola during their work in Africa and exported the disease to their homeland, infecting additional health care workers. The high morbidity and mortality associated with VHFs and the lack of effective treatment led the Centers for Disease Control and Prevention (CDC) to list most hemorrhagic fever viruses as Category A bioweapon agents (CDC, n.d.).

The United States, Russia, and the Soviet Union weaponized several hemorrhagic fever viruses. Russia and the Soviet Union produced large quantities of Ebola, Marburg, Lassa, Junin, and Machupo as bioweapon agents until 1992 (Alibek & Handelman, 1999; Miller, Broad, & Engelberg, 2002). Based on unconfirmed reports by leadership from within the Soviet biological weapons establishment, Ebola was one of several viruses that may have been altered to greatly enhance transmission among humans (Alibek & Handelman, 1999).

TOXINS

A toxin is any toxic substance of natural origin, produced by bacteria, marine life, fungi, plants, and animals. Toxins can be proteins or nonproteins that interfere with proper biological functions. Unlike bacteria and viruses, toxins do not replicate. Toxins are not a persistent threat in the environment and are not contagious. Toxins can be destructive through most forms of exposure, but very few toxins present a threat by skin contact, such as mycotoxins from fungi.

Exotoxins are released from bacteria during cellular processes (extracellular toxin) and endotoxins are released during cell death (lysis). Toxins are among the most toxic substances on a by-weight basis. Many toxins are lethal at microgram (μg) doses and incapacitating at nanogram (ng) doses. To put this in perspective, a single grain of sugar weighs 625 μg or 625,000 ng. A common example is that the amount of purified botulinum toxin that can fit on the head of a pin is enough to kill 100,000 people. While this example assumes an unobtainable means of delivery, consider the Iraqi biological weapons program that produced 4,900 gallons of weaponized botulinum toxin (Alibek & Handelman, 1999; Council, 1995; Zilinskas, 1997). That is a lot of pinheads. Some toxins, such as ricin and saxiotoxin, appear on both the chemical and biological select agent lists (OPCW, n.d.).

Botulinum toxin is produced by the bacteria *Clostridium botulinum* (*C. botulinum*). Botulinum toxin is the most toxic substance known to exist and manifests as the neuroparalytic disease of botulism. The natural function of this extracellular neurotoxin is unknown. Botulism occurs in three forms, dependent on the route of exposure: inhalational, foodborne, and wound. Infantile botulism is a special foodborne case that occurs most commonly when infants are given honey containing botulinum spores.

Botulinum toxin has seven forms (serotypes) but all produce similar symptoms. Botulism is similar to the familiar disease tetanus (30–40 percent homology), which is produced by the bacteria *Clostridium tetani*. Botulinum toxin interferes with the proper signaling through neurological pathways by blocking the release of neurotransmitters. This occurs when the toxin cleaves proteins that are required for the release of acetylcholine within the synaptic cleft. This classically results in descending flaccid paralysis and can be fatal when respiration becomes involved (Dembek & Lenhart, 2007). When the diaphragmatic muscles are paralyzed, patients should be treated with respiratory care through mechanical ventilation and feeding tubes. Antitoxins may be administered as soon as possible to exist to halt the progress of paralysis but they do not reverse existing symptoms (Dembek & Lenhart, 2007). If stabilized, patients can recover as the toxin naturally degrades and is metabolized.

Symptoms of botulism are essentially the opposite of early acute nerve agent exposure. Using the "on-off switch" parallels from Chapter 9, Chemical Agents, botulism creates an "always-off" situation, whereas nerve agents were "always-on". Acute nerve agent toxicity eventually fatigues the muscular system and results in respiratory failure similar to botulism.

Prions are not formally listed as biological agents and scientific knowledge on prions is relatively undeveloped. Prions are misfolded proteins that cause infection in mammals. The name "prion" comes from proteinaceous infectious particles (Prusiner, 1982). Most people would recognize the prion disease "Mad Cow disease" which was brought to the public light through media coverage of widespread cattle infections in the United Kingdom, beginning in 1986. In this epidemic, cattle were exposed to prions when fed with infected remains of other cattle as a protein supplement. Prions are extremely resistant to disinfectants, food processing, and typical sterilization techniques.

Mammalian prion diseases damage the brain or other neural tissue, are currently untreatable, and are always fatal (Prusiner, 1998). The onset of symptoms for many prion diseases is very long (5–20 years) but once symptoms appear little can be done to slow the progress of the disease. Due to the long delay of onset, prions are not considered useful as biological weapons.

One critical distinction between toxins and prions are that toxins do not replicate/propagate, whereas prions do. The ability for prions to increase in number within a host defies the central dogma of microbiology (Figure 10.1). Since prions multiply without the use of nucleic acid (DNA or RNA), researchers have developed multiple controversial theories about this mechanism. Most theories involve the reforming of existing proteins, which is catalyzed by infectious particles. As a greater number of existing proteins are misshapened from this action, they cannot perform their intended functions and result in the presence of disease symptoms.

On the larger scale, prion infection can give normal brain tissue a spongy texture. In cattle, this led to the common name as Bovine Spongiform Encephalopathy. Contact with prion-infected meat can cause diseases such as Creutzfeldt-Jakob disease in humans (Ironside, 2006).

PATHOGEN NAME VERSUS DISEASE NAME

Based on inconsistencies in popular media and common reporting errors, it is pertinent to review proper naming conventions of pathogens and the physiological disorders they cause. It should go without saying that biological agents can cause disease. People and animals are exposed to the pathogen, which creates signs and symptoms of a particular disease. If someone is exposed to the bacteria *B. anthracis* (the pathogen), they may contract a form of anthrax (the disease). The opposite convention is incorrect; someone cannot be exposed to anthrax. If an infant is fed honey that contains spores from *C. botulinum* (the pathogen) he will likely develop infant botulism (an intoxication, "the disease"). The infant was not exposed to botulism; he contracted it through a food source contaminated with the pathogen (sporulated *C. botulinum*).

In this manner, clinical symptoms (disease) are due to the pathogenic mechanisms of a causative agent (bacteria, virus, etc.). One exception is viral infections. Since the species' name of a virus is typically the same as the clinical name of the symptoms of infection, someone can be exposed to Ebola (the pathogen) and also "have" Ebola. In this situation, it would be more proper to say someone was exposed to the Ebola virus and contracted the Ebola virus disease, but this is rarely adhered to outside technical publications.

Additionally, when one is referring to a single bacterial cell, it is proper to use the term "bacterium." "Bacteria" is plural for bacterium and can refer to a specific species or the entire biological domain of bacteria. A single virus particle would be referred to as a virion or a virus particle. The term "virus" typically refers to a specific species or the entire pathogenic category.

REFERENCES

Alibek, K., & Handelman, S. (1999). *Biohazard: The Chilling True Story of the Largest Covert Biological Weapons Program in the World. Told From the Inside by the Man Who Ran It.* New York: Random House.

BBC. (2014). Ebola: Mapping the Outbreak. Retrieved from http://www.bbc.com/news/world-africa-28755033

Cann, A. J. (2012). *Principles of Molecular Virology* (5th ed.). Oxford: Academic Press.

CDC. (n.d.). Emergency Preparedness and Response: Bioterrorism Agents/Diseases. Retrieved from http://www.bt.cdc.gov/Agent/agentlist-category.asp

CDC. (2010). 2009 H1N1 – Overview of a Pandemic. Retrieved from http://www.cdc.gov/h1n1flu/yearinreview/yir1.htm

CDC. (2013). Anthrax: Symptoms. Retrieved from http://www.cdc.gov/anthrax/basics/symptoms.html

Council, U. N. S. (1995). *Tenth Report of the Executive Chairman of the Special Commission Established by the Secretary-General Pursuant to Paragraph 9(b)(I) of Security Council Resolution 687 (1991) and Paragraph 3 of Resolution 699 (1991) on the Activities of the Special Commiss.* New York. Retrieved from http://fas.org/news/un/iraq/s/s1995-1038.htm

Dembek, Z. F., & Lenhart, M. K. (Eds.). (2007). *Medical Aspects of Biological Warfare.* Washington, DC: Office of The Surgeon General.

Drexler, M. (2002). *Secret Agents: The Menace of Emerging Infections.* Washington, DC: Joseph Henry Press.

Guillemin, J. (1999). *Anthrax: The Investigation of a Deadly Outbreak.* Los Angeles, CA: University of California Press.

Hogan, C. M. (2014). Biodiversity: Bacteria. Retrieved from http://www.eoearth.org/view/article/150368/

Hugh-Jones, M. E., & de Vos, V. (2002). Anthrax and Wildlife. *Revue Scientifique et Technique (International Office of Epizootics), 21*(2), 359–383. Retrieved from http://www.ncbi.nlm.nih.gov/pubmed/11974621

Ironside, J. W. (2006). Variant Creutzfeldt-Jakob Disease: Risk of Transmission by Blood Transfusion and Blood Therapies. *Haemophilia: The Official Journal of the World*

Federation of Hemophilia, 12(Suppl 1), 8–15; discussion 26–8. doi:10.1111/j.1365 -2516.2006.01195.x

Miller, J., Broad, W. J., & Engelberg, S. (2002). *Germs: Biological Weapons and America's Secret War* (Reprint.). New York: Simon & Schuster.

Nuclear Threat Initiative. (n.d.). About NTI. Retrieved October 15, 2015, from http://www.nti.org/about/

OPCW. (n.d.). *Chemical Weapons Convention*. Retrieved from https://www.opcw.org/chemical-weapons-convention/

Prusiner, S. B. (1982). Novel Proteinaceous Infectious Particles Cause Scrapie. *Science (New York, N.Y.)*, *216*(4542), 136–144. Retrieved from http://www.ncbi.nlm.nih.gov/pubmed/6801762

Prusiner, S. B. (1998). Prions. *Proceedings of the National Academy of Sciences of the United States of America*, *95*(23), 13363–13383. Retrieved from http://www.pubmedcentral.nih.gov/articlerender.fcgi?artid=33918&tool=pmcentrez&rendertype=abstract

U.S. Department of State. (2002). *Patterns of Global Terrorism 2001*. Retrieved from http://go.usa.gov/QbaF

Wessely, S., Hyams, K.C., Barthelolomew, R. (2001). Psychological Implications of Chemical and Biological Weapons. *BMJ* 323 (October), 878–879.

World Health Organization. (1970). *Health Aspects of Chemical and Biological Weapons*. Retrieved from https://extranet.who.int/iris/restricted/bitstream/10665/39444/1/24039.pdf

Zajtchuk, R. (1995). *War Psychiatry* (R. F. Bellamy, Ed.). Washington, DC: Office of The Surgeon General, United States of America.

Zilinskas, R. A. (1997). Iraq's Biological Weapons. The Past as Future? *JAMA*, *278*(5), 418–424. Retrieved from http://www.ncbi.nlm.nih.gov/pubmed/9244334

11

Radiological and Nuclear Weapons

Kelley J. Williams

Radiological dispersal/exposure devices cause unwanted exposure to potentially harmful sources of radioactivity. Several classes of radiological weapons exist, but this text refers to a radiological dispersal device (RDD) as one that uses conventional explosives to disperse radiological material. The health and destructive effects of an RDD are vastly different from those of a nuclear weapon. The primary hazard of an RDD is the explosive blast, shrapnel, and fireball in the immediate vicinity of the detonation. The secondary threat of an RDD is from the radiation component. The radiation hazard severity is highly dependent on the type and amount of radiological material in the device and the efficiency of its dispersal during the explosion. While the explosive effects of an RDD are short-lived, the radioactive material can contaminate large areas for many years. Although not commonly explored, a radiological weapon could expose victims to radiation through aerosols, direct injection, or a static source.

Nuclear weapons present the only true threat of mass destruction. Unlike chemical, biological, radiological, and conventional explosive weapons, which threaten individuals or buildings, nuclear weapons hold entire cities and nations at risk. Nuclear weapons represent the pinnacle of man's scientific and engineering marvels but also their propensity for self-destruction. Nuclear weapons utilize highly refined natural and man-made isotopes of uranium, plutonium, and other elements. Most modern nuclear arsenals are 10–20 times more powerful than the device used by the United States against the Japanese city of Hiroshima on August 6, 1945. This attack killed up to 80,000 people immediately and destroyed 5 square miles of the city (Woodruff, Alt, Forcino, & Walker, 2012).

> With modern weapons-grade uranium . . . terrorists . . . would have a good chance of setting off a high-yield explosion simply by dropping one half of the material onto the other half . . . even a high school kid could make a bomb in short order. (Alvarez, 1987)

Radiological and nuclear weapons are very different in the spectrum of potential destruction and severity of injuries they may cause. They differ greatly in the cost and amount of technical expertise required for their development and successful use. Although radiological and nuclear weapons are unique threats, it is helpful to discuss them together to highlight these distinctions and common radiation effects without redundancy.

Why would a terrorist or weapon of mass destruction (WMD) criminal choose radiological or nuclear weapons? There is no single weapon that imparts greater destructive power than a nuclear explosive. First-generation nuclear devices created 16–20 kT (TNT) of explosive power. These weapons, if detonated in modern metropolitan areas such as Los Angeles, could kill 60,000 and expose 150,000 to hazardous radiation levels; 600,000 homes would be lost, and several million people would be displaced (Becker, 2012). Acquiring a nuclear weapon for terrorist use, however, would likely prove exceedingly difficult unless supported by a nuclear capable nation. There is a differentiation between *acquiring* an existing weapon and *constructing* a weapon. "Acquiring" could mean a weapon was given by a sympathetic nuclear-armed state (support) or simply stolen from *any* nuclear state (no support). Nuclear capable nation could be any nation in possession of a nuclear stockpile or the ability to build weapons if desired, as with the nations of Japan, Germany, and Canada.

Radiological weapons are intended to expose people and materiel to radioactive isotopes. These are commonly referred to as radiological dispersal devices (RDDs) but could also be radiological exposure devices (REDs). An RDD, also known as a "dirty bomb," uses conventional explosives to disperse radioactive material. The immediate destruction of an RDD comes from the explosion's blast, fireball, and accompanying shrapnel. Depending on the type of radiation source used, the contamination could present hazardous levels and turn city blocks into radiation hot zones for years. Radiological weapons are likely candidates for use when a terrorist group has access to radioisotopes and wants to create immediate and residual hazards while capitalizing on the public's lack of understanding and abundance of fear regarding radiation hazards.

Unfortunately, a summary of radiological and nuclear weapons requires a specific vocabulary and basic understanding of radiation. If you were comfortable with high school nuclear physics, this will serve as a brief review.

The definition of "radiation" covers a wide spectrum of natural phenomena that can be classified as ionizing, nonionizing, or cosmic radiation (Table 11.1). The most significant type of radiation that occurs in a radiological incident (accidental or weaponized) or during nuclear weapon detonation is ionizing radiation. The types of ionizing radiation that occur during nuclear or radiological incidents (alpha, beta, gamma, X-ray, and neutron) will be detailed later in this chapter as they relate to weapon effects. The discussion of radiological and

Table 11.1
Radiation spectrum and the types of radiation associated with radiological and nuclear weapon use

Radiation Category	Examples	Source
Ionizing	Alpha particles	RDD and nuclear
	Beta particles	RDD and nuclear
	Gamma rays	RDD and nuclear
	Neutrons	RDD and nuclear
	X-rays	Nuclear
	Ultraviolet	
Non-ionizing	Visible light	
	Infrared (IR)	
	Microwaves	
	Radio waves	
	Thermal (heat)	
Cosmic	High-energy particles from the sun or deep space	

nuclear weapons can be simplified by thinking of ionizing radiation as the release or transfer of energy.

Atoms are composed of electrons, protons, and neutrons. In a traditional cartoon of an atom, protons and neutrons are clustered in the nucleus and surrounded by a cloud of electrons that orbit the nucleus (Figure 11.1). Ionizing radiation presents enough energy to liberate electrons from other molecules or atoms (ionization). Ionization sources often include accelerators such as X-rays, fusion neutrons, protons, and alpha particles.

If an event causes an electron to leave its nuclear orbit, that atom has been ionized. If an event causes the atom to be split into (generally) two nuclei of lighter elements, this event is called fission, and these new nuclei are called fission fragments. Only certain heavy elements (nuclides) are capable of undergoing a fission event and are known as fissionable materials. Special elements that can sustain a nuclear reaction are known as fissile materials and are the fuel for nuclear weapons.

As you would hope, this special nuclear material is both difficult and expensive to acquire and is highly protected. In the case of uranium-235 (U235) (Figure 11.2), a neutron may cause induced fission, splitting the uranium atom (momentarily U236) and creating two lighter nuclei and two or three free neutrons. These neutrons then go on to induce more fission reactions, and so on.

Figure 11.1
Basic atomic structure. (Courtesy of Kelley Williams)

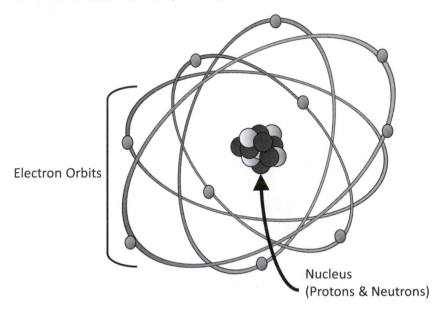

Electron Orbits

Nucleus
(Protons & Neutrons)

This is the same reaction that occurs in most nuclear power reactors but at a controlled slower rate. Each fission event releases an astonishing amount of energy. The complete fission of 1 pound of uranium releases the same explosive energy as 8,000 tons of TNT! It can be said that the only difference between a nuclear power reactor and nuclear weapons is the rate of reaction, the energy of the neutrons causing the fissions, and the density of the critical mass. If a certain amount of fissile material is combined into a single mass, it will be able to sustain a chain reaction, where the number of fissions occurring per second remains constant. This is known as a critical mass. If the fissile material is below this level (subcritical mass), it will not sustain a chain reaction. If more material than necessary for a critical mass is assembled into a supercritical mass, the number of fission reactions per second will increase exponentially.

Nuclear weapons employ various tactics to rapidly create a supercritical mass from one or more subcritical masses of fissile material. In the detonation of a nuclear weapon, the exponential growth of this reaction through the mass of fissile material is responsible for weapon yields that can destroy entire cities.

When an event causes two lighter nuclei combine to produce one heavier nucleus and possibly a free neutron, this is called fusion and is accompanied with an enormous release of energy.

Figure 11.2
Induced fission example. (Courtesy of Kelley Williams)

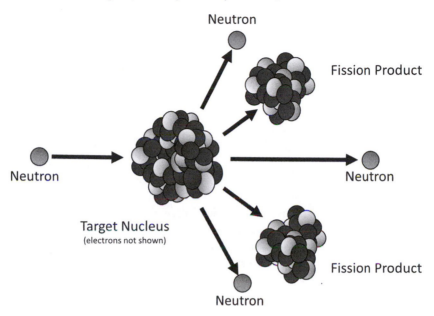

Fusion reactions occur at 50,000,000°C or 90,000,000°F. By any scale, this is the hottest natural phenomena known and occurs only in stars, particle accelerators, and the detonation of modern nuclear weapons. Nuclear weapons that utilize fusion reactions are also known as thermonuclear weapons. There is no theoretical limit to the explosive yield of these weapons. The largest nuclear bomb ever detonated was called Tsar Bomba, detonated by the USSR in October 1961. With an estimated yield of 50–58 MT (1 megaton = 1,000 kilotons), this single explosion was 10 times greater than the combined explosive ordnance used in WWII and over 1,000 times more powerful than either of the nuclear bombs used against Japan.

An element is typically identified by the number of protons and neutrons in the nucleus. Elements can exist in different configurations (isotopes), depending on the number of neutrons that accompany the protons in the nucleus. For example, U238 contains 92 protons and 146 neutrons in its nucleus. U235 will still have 92 protons in the nucleus, but only 143 neutrons. There is only a 3-neutron difference between U238 and U235, but U235 can sustain a nuclear reaction (fissile material) and U238 cannot. Some isotopes are stable and some are unstable and may emit ionizing radiation as they strive to achieve a more stable nuclear configuration. For example, carbon-12 and carbon-13 are stable isotopes of carbon, but carbon-14 is unstable and spontaneously radioactive (a radionuclide).

The types of ionizing radiation that occur during nuclear or radiological incidents are alpha, beta, gamma, X-ray, and neutron. Radiation hazards have different properties such as their speed and penetrating power, their ability to ionize other material, and the materials required to shield the hazard.

The radiation hazards from a nuclear weapon detonation are complex and depend on the height of burst and type of weapon used. Radiation hazards are also defined as prompt radiation (moment of blast) and residual radiation (fallout), which may last many years. In general, the greatest radiation hazards are gamma rays and neutrons from prompt radiation. In fallout, the greatest hazards are alpha and beta emitters. Alpha and beta particles are only a small fraction of the hazard and are often not addressed as nuclear weapon radiation hazards relative to the other destructive effects. Radiation hazards from an RDD depend on the source used but will likely create alpha, beta, gamma, and possibly neutron hazards.

Alpha particles are essentially a helium nucleus (2 protons and 2 neutrons). "Alphas" are relatively slow, have little penetrating power, and only travel up to 5 cm in air. Alphas can be shielded by a piece of paper or human skin. It is very effective at directly ionizing the bonds in DNA (deoxyribonucleic acid), potentially leading to cell death, mutation, or cancer. Alpha is only hazardous if it is ingested, inhaled, or embedded in a wound. In these situations, the accumulated dose of radiation will increase until the material is excreted from the body. For this reason, RDDs may be assembled with prominent alpha emitters. Areas contaminated with alpha radiation could remain hazardous for years. Sources of alpha radiation include the decay of uranium, plutonium, fission fragments, and other radioisotopes.

Beta particles are fast-moving electrons that can travel up to 5 meters in air. They have less potential to ionize other materials but can penetrate further, passing through several layers of skin. Betas can be shielded by a few millimeters of aluminum or several layers of clothing. The biological hazard of beta radiation is mainly superficial skin injuries. Beta radiation is also known as beta decay as it comes primarily from the decay of fission products. The process of beta decay is usually accompanied by some level of gamma radiation.

Gamma rays are electromagnetic energy waves, not particles. Since gamma travels at the speed of light it does not ionize material directly, but creates a series of events that indirectly ionizes DNA. Gamma can be shielded by a few inches of lead and will pass through people and structures for up to 500 meters depending on their level of energy. A person or structure cannot be "contaminated with gamma." It is possible to have contamination from radioactive material that emits gamma rays, but once the source is removed, the gammas go with it. Exposure to gamma radiation is known to create dose-dependent whole-body injuries. Gamma rays are produced when excited particles achieve a more relaxed state, such as after fission or fusion reactions, or following emission of an alpha or beta particle. Gamma rays are often referred to as nuclear radiation since they originate from an atom's nucleus.

Neutrons are particles that are dislodged from nuclei during nuclear fusion and fission reactions. Their energy and speed vary, but do not travel as far as gamma. Like gamma rays, neutrons have a great ability to penetrate tissue and can cause whole-body injuries. Neutron hazards would not be expected from an RDD explosion.

X-rays are the most distinctive feature of nuclear detonations and are responsible for up to 70 percent of a weapon's initial yield (Glasstone & Dolan, 1977). X-rays are similar to gamma rays but originate from the outer electrons of an atom, not the nucleus. For this reason, X-rays are often referred to as atomic radiation. To describe the function and effect of high-energy X-rays during nuclear detonations, a distinction must be made between atmospheric bursts and those in space (exoatmospheric).

During an atmospheric burst, X-rays from the weapon rapidly ionize the atoms present in the air. This ionization creates extreme heat and pressure. Therefore, X-rays are the driving force behind the fireball and blast wave that create havoc on people and structures. During an exoatmospheric burst, there is no interference from the air, so X-rays travel across the vacuum of space and can destroy satellites and possibly other (enemy) nuclear warheads. X-rays are exclusive to nuclear weapons and are not a hazard of RDDs.

ROADMAP TO NUCLEAR WEAPONS

There are no secrets to making a basic nuclear weapon. A strong suicidal person could simply drop 100 lbs of weapons grade U235 onto another 100 lbs of the same and experience a reasonable probability of nuclear fission before an untimely death. The processes required to make a very powerful, reliable, and accurate nuclear weapon are shielded in heavy secrecy by nuclear-capable nations. The most significant obstacle a nuclear proliferator faces is the acquisition of fissile material in sufficient quantities to fuel a nuclear weapon. Nuclear weapon proliferators must either produce, steal, purchase, or be given nuclear weapon fuel to engage in weapon development. U235 is the only naturally occurring fissile material, but only occurs in 0.7 percent of uranium ore. The remaining 99.3 percent is U238.

Nuclear reactors for electrical power generally use low enriched uranium (LEU) of 3 percent. The designation of highly enriched uranium (HEU) is given to uranium that is 20 percent U235 or greater. Weapon-grade (WG) uranium is at least 90 percent U235. The exceedingly expensive and laborious process of taking uranium ore (0.3 percent U235) to higher proportions of U235 is called enrichment. Obviously, enrichment to 3 percent LEU reactor fuel is faster than enrichment to 90 percent WG fuel. If international verification teams sample output from a reportedly peaceful process and discover greater than 19.8 percent U235, the enrichment process is very likely in violation of international agreements and creating fuel for use in nuclear weapons.

Various techniques are used to enrich uranium in large volumes, but all are very expensive (often over $100 million) and require extensive processing facilities. In each technique, uranium ore is processed into a form called yellow cake. Next, fluorine is added to create uranium hexafluoride ("hex"). Hex is the gaseous form of uranium that is enriched to make fuel for reactors and nuclear weapons. Enrichment occurs by "simply" separating the isotopes U235 and U238, where the enriched U235 is kept for fuels and the depleted U238 is reprocessed or used in other military or industrial capacities.

Uranium enrichment has occurred through several methods of isotope separation, notably thermal diffusion, electromagnetic, gaseous diffusion, gas centrifuge, and aerodynamic nozzle. The most common enrichment method is by gas centrifuge. Abdul Qadeer Khan is the father of the Pakistani nuclear weapons program and known as the greatest source of nuclear weapons proliferation in the world. He sold gas centrifuge equipment and offered skilled labor to North Korea, Iran, and Libya, which permitted these nations to begin their nuclear weapons programs with greater probabilities of success. The very photos and news releases that Iran made public to demonstrate it is pursuing peaceful uses for nuclear power also indict them for enriching beyond legal limits permitted by treaties to which they are signatories (UN Security Council, 2015).

Several methods of isotope separation have been tested but not used by any nation for fuel purposes: molecular laser isotope separation (MLIS), atomic vapor laser isotope separation (AVLIS), and chemical isotope separation. These techniques permit more efficient enrichment in much smaller facilities with less hazardous materials. If these methods are perfected and become available, they could pose significant challenges to the nuclear nonproliferation community.

Plutonium is created through a process called transmutation. In standard nuclear power reactors, the fuel (97 percent U238, 3 percent U235) captures neutrons over time, thus turning U238 into U239 (Bridgman, 2013). This U239 is unstable and transmutes to plutonium-239 (Pu239). Pu239 is stable and fissile but a greater radiation hazard than U235 or U238. Plutonium has degrees of "purity" similar to the LEU, HEU, and WG ratings of uranium. Uranium is measured with respect to the desirable isotope, U235. Plutonium is measured by the percentage of higher plutonium isotopes (Pu240–Pu242). Reactor grade plutonium contains a 19 percent or greater content of Pu240–Pu242. WG plutonium has 7 percent or less Pu240–Pu242. Pu240, Pu241, and Pu242 are created when Pu239 captures one, two, or three, respectively, additional neutrons during the course of normal reactor operation. Pu240 and Pu242 are considered undesirable impurities since their high rates of spontaneous fission create instabilities and are not fissile contributors to the power of a nuclear weapon. Pu241 is stable and fissile, which adds to the explosive yield, but is relatively rare. Reactor operation time is a key metric of nuclear intentions. Reactors that shut down for fuel replacement after only 1,000 hours or less are clearly intended to produce plutonium for weapon sources (Bridgman, 2013). For this reason, nuclear power facilities and test reactors that permit easy removal of spent fuel are closely monitored for potential plutonium production and the processing steps required to extract the plutonium from the spent fuel.

Discussion of uranium and plutonium as nuclear fuel relates to fission reactions in very heavy elements, which are propagated by free neutrons. Fusion reactions increase the yield of nuclear weapons by adding neutrons late in the fission reaction ("boosting") and utilize light elements as fuel, mainly tritium and deuterium. Deuterium (H2) is one of two stable isotopes of hydrogen and contains one proton and one neutron. It is abundant in nature, easily isolated, and is responsible for the term "heavy water" ($2H_2O$). Tritium (H3) is not available in nature and must be produced by the neutron bombardment of lithium-6 in a reactor. The production of tritium by a potential nuclear weapon proliferator would be a clear intent to produce boosted weapon.

There are also concerns over the potential use of uncommon fissile materials. If thorium-232 is bombarded with free neutrons, it can become U233 in a process similar to the production of plutonium (Bridgman, 2013). While it is possible to utilize U233 as nuclear weapon fuel, it creates challenging conditions that should dissuade interested proliferators. U233 is radioactive to the degree that

Figure 11.3
Nuclear weapon development cycle. (Courtesy of Kelley Williams)

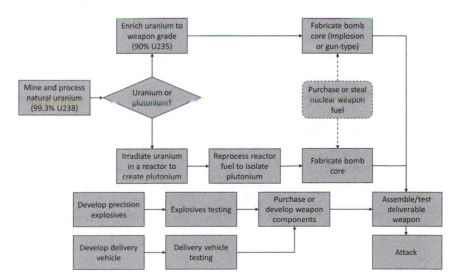

Figure 11.4
Potential clandestine nuclear weapon development cycle. (Courtesy of Kelley Williams)

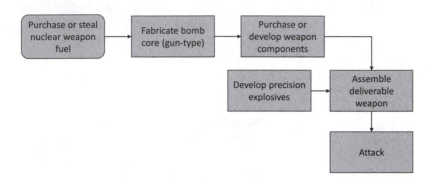

it cannot be safely handled in typical facilities as U235 and Pu239 could. An additional problem with U233 is that the rate of spontaneous fission could create instability (i.e., premature detonation) if used in a weapon.

The development of a modern nuclear weapons program that leads to an arsenal of weapons that can be delivered by ballistic missiles would take decades and billions of dollars to complete (Figure 11.3). Additionally, significant international pressure would deter and complicate this process. Since this process is monumental, many strategists predict that the greater nuclear weapon threat may come from a clandestine program (Figure 11.4). Creating a single rudimentary gun-type nuclear weapon removes the requirements to personally enrich nuclear fuel and test complex timing explosives, and delivery systems. The first nuclear weapon used in WWII against Hiroshima, Japan, was a gun-type weapon called Little Boy. This weapon was considered to be a guaranteed success to the degree that it was not tested before use. The process to developing such a clandestine weapon is only prevented by denying the proliferator acquisition of highly enriched uranium.

NUCLEAR WEAPONS 101

We have mentioned the basics of nuclear fission and the common materials used to fuel these reactions. It is helpful to understand the unclassified basics of nuclear weapons such as their basic designs, relative power, and delivery methods. Nuclear weapons create a supercritical mass from one or more subcritical (stable) masses of fissile material in either a gun-type or implosion weapon design.

The most basic type of nuclear weapon is called a gun-type weapon. This design uses high explosives to force two subcritical masses together within the weapon casing. This must be accomplished in a very short period to prevent the weapon blowing itself apart before developing maximum explosive pressure. Little Boy used uranium-only (>80 percent U235) weapon whose official yield estimate is 15 kT (DOE/NV, 2000). Hiroshima had a population of nearly 300,000 on August 6, 1945. Little Boy killed 70,000 people (including 20 American POWs) and injured 70,000. The official death toll from this attack grew to 140,000 by the end of 1945 and to 200,000 within five years (Graham et al., 2009). A gun-type weapon can use lower grade uranium (20–80 percent HEU) but will be large and have low fission efficiency. Due to the rate of spontaneous fissions, Pu239 and U233 are not suitable fuels for a gun-type weapon. Due to the low relative complexity, the gun-type weapon is more probable in clandestine or nonstate-sponsored weapon programs.

Implosion weapon designs use a mass of fissile material(s) that is in a noncritical geometry, for example, a hollow sphere. Explosives that surround the fissile material (plutonium and/or uranium) compress the core into a supercritical mass, which leads to the fission chain reaction. Devices called "spark plugs" assist the chain reaction by providing an initial source of free neutrons to provide precisely timed fissions. Implosion weapons may also include gas boosting through fusion reactions.

Implosion weapons include all weapon designs since Little Boy but vary greatly in size, power, and specific design. Great scientific advances led to smaller, more powerful weapons between 1945 and 1992. The greatest advancement came in 1952 when the first thermonuclear weapon was detonated. This device, called "Ivy Mike," was the first nuclear weapon to include staged implosion and utilized fusion as a source of enhanced yield (10.4 MT). Throughout the history of the U.S. nuclear weapons program, devices were created that range in power from 1 kT to 15 MT. The 1963 Limited Test Ban Treaty addressed the growing environmental concerns of nuclear tests and prohibited nuclear detonations in the atmosphere, outer space, or under water (UN Security Council, 1963).

Improvised nuclear devices (INDs) are a hypothetical threat category that deserves attention. Although none are known to exist, an IND is a nuclear weapon that was produced in a clandestine fashion with illegally acquired materials or an existing weapon modified for unintended use. Five nations are recognized under the NPT as nuclear weapon states (NWS): United States, Russia, France, China, and the United Kingdom. Three other nations are known to have nuclear weapons but are not recognized under the NPT: India, Pakistan, and North Korea. These are referred to as nonnuclear weapon states. Israel holds the official position that it will not declare if it does or does not have a nuclear weapon arsenal.

It is possible that a terrorist group would attempt to steal an intact nuclear weapon from an existing arsenal. This is a highly unlikely scenario since the security around nuclear weapons is a significant deterrent. Nuclear weapons held in NWS arsenals are not shiny bombs with a large red "Do not push!" button on top. Significant physical and digital security measures are in place to ensure only authorized personnel are able to arm and detonate these weapons. While there are significant obstacles to the stolen-weapon scenario, it cannot be ruled out because insider involvement, political instability, and human coercion could permit unauthorized access and breaches of security.

INDs are also weapons of rudimentary nature, constructed from purchased, stolen, or illegally provided fissile material and nuclear weapon components. In the United States, emergency responders and national security personnel routinely train for the detonation of a 10 kT IND in metropolitan areas. Less than a year before his death in 1987, Dr. Luis Walter Alvarez presented the famous statement that "with modern weapons-grade uranium, the background neutron rate is so low that terrorists, if they have such material, would have a good chance of setting off a high-yield explosion simply by dropping one half of the material onto the other half. Most people seem unaware that if separated U235 is at hand it's a trivial job to set off a nuclear explosion ... even a high school kid could make a bomb in short order" (Alvarez, 1987). It should not be understated that for this reason the international nonproliferation community is heavily focused on the monitoring the production and security of nuclear materials.

DEFINING THE RDD THREAT

Discussions of RDDs are more academic than historical. Several RDD threats in the United States were stopped by law enforcement, but none has occurred. There is no blueprint for an RDD as they are improvised devices that could vary greatly in power and effectiveness. An RDD is not a "poor man's nuke" or an IND although nuclear weapons can disperse radiation hazards. Nuclear weapons use the uncontrolled release of energy from fissile material to create extreme damage. RDDs use conventional explosives to disperse radioactive material, creating hazards through the explosion and contamination from the radioactive debris. However, it is conceivable that a weapon intended as an IND could malfunction or have such poor yield that the fissile material is spread to the immediate area, creating an unintentional RDD incident. The "dirty bombs" portrayed in popular culture media typically present images of citywide devastation and civilian masses that suffer from radiation sickness and rapid death. The reality of an RDD detonation is expected to be quite different.

RADIOLOGICAL ATTACK SCENARIO

An astute RDD proliferator is expected to realize RDDs may not have the mass destruction and social disruption effect they intend. This is one reason

Homeland Security strategists forecast complex distributed attacks. Dr. Steven M. Becker described a scenario where a series of coordinated RDD attacks on key commercial, governmental, or military infrastructure would result in civilian and military casualties as well as radioactive contamination left by the attacks. This would feed public apprehension about real and perceived dangers, could lead concerned individuals to flood medical facilities, hobble administrative and business centers, and even paralyze entire sections of cities (Becker, 2012).

There are several physical and psychological hazards of RDDs. Psychologically, most people report they have little knowledge about radiation and its effects. Similar to biological weapons, people fear a threat they cannot immediately detect with their senses. As previously mentioned, the greatest physical hazard of a conventional RDD is the explosive blast. The radiation hazard would depend largely on the radioisotope used and would not likely be discovered until emergency responders arrive and their radiation monitors start alarming. Radioactive particles would likely be dispersed throughout the dust cloud created by the explosion and inhaled by victims. Radioactive material would also likely become embedded in the wounds created by shrapnel and debris for victims near the explosion. Radiation that is internalized presents significant hazards because the accumulated dose could reach dangerous levels and remain in the body for long periods of time. The contaminated dust cloud would follow the wind and eventually settle, creating a radiation hot zone. Depending on the type of radiation, the contamination could present hazardous levels and close multiple city blocks for years (Table 11.2). Fortunately, unless radioactive material or particles (alpha and/or beta) is internalized, there is little likelihood that the radiation from an RDD would actually cause radiation sickness. The acute doses of radiation received by victims would not likely be intense enough to cause injuries similar to those experienced at Hiroshima, Nagasaki, Chernobyl, and in numerous radiation accidents.

Table 11.2
Radiological isotopes

Radionuclide	Half life	Use
Americium-241	432 years	Household smoke detectors
Cesium-137	30 years	Medical source Food irradiation
Cobalt-60	5 years	Cancer therapy
Iodine-131	8 days	Cancer therapy
Iridium-192	74 days	Medical source Industrial radiography
Plutonium-238	88 years	Satellite power souce
Strontium-90	29 years	Radio-thermal generator

Approximately 5,000 natural and "man-made" radioisotopes are known to exist. You have likely experienced the benefits of radioisotopes by using smoke detectors in your home and through medical imaging techniques. Unfortunately, the same sources for radiation that are helpful in modern life can also be utilized as the radiation component of a radiological weapon.

EXPECTED RESULTS OF MODERN NUCLEAR ATTACKS

Nuclear weapons cause destruction through thermal, blast, and radiation effects. These effects are generally classified as either prompt or residual effects. To illustrate these effects, we will describe a somewhat chronological series of events beginning with the detonation of a 35 kT weapon (gun-type, non-boosted) at ground level of a modern metropolitan city. The following paragraphs summarize the thermal, blast, and radiation hazards that occur in the first 7 seconds after detonation and the residual hazards that would remain for weeks. Calculations for each effect were computed by the author using unclassified standard equations and charts for nuclear weapon effects (Glasstone & Dolan, 1977).

As previously described, a supercritical nuclear fission reaction creates more generations of fission reactions and free neutrons. This process generates very high energy X-rays that ionize the materials within the weapon even before the weapon casing is ruptured. In less than one microsecond, the X-rays ionize the existing material in the weapon and begin to leak out of the case. As the X-rays leak out they ionize and heat the surrounding air, which we interpret as a growing fireball. After 0.075 milliseconds the fireball would be about 100 meters in diameter and over 0.5 million degrees. As the fireball grows its expansion also decelerates. After 1.4 milliseconds the fireball is about 200 meters in diameter and "cooling" to several hundred thousand degrees. At about this point, a phenomenon known as hydrodynamic separation occurs. In this event, a supersonic shock wave escapes the X-ray-heated fireball that carries enough energy to also heat the surrounding air (shock heating) but to a lesser degree. To a distant observer this would appear as a second fireball that passes through the first.

Exposed people within about 1.5 miles from ground zero would receive third-degree burns and first-degree burns would occur beyond 2 miles. People who witness the detonation within 10 miles could suffer flash blindness and retinal burns. Within a 2-mile radius from ground zero, most structures and vegetation would receive sufficient radiant exposure to instantly ignite, causing widespread fires. Just over 1 mile from ground zero, most clothing will ignite. The same weapon, if detonated at 10,000 feet altitude, would produce these thermal effects in about 2–3 times greater magnitude.

Those people and structures that survived the prompt thermal effects will then face the shock and blast of the detonation. The terms "shock" and "blast" refer to two related but different events. Shock is used to describe the supersonic pressure wave that expands spherically from the point of detonation and is amplified by reflections with the ground. This is the force that ruptures eardrums, breaks windows, and knocks over structures that are now likely on fire from the thermal effects. Blast refers to the high-speed winds that follow the blast front, applying drag force on structures similar to a tornado. Blast is the pushing force that knocks over wood buildings, powerlines, trains, and cars.

Unlike a tornado, once the blast wave passes (positive phase), a low pressure center causes the winds to rush back in the opposite direction (a negative phase). This negative phase loading on structures is devastating since structures are typically weakened from the initial blast and are not capable of withstanding the rapid loading in the other direction. Blast effects also generate deadly debris clouds as objects are carried away at hundreds of miles an hour. Relating this example to the Enhanced Fujita scale tornado categories, winds over 135 mph (EF-3 tornado) would be experienced 1 mile from ground zero (NOAA, 2007). EF-5 tornado (most severe) winds would occur at 0.75 miles away. The winds would be supersonic (over 760 mph) beyond 0.33 miles away, but we've already mentioned people would be dead from thermal exposure well beyond these distances. These strong winds will cover the first 2 miles from ground zero in about 7 seconds.

Robust steel and concrete buildings would receive severe shock and blast damage over 0.5 mile away and moderate damage at twice that distance. This weapon would create a crater that is over 170 feet wide and 80 feet deep. Due to the size of this crater, over 163,000 cubic feet of earth would be displaced. Aircraft in the takeoff and landing sequence (below 1,000 feet) could be knocked from the sky due to the blast overpressure up to 1 mile away.

Some people near the blast will likely be indoors and receive shielding from the great thermal radiation. These buildings may also withstand the shock and blast effects (positive and negative phases), possibly because there were other buildings between them and the blast. People in these buildings may still be at risk. Within 0.25 mile, there is a very high probability that people will experience lethal overpressure moves through the interior of these structures. Death can occur within a few minutes from air embolic obstruction of the vessels of the heart or brain from suffocation caused by the lung hemorrhage or edema. Similar "survivors" at almost 0.5 mile away will likely receive severe lung damage from the overpressure.

Initial radiation is the next killer in line. If someone was fortunate enough to survive the direct and indirect effects of thermal radiation, shock, and blast, the initial radiation might punch their ticket. Through this example, it should be quite clear that people within 0.5 mile of this "low yield" nuclear device should have their living will and testament up to date. Initial radiation includes that which is emitted within the first minute after detonation (Glasstone & Dolan,

1977). This includes gamma rays and neutrons, which reach targets almost instantaneously, penetrating soft tissue and ionizing DNA which leads to cell death. Initial radiation does not include alpha and beta particles since they have such short range at this point (several yards) and are vastly overpowered by other effects. Unless someone is several feet underground and at least 0.5 mile away at the time of the blast, death from radiation sickness is a threat up to 0.75 miles away. Inside this range, the effects of radiation will take their toll in a well-known dose-dependent manner. Within 0.5 mile death is expected within 1–2 days. At 0.75 miles, death is likely from 2–14 days (unshielded person) out to 2–12 weeks (person in a basement). Beyond 1 mile there is little expectation of experiencing clinical symptoms of radiation sickness.

People farther from the detonation that do not experience the various initial effects will have to contend with residual radiation and radioactive fallout. Residual radiation is defined as that which is emitted more than 1 minute after detonation (Glasstone & Dolan, 1977). The primary hazard of residual radiation is the creation of fallout particles. Because of the intense heat during the explosion, some of the soil is vaporized and taken into the fireball. This material combines with radioactive fission products and cools into a wide range of particles sizes. Some of this material is pulled outward by the blast winds but much of it is carried up in the telltale mushroom cloud. In this example, the cloud would reach a height of almost 30,000 feet. Estimating the plume dispersion with standard atmospheric conditions throughout that altitude, unprotected people up to 22 miles downwind (prevailing) could receive such high doses of radiation that death could occur between 2 and 12 weeks. People in standard family homes could be in danger out to 9 miles. People who shelter-in-place in basements and underground structures may experience an excessive reduction in their white blood cell count (leukopenia) but should fully recover.

Since people most near the blast have much less probability of survival for a myriad of reasons explained above, rescue personnel should focus their efforts in an outside-in manner. People outside the 75 mile radius could be assisted immediately, but other groups closer to ground zero may receive delayed care. This is because emergency responders must wait for background radiation levels to drop to a point that permits a safe work period for a specified length of time, say a 4-hour shift. Due to the predicted radiation dose rates after the blast, responders may not be permitted to help people at the 20-mile mark for 3–5 hours. This time increases as workers approach ground zero, causing victims within 5 miles to possibly wait 1–2 days for support. These estimates assume emergency responders are available and under positive control. As witnessed in Hiroshima, the thermal effects could cause a widespread firestorm that moves through the city beyond initial thermal effects and complicates further rescue operations. This cascade of effects could be accomplished with only 62 pounds (28 kg) of weapons grade U235 with 7 percent fission efficiency, using a gun-type (first-generation) device. If this low fissile mass does not seem alarming, consider that because of U235's high density, this is equivalent to a 5.5 inch diameter solid sphere.

REFERENCES

Alvarez, L. W. (1987). *Adventures of a Physicist*. New York: Basic Books.

Becker, S. M. (2012). Psychological Issues in a Radiological or Nuclear Attack. In A. B. Mickelson (Ed.), *Medical Consequences of Radiological and Nuclear Weapons* (pp. 171–194). Fort Detrick: Office of The Surgeon General Department of the Army, United States of America. Retrieved from http://www.cs.amedd.army.mil/borden/FileDownloadpublic.aspx?docid=97c4ef32-c8c3-44cf-bf3b-ec325372b4f2

Bridgman, C. (2013). *Nuclear Fuel Cycle*. Personal Collection of Charles Bridgeman. Dayton, Ohio: Air Force Institute of Technology.

DOE/NV. (2000). *United States Nuclear Tests: July 1945 through September 1992*. Retrieved from http://www.nv.doe.gov/library/publications/historical/DOENV_209_REV15.pdf

Glasstone, S., & Dolan, P. J. (1977). *The Effects of Nuclear Weapons* (3rd ed.). Washington, DC: United States Government Printing Office.

Graham, J. S., Stevenson, R. S., Mitcheltree, L. W., Hamilton, T. A., Deckert, R. R., Lee, R. B., & Schiavetta, A. M. (2009). Medical Management of Cutaneous Sulfur Mustard Injuries. *Toxicology, 263*(1), 47–58. doi:10.1016/j.tox.2008.07.067

12

Explosive Weapons

Kelley J. Williams

In the context of CBRNE (chemical, biological, radiological, nuclear, and explosive), the "E" refers to *high-yield explosives*. Common case studies of high-yield explosives include the 1983 bombing of the U.S. Marine barracks in Beirut, the 1993 World Trade Center bombing, the 1995 bombing of the Alfred P. Murrah Federal Building in Oklahoma City, and the 2013 Boston Marathon bombing. Explosives are powerful and accessible, and serve as brutal weapons of mass psychological destruction. These attacks involved the use of weaponized commercial explosives rather than military munitions.

WHY WOULD A TERRORIST OR WMD-CRIMINAL CHOOSE EXPLOSIVE WEAPONS?

Explosive weapons are easier to acquire and employ than other weapons of mass destruction (WMDs). The use explosives and firearms create immediate death and destruction that achieves common terrorist goals of generating mass media coverage for their cause. Additionally, the general public readily empathizes with victims of explosive weapon attacks even if they have never experienced them personally. People tend to possess a level of fear that relates to the threat of guns and bombs more easily than chemical or biological agents.

Firearms (pistols, rifles, shotguns) are not considered high-yield explosives or WMDs. However, the frequent and apparently random use of firearms in public attacks causes great fear and destruction. Under these conditions, firearms could be considered weapons of mass psychological destruction (WMPDs). Public schools do not employ chemical agent detectors, biological sampling equipment, or radiation monitors. Many schools have installed metal detectors due to the perceived threat of firearms. This simple example demonstrates that firearms are considered a legitimate threat to school systems, whereas chemical, biological, and radiological are not. This perceived threat is likely due to the historic use of firearms in school shootings and the magnified defensive perspective of parents. From 1992 to 2004, there were 75 gun-related homicides on school campuses (0.02 per 100,000 students) (Centers for Disease Control, 2008). While these school shooting statistics would suggest students are safe, the psychological impact of these horrific incidents has led many school districts to enhance physical security measures that address the real and psychological threats of firearms use.

PROPERTIES OF CHEMICAL EXPLOSIVES

Chemical explosives possess a great amount of potential energy per-unit mass. Energy is contained within the chemical bonds of the material. This energy is liberated by rapid decomposition or expansion and known as an explosion. The most significant difference between chemical and nuclear explosives is that chemical explosions convert potential energy stored between atoms and nuclear explosions release potential energy from within the elements (atoms) themselves.

The release of energy by chemical explosives requires three components: fuel, oxygen, and an ignition source. The release of energy from explosive material commonly produces blast pressure, sound, heat, and light. The significance of these events is correlated with the mass and configuration of the explosive material at the time of the explosion.

Explosions are grouped into three categories based on the speed of expansion. "Detonation" refers to an explosion that expands faster than the speed of sound (above 5,000 feet per second). Detonations can produce great damage to people and structures by the difference in pressure across the expanding blast wave. Materials that can detonate are known as high explosives. Explosive materials that expand below the speed of sound (below 5,000 feet per second) and cannot sustain a detonation wave under any condition are said to deflagrate and are known as low explosives. Materials that burn without significant expansion are considered combustible or flammable.

Explosives are also categorized by sensitivity. Primary explosives are initiated by low levels of heat, friction, or pressure. Secondary and tertiary explosives require considerably less energy to initiate an explosion. For safety, it is desirable to initiate relatively large amounts of secondary explosives with small amounts of primary explosives. In this example, the secondary explosive contributes the majority of the explosive effects once initiated by the primary explosive. Primary explosives are most commonly used in blasting caps that can cause short-range damage on their own.

In addition to the speed of decomposition and sensitivity, explosives are categorized by the strength of the explosion they produce through detonation pressure. Strength is measured with the metric of *brisance*, which is French for "to break or shatter." Explosives with high brisance are effective when cutting steel or shattering dense objects. High-brisance explosives are often are commonly used in "shaped charges" in order to focus the cutting power of the explosion. Low-brisance explosives are better at pushing than cutting. Low-brisance explosives are common in mining and demolition due to their ability to shatter and move large masses of earth.

Explosives are commonly portrayed in movies and television as sticks of dynamite or clay-like plastic explosives. Explosives exist in many forms, which allow explosive materials to be used in a wide variety of applications. The potential form a particular explosive may be used in is often a factor of the materials properties and expected uses in commercial or military applications. Forms of explosives include:

- Pressings
- Castings
- Plastic or polymer bonded
- Putties (AKA plastic explosives)
- Rubberized
- Extrudable
- Binary
- Blasting agents
- Slurries and gels
- Dynamites

EXPLOSIVES REGULATION

Federal regulations on explosives in the United States are controlled by Title 18 of the United States Code and Title 27 of the Code of Federal Regulations. 18 U.S.C. Chapter 40 covers the "Importation, Manufacture, Distribution and Storage of Explosive Materials" and 27 C.F.R. Chapter II, Part 555 outlines "Commerce in Explosives." The use of explosives to attack the public or infrastructure is considered an unlawful act with use of a WMD. The Federal Bureau of Investigation maintains jurisdiction over domestic WMD incidents (REF).

FORMS OF EXPLOSIVES

Military explosive ordnance includes bombs, rockets, missiles, mines, artillery, mortars, grenades, and others. Military munitions are designed to achieve the greatest explosive effects possible for a device of a given size. Military explosive projectiles contain, at a minimum, a projectile shell that is filled with high explosives and fitted with a fuze. Ordnance may be delivered to a target by internal or external propellant (e.g., missiles and artillery), gravity (e.g., bombs), or hand-thrown (e.g., grenades). Ordnance detonation is initiated by the fuze when certain criteria are met, such as point-impact, passage of time, altitude, radar vicinity, pressure sensitivity, magnetic field, or GPS location. The explosives in military munitions are very efficient and safe when stored and used properly. Developed nations tend to place great levels of security around storage depots to prevent unauthorized access, theft, and exposure to the elements. Military explosives are usually composed of high-brisance materials, which shatter the weapon's shell and produce shrapnel in addition to common explosive effects.

Commercial explosives are most commonly used in mining and demolition. Commercial explosives are not designed to produce shrapnel and are typically assembled at the site of use. There is a larger selection of commercial explosives than in military applications. Mining applications typically use low-brisance explosives that are designed to crack layers of the earth and move large volumes of material. This process increases the efficiency of material removal by digging equipment and earth movers.

An *improvised explosive device* (IED) does not take a common form or application. IEDs are illegal explosive devices that fall outside of legitimate military or commercial uses. Regardless of size and complexity, every IED contains an explosive component and a source of initiating the explosion. IEDs range in size from several ounces to thousands of pounds. Although IEDs are commonly thought of as homemade bombs, an IED could also be used to disperse chemical, biological, or radiological hazards. IEDs can range in complexity from homemade explosives and a sparkler to military munitions with complex fuzes and remote detonation systems.

IEDs have been used to assassinate individuals and destroy large buildings. IEDs presented the greatest threat to military service members in Iraq and Afghanistan due to their nonstandard appearance and use. Most static IEDs were never seen before detonation as they were hidden in trash, buried under the roads, cast into sections of concrete curbing along streets, placed inside animal carcasses, or placed under bridges for passing vehicles.

IEDs are often placed in vehicles to deliver the explosives to a target. These devices are known as vehicle-borne IEDs (VBIEDs). IEDs have been placed in the frames of motorcycles and bicycles, and even in the saddlebags of living livestock. VBIEDs possess several advantageous characteristics from an attacker's perspective that made them difficult to defend. By definition, a VBIED is mobile and can deliver an explosive payload to a target without the target passing a stationary IED. This gives the attacker a choice of time and location for the detonation. Vehicles can carry large amounts of explosives without visual clues. Vehicles provide attackers with moderate protection from small arms fire and can be lightly armored. VBIEDs have the potential to breach outer layers of security by driving around or through obstacles, thereby decreasing the distance from the target and the explosives. Some VBIEDs were armed to detonate even if the driver was killed or could be detonated remotely by phone or timed fuze. Often, VBIEDs were used in a suicide attack where the driver initiated (command detonated) the explosion while still within the vehicle. This should certainly be viewed as a critical flaw of VBIEDs.

VBIEDs contributed a great deal of psychological stress to military service members serving in Iraq and Afghanistan. The persistent threat of VBIEDs caused many to view each vehicle as a potential weapon. This stress even leads to posttraumatic stress disorders (PTSD) even among troops that did not experience direct attack.

Incidents involving *homemade explosives* (HMEs) are increasing in frequency and destructive power. HMEs include mixtures of fuels and oxidizers whose intended use is source of energy for an explosive device. HME is often used in IEDs when military or commercial explosives are either not available through theft or illegal acquisition. Explosives are, by definition, unstable energetic materials. HME presents great risks of safety hazards since the methods and materials utilized in the production process often contribute to material instability. As the name implies, HME is commonly produced from commercially available materials and equipment.

HME proliferation is exacerbated by the Internet. Many Web sites post detailed information on HMEs. These sites include recipes, where to find the materials, various production processes, and employment techniques. The information found online often contains critical errors that lead to material instability and can cause injury or death to the user. Several popular HMEs include:

- TATP (triacetone triperoxide)—This primary high explosive is also known as "Mother of Satan" or simply acetone peroxide. TATP is extremely unstable and powerful in gram-quantities. TATP was used in the 2005 London bombings, numerous suicide bombings in Israel, and Richard Reid's failed 2001 "shoe bomb" attempt aboard an international flight. TATP is made with acetone and peroxide yet contains almost as much explosive power as TNT (trinitrotoluene). Both precursors are commercially available at mass retail and cosmetic stores and no special equipment is required for the production process. Most injuries involving TATP occur during production or placing the final product into a compact prior to use. TATP is very sensitive to friction and heat. Impurities in the mixture or slight errors during production have led to spontaneous ignition in many cases.
- HMTD (hexamethylene triperoxide diamine)—HMTD is less sensitive than TATP but is still very powerful. HMTD is prepared with hydrogen peroxide, strong acids, and hexamine. Hexamine is found in several fuels for camping stoves but not readily found in large quantities. HMTD was used in several terrorist plots such as the London bombings in July 2005 (Kelly, 2005)
- ANFO (ammonium nitrate fuel oil)—ANFO is widely available as a commercial explosive with valid permits. Commercial ANFO could be stolen but is also easy to produce. Whereas TATP and HMTD require high school–level chemical reactions and processes, ANFO is produced by simple mixing. The primary obstacle to making ANFO is the acquisition of the proper mixture of ammonium nitrate. Following the Oklahoma City bombing of the Murrah building, ammonium nitrate fertilizers came under strict control. In June 2005, the U.S. Senate approved measures to place chemical taggants in commercial explosives and urged the same for

ammonium-based fertilizers (Gray, 1995). The Department of Homeland Security also proposed the Ammonium Nitrate Security Program to regulate the sale, transfer, and uses of ammonium nitrate to prevent the use of such materials in acts of terrorism (121 STAT. 2084, Public Law 110-161, Dec. 2007).

CASE STUDY SUMMARY—OKLAHOMA CITY BOMBING (HIGH-YIELD)

On April 19, 1995, Timothy McVeigh and Terry Nichols attacked the Alfred P. Murrah Federal Building in Oklahoma City with high explosives. Their bomb was delivered to the target in a Ryder rental truck, utilized nearly 5,000 pounds of nitromethane-boosted ANFO (ANNM), and initiated by timed fuzes (FBI, 2015). The bomb created a crater that was 8 feet deep and 30 feet wide (City of Oklahoma City Document Management, 1996). The explosion was massive, collapsing 30 percent of the Murrah building, severely damaging 324 other buildings, and breaking windows of 258 surrounding buildings (Oklahoma Department of Civil Emergency & Management, 1995). A total of 168 people were killed and 680 were injured (FBI, 2015). This was the largest domestic terrorist attack the United States had experienced (Nixon, Vincent, Krug, & Pfefferbaum, 1998).

A comprehensive study by Carol S. North et al. revealed the psychological impact of this attack on survivors. Approximately six months following the Murrah building bombing, 255 eligible survivors were interviewed. Over 34 percent of the respondents had PTSD and 76 percent of those reported same-day onset of symptoms (North, 1999). Common symptoms between the reports included intrusive re-experience and hyperarousal.

CASE STUDY SUMMARY—BOSTON MARATHON (IED, LOW-YIELD)

On April 15, 2013, Chechen brothers Dzhokhar and Tamerlan Tsarnaev attacked the 117th Boston Marathon with two IEDs. Two pressure cookers were filled with black powder from fireworks (low-energy propellant) as well as ball bearings (BBs) and nails to create shrapnel (United States District Court for the District of Massachusetts, 2013). The anti-personnel bombs used modified Christmas lights as fuzes and were activated from a distance with remote controlled toy parts. Three people in close range to the bombs were killed and approximately 264 others were maimed, burned, or otherwise injured (Malone, 2013). This attack is a good example of the threat presented by readily available commercial products and relatively low levels of sophistication. Use of pressure cookers enhanced the blast pressure and shrapnel effects of a low-energy propellant.

Although no structural damage occurred, it generated large amounts of psychological distress with survivors and the general public (Conner, Black, &

Reuters, 2013). While the attack was small, the law enforcement response was significant. Martial law was declared by Boston law enforcement and a large interagency task force engaged in a manhunt to find the remaining suspect, Dzhokhar Tsarnaev (Dahl, 2013). Under martial law, families were removed from their homes at gunpoint while their homes were searched without warrant or probable cause. Congressman Ron Paul criticized the response as being more frightening than the attack itself (Siddiqui, 2013). Rep. Paul felt the response violated civil liberties and was ultimately unsuccessful, but the Massachusetts governor and State Police defended their actions as acting in the best interest of public safety.

This incident demonstrated a psychological response that was magnified by public fear. This heinous attack potentially sent the message to other would-be terrorists that a small attack can wreak widespread civil distress and economic loss (Cohen, 2013). Dzhokhar Tsarnaev was charged and convicted on 30 crimes related to terrorism, including use of a weapon of mass destruction (United States District Court for the District of Massachusetts, 2013).

REFERENCES

Centers for Disease Control. (2008). School-Associated Student Homicides: United States 1992–2006. *Morbidity and Mortality Weekly Report, 57*(2), 33–36.

City of Oklahoma City Document Management. (1996). *City of Oklahoma City Final Report, Alfred P. Murrah Federal Building Bombing, April 19, 1995* (1st ed.). Oklahoma City: Fire Protection Publication.

Cohen, M. (2013). Why does America Lose its Head Over "Terror" but Ignore its Daily Gun Deaths? Retrieved April 28, 2015, from http://www.theguardian.com/commentisfree/2013/apr/21/boston-marathon-bombs-us-gun-law

Conner, T., Black, J., & Reuters. (2013). Explosions Rock Finish of Boston Marathon; 3 Killed and Scores Injured.

Dahl, J. (2013). Boston Marathon Manhunt: Search for Bombing Suspect is Law Enforcement's First Major Test of Post-9/11 Training. Retrieved April 28, 2015, from http://www.cbsnews.com/news/boston-marathon-manhunt-search-for-bombing-suspect-is-law-enforcements-first-major-test-of-post-9-11-training/

FBI. (2015). The Oklahoma City Bombing 20 Years Later. Retrieved April 27, 2015, from https://stories.fbi.gov/oklahoma-bombing/

Gray, J. (June, 1995). Senate Votes to Aid Tracing of Explosives. *NY Times.* New York.

Kelly, R. (2005). London Bombers Used Everyday Materials. Retrieved April 28, 2015, from http://www.redorbit.com/news/general/197067/london_bombers_used_everyday_materialsus_police/

Malone, S. (2013). Boston Marathon Bombing Injury Total Climbs to 264, Officials Say.

Nixon, S. J., Vincent, R., Krug, R. S., & Pfefferbaum, B. (1998). Structure and Organization of Research Efforts Following the Bombing of the Murrah Building. *Journal of Personal and Interpersonal Loss.* doi: 10.1080/10811449808414432

North, C. S. (1999). Psychiatric Disorders among Survivors of the Oklahoma City Bombing. JAMA, *282*(8), 755. doi: 10.1001/jama.282.8.755

Oklahoma Department of Civil Emergency, & Management. (1995). *After Action Report: Alfred P. Murrah Federal Building Bombing 19 April 1995 in Oklahoma City, (April)*, 77. Oklahoma City, Oklahoma: Department of Central Services Central Printing Division.

Siddiqui, S. (2013). Ron Paul: Shutdown after Boston Bombings More Frightening than Attack Itself. Retrieved March 28, 2015, from http://www.huffingtonpost.com/2013/04/29/ron-paul-boston-bombings_n_3179489.html

United States District Court for the District of Massachusetts. (2013). Dzhokhar Tsarnaev Criminal Complaint, 91. Retrieved from http://www.justice.gov/iso/opa/resources/363201342213441988148.pdf

Part IV

Prevention and Policy

13

Weapons of Mass Psychological Destruction: Policy and Prevention

William O'Donohue

Terrorism has had a personal and psychological effect on millions of people around the world. In this book, a collection of nationally recognized experts have discussed a variety of pivotal areas in regard to how terrorists utilize the mind, psyche, or the psychology of terrorism to impose their will and harm innocent people. The present chapter will examine the prevention and policy efforts that can decrease the likelihood of terrorist attacks in the future. This chapter is ideal for government officials, community leaders, the law enforcement community, and homeland and national security executives to assist them in acquiring the needed steps to prevent and combat terrorism.

WEAPONS OF MASS PSYCHOLOGICAL DESTRUCTION: POLICY AND PREVENTION

Terrorists, by definition, seek not solely to kill their perceived enemies but to instill terror in groups that they oppose. Terror is a psychological state. Thus, a key goal—perhaps the key goal—of terrorist organizations is a psychological one—the murdering and maiming is secondary to the psychological harm they want to cause their opponents. Those harmed psychologically far outnumber those harmed physically; thus, terrorists commit a variety of acts that can make their perceived enemies feel threatened, angry, stressed, unsafe in their everyday activities, worried about the safety of their loved ones, not confident in the economy, uncertain about the future, doubting whether mundane activities can be successfully completed, and doubts about the competence and wisdom of their society's leaders and institutions. And a unique and appalling aspect of these terrorist organizations is that their physical and psychological targets are usually civilians—including children—individuals usually regarded as protected in armed conflicts between civilized nations. Of course there have been a wide variety of terrorist organizations operating over various times and in various places and political contexts from the Irish Republican Army to the Red Brigade to the Ku Klux Klan. However, currently it is fair to say that the majority of the terrorist threats both to the United States and to the world are associated with radical Islam and jihadists. This chapter will focus on this terrorist threat.

If and when terrorists are successful at instilling these psychological states in their opponents, there are a variety of additional negative outcomes that can then result in a cascading causal chain:

1. curtailed activities of normal daily life
2. decreased enjoyment of everyday activities
3. increased suspiciousness and hypervigilance
4. decreased economic activity
5. decreased population health and fitness
6. increased inconveniences such as those experienced in airports
7. political dissent and disarray
8. increased expenditures on safety, defense, and antiterrorist measures that decrease expenditures in other areas that can benefit society (i.e., the classic "guns or butter" trade-off in economics)

It is important to note that these outcomes can contribute to further states of affairs that have additional negative psychological consequences such as depression and unemployment or stress associated with a variety of medical problems. Thus, terrorists can attempt through their acts to initiate a long and complex causal chain of negative psychological and behavioral consequences.

For example, Osama bin Laden stated that one of his aims was to ruin the U.S. economy. He was not successful but the economic and resultant psychological costs were significant. Bloom (2007) found that the uncertainties created by the terrorist attacks on 9/11 resulted in the first three months after 9/11 a loss of 1 million jobs and 3 percent decrease in the gross domestic product. Of course, the increased rates of a variety of psychological problems such as depression, stress, anxiety, divorce, and substance abuse are well-known consequences of job loss and reduced financial circumstances. After these first three months there were a number of other negative economic effects on the airline industry, the travel and tourism industry in general. The insurance industry faced nearly $33 billion in claims.

Individuals, rationally, perceived a new set of real and potentially devastating risks. According to Jasen (2011)

> The financial impact of the attacks forced the industry to reconsider how it looks at risk. "Nobody had imagined anything on the scale of 9-11," said Steven Weisbart, senior vice president and chief economist at the Insurance Information Institute. Prior to 2001, terrorism insurance didn't exist as a separate category but was included as part of standard commercial policies. Some 61 percent of companies

purchased terrorism insurance in 2009, including 80 percent of utilities, according to a 2010 report from the Institute. Power plants, ports, airports, sports stadiums, shopping malls, and "almost every tourist attraction you can think of" are insured, Robert Hartwig, president of the Institute said in a video on its website. "Everyone who wants terrorism insurance can get it."

However, it is also commonly said that 9/11 "changed life forever" or created a "new normal." This seems fair: 9/11 certainly left Americans feeling more vulnerable. In mental health terms, the most common diagnosis after 9/11 was posttraumatic stress disorder (PTSD), a DSM anxiety diagnosis that is characterized by significant fear, hypervigilance, nightmares and other recurring intrusive recollections, avoidance of stimuli that provide a reminder of the trauma, and disturbances in functioning. Fortunately, there was some relatively good news in the prevalence of PTSD after 9/11. PTSD was largely confined to those who had direct experience with the terrorist acts or its consequences—survivors and first responders. There were clinical and subclinical "spillover" effects on those who were distant and who simply watched the events on television. Galea et al. (2003) documented prevalence of probable PTSD in residents in Manhattan at 7.5 percent one month after 9/11, with sharp declines at six months (0.6 percent). Even in those with high levels of exposure to the World Trade Center attacks, where rates of PTSD were about 25 percent, resilience (defined by no more than one symptom of PTSD at any point during the first six months after the attack) continued to exceed 50 percent (Bonanno, Galea, Bucciarelli, & Vlahov, 2006, 2007).

In addition, Perlman et al. (2011) examined all the published scientific literature on the psychological effects of 9/11 in articles reviewed by PubMed and found the following:

1. Measurements taken 3–5 days after 9/11 suggested that 44% of the adult U.S. population experienced substantial stress. Findings from subsequent national studies also showed that individuals across the country experienced fear and insecurity, and had increased rates of post-traumatic stress (PTSD) symptoms 2 months later.
2. [The] prevalence of PTSD 2–3 years after 9/11 was 12.4% in rescue and recovery workers and volunteers, with a range from 6.2% for police to 21.2% for unaffiliated volunteers.
3. The severity of children's reactions has been positively correlated with parental distress (parental posttraumatic stress and crying in front of the child) and with the number of graphic images seen on television.
4. In enrollees in the WTC Health Registry who screened positive for chronic PTSD symptoms after the disaster, a third also reported a diagnosis of depression since 9/11.
5. Responders with probable PTSD had 13.9 times higher odds for probable depression and 9.2 times higher odds of panic disorder than those without PTSD; comorbid responders were 40–86 times more likely to have emotional disruption of function [. . .] than were those without PTSD, panic disorder, or depression.

6. In people [. . .] who did not report a PTSD diagnosis before 9/11, the prevalence of the disorder was higher 5–6 years after the attacks (19%) than after 2–3 years (14%). Late-onset PTSD (a report of symptoms consistent with PTSD in the 2006–07 survey, but not in the 2003–04 survey) had developed in 10%.

Of course, these terrorist attacks were also related to decisions to engage in war, in decisions on deployment of troops, in energy policy, and in diplomatic and geopolitical alliances. It is thus fair to say that these terrorist attacks have numerous effects at a variety of levels in a variety of contexts that change the psychological and behavioral conditions for the populations that are targets.

A final negative psychological consequence of terrorism that needs to be mentioned is the psychological effects of increased government intrusion in the lives of citizens. Newspapers carry reports of telephone surveillance, cameras are installed to monitor the behavior of citizens in public places, government employees search bags, and people are even patted down before entry to public events or airline terminals. Citizens can feel the increased presence of "Big Brother" and a decrease in the sense of privacy and freedom. Huddy and Feldman (2011) found evidence for changes in political beliefs:

[S]ubjective reactions to terrorism played an important role in shaping support for national security policy in the wake of 9/11. Support for a strong national security policy was most pronounced among Americans who perceived the nation as a threat from terrorism and felt angry with terrorists. In contrast, Americans who were personally affected by the attacks were more likely to feel anxious about terrorism, and this anxiety translated into less support for overseas military action. In addition, Americans who felt insecure after the 9/11 attacks and perceived a high future threat of terrorism were more likely than others to support strong foreign and domestic national security policies. Overall, research on American political reactions to 9/11 suggests that support for a strong government response to terrorism is most likely when members of a population perceive a high risk of future terrorism and feel angry at terrorists.

This chapter will focus on this question, "Given these significant negative psychological consequences of terrorist attacks, what policies ought to be considered and implemented to prevent or reduce these?" This chapter will argue that the answer to this question is complex and a policy to prevent or minimize the negative psychological effects of terrorists' acts needs to be multidimensional. In addition, the policy needs to operate in a context in which (1) epistemic sophistication is valued and decisions are evidence based including lessons learned and are gathered from professionals in nations that have more experience with these problems, such as Israel; (2) professional mental health services delivered are consumer centric so that consumer literacy and choice can be maximized; (3) services are evidence based; and (4) research and quality improvement frameworks are designed so that these professional efforts and judgments can be constantly evaluated, improvements assessed, and realistic effectiveness data can be gathered.

A related question becomes, what organizations ought to be charged with developing and carrying out these policies and procedures? To date, professional organizations such as the American Psychological Association have done little that is proactive along these lines, and instead either nothing is done or governmental agencies are carrying out these tasks. To be sure, some of this is due to funding issues, but again, it is perhaps a part of the advocacy mission of these professional organizations to seek the necessary funding. Thus, a second agenda that needs to be undertaken is to energize these organizations to orient toward this problem. It should be a priority for every mental health organization to work together to develop comprehensive and effective policies concerning this matter.

DIMENSIONS OF THE POLICY

Again, any policy has to be multidimensional, given the complexity of the problem. This chapter will divide policy dimensions along two broad lines: the *rational* by which it is meant policies concerning methods in which a rational agent can be influenced positively and the *irrational*, which involves the opposite— ways in which policy needs to intersect and influence irrational ways of appraising aspects of the problem.

The Rational

A comprehensive policy ought to have at least the following dimensions:

1. *The development of information sources so that citizens can rationally appraise international successes in reducing terror threats.* The informed citizen needs to rationally appraise this threat of terrorism. However, most of the current information is piecemeal, disorganized, and perhaps sensationalized or politicized in the media. It would be useful to present consumer-centric, user-friendly information concerning this. Of course the information would need to be accurate and trustworthy. But even "bad news" could be valuable—that is, an increase in the threat of terrorist activity as informed citizens could take rational precautions during this time. The goal here is to provide accurate, easily attainable, and personally relevant information on the international terrorist threat to the notion that most individuals can align their emotions with a realistic appraisal of threats. For example, the question ought to be addressed, what is the current status of ISIS and what does that mean for my safety? Of course the answer might be complex—it can vary from month to month and it can vary whether one is an employee at the Mall of America or whether one lives in Manhattan; however, we ought to have enough resources to devote to this important task.
2. *The development of information sources so that informed citizens can rationally appraise domestic successes at reducing terrorist incidents.* Currently, there is no source. There

was some vague color coding of threats (an "orange" threat level) that few people really understood. If we are to minimize the psychological damage of the threat of terrorism or actual incidents of terrorism, accurate information about terrorist activities and their detection and suppression needs to be available to citizens. Again, this can allow citizens to titrate their emotions to rational threat assessment instead of their use of problematic heuristics or biases. Again, this information might have to be parsed in important ways, but the information vacuum that is currently present does not aid in rational reactions to this situation.

3. *Have government agencies explain and justify steps so that citizens can agree in their democratic processes the cost and benefits of increased defense, security, and surveillance operations.* Again, for many, the threat of terrorism and terrorists acts comes with a psychological cost. There are also concerns regarding a decrease in privacy and freedom and, for other individuals, there are personal costs in health, life, and family stress when they serve in the armed forces. The government should explicate what it is doing and justify these actions by a clear and rational evaluation of costs and benefits. Again, these have to be user-friendly. For example, "Yes, some phone conversations are being monitored, but these are confined to those using certain phrases associated with terrorism, or those emanating from certain countries, or those who have been rationally profiled as having a high risk of being associated with terrorism. Your phone calls to your friends, stock broker, or significant other are not being monitored." This again will allow more rationally informed emotions to be displayed.

4. *Develop a mental health media policy for postevent terrorist events.* There ought to be a proactive plan to respond well to postdisaster media inquiries that can be predicted: "What are the effective interventions for stress?" or "What can parents do when their children see these events on television?," and so on. Also a series of public service announcements can provide useful information on psychological consequences and their mitigation.

5. *Develop a policy on restoring and healing communities.* It is commonly observed that communities are brought together after terrorist attacks, but some communities can be disproportionately harmed by an attack as the firefighters and police were in Manhattan after 9/11. There ought to be explicit plans for helping to restore these affected communities psychologically. According to Watson, Brymer, and Bonanno (2011) the major principles in accomplishing this are: (a) promoting a sense of safety, (b) promoting calming, (c) promoting a sense of self-efficacy and community efficacy, (d) promoting connectedness, and (e) instilling hope. Plans to mobilize resources to do this need to be in place before these disasters occur. In addition, there should be a research agenda to test the effectiveness of these interventions.

6. *Develop funding priorities, mechanisms, and quick dissemination of funds.* This also should be done proactively. There ought to be funding mechanisms ready to disseminate for increased provision of disaster psychological services (that will be described more fully below) as well as funding to evaluate these and address other key questions such as resilience and unaddressed needs.

7. *Have major mental health organizations form explicit expert consensus policies, procedures, and emergency plans.* These again can be proactive and reviewed ahead of time for their comprehensiveness and likely efficacy. All stakeholders ought to have

a role in these and a variety of stepped care approaches ought to be considered (e.g., psychological help integrated at primary care medical sites, Web sites and social media, books and pamphlets, and public service announcements).

8. *Develop a harm reduction orientation.* The harm reduction model can be very useful. Some may think that once a horrible terrorist event or events have occurred, the harm has already been done and there is little that now can be done. This view needs to be replaced with a more hopeful and instrumental orientation whose core is reducing the harm that has begun. In addition, target resources where these can reduce the most harm. For example, in a review of the literature, Watson et al. (2011) suggested that certain populations have shown much more resiliency post disaster than others: the risk factors that appear strongest are severe exposure to the disaster (especially injury, threat to life, and extreme loss), living in a highly disrupted or traumatized community, female gender, age in the middle years of 40 to 60, little previous experience relevant to coping with the disaster, ethnic minority group membership, poverty or low socioeconomic status, the presence of children in the home, psychiatric history, secondary stress, weak or deteriorating psychosocial resources, avoidance coping, and assignment of blame. Of particular relevance for potential early intervention are postevent risk factors, such as the absence of or negative social support, higher levels of contextual life stress (Brewin, Andrews, & Valentine, 2000), lack or loss of both practical and social resources (Hobfoll et al., 2007; Kaniasty & Norris, 2009; Neria et al., 2010), people's negative coping strategies (e.g., self-blame), and their negative appraisals about the event, their role in it, their reactions, and their potential future risk (Ehlers et al., 2003; Holman & Silver, 2005; Silver et al., 2002). Disaster studies among children and adolescents have documented a variety of risk and protective factors, including child and family predisaster functioning, parental disaster response, religion, sex, age, influences of peers and school, degree of loss, being evacuated or displaced, separation from a primary care giver, extent of postdisaster stresses and adversities, frequency of exposure to trauma and loss reminders, and ongoing exposure to media coverage (Brymer, Steinberg, Watson, & Pynoos, in press; Goenjian et al., 2005; Pfefferbaum et al., 2001; see also Eisenberg & Silver, 2011).

9. *The development of a detailed policy and implementation plan for mobilizing services.* A comprehensive listing of professional mental health services includes: developing and implementing metrics regarding needs assessment both at the individual and at the community levels. Because past research has shown that universal interventions are not needed, implementing effective mental health screening procedures are required for targeted high-risk populations. In addition, the development and implementation of surveillance procedures to detect later developing problems would be important. Communication and clarifying risk and resilience factors, particularly as these relate to varying outcome trajectories for survivors and inform intervention for these groups are essential. The development and implementation of evidence-based early, midterm, and late interventions for children, adults, and families would be another important step. Most of these are cognitive behavioral and their evidence base is relatively well known (see Fisher and O'Donohue, 2009). Strategies to mobilize and expand access to postdisaster mental health services including ehealth, telehealth, and stepped care services would also be important of a systematic response (see O'Donohue & Draper, 2011). Finally the enhancement of training methods

and educational platforms for workforce development among psychologists, paraprofessionals, and other disaster responders. would need to be accomplished. Watson et al. (2011) provide a useful table (Table 13.1) for the fuller context of these services.

Table 13.1
Expert consensus efforts on disaster behavioral health intervention

Be proactive/prepared ahead of time, pragmatic, flexible, and plan on providing the appropriate services matched for phase across the recovery period.

Promote a sense of safety, connectedness, calming, hope, and efficacy at every level.

Do no harm, by:

- Participating in coordination of groups to learn from others and to minimize duplication and gaps in response;

- Designing interventions on the basis of need and available local resources;

- Committing to evaluation, openness to scrutiny, and external review;

- Considering human rights and cultural sensitivity;

- Staying updated on the evidence base regarding effective practices.

Maximize participation of local affected population, and identify and build on available resources and local capacities (family, community, school, and friends).

Integrate activities and programming into existing larger systems to reduce stand-alone services, reach more people, be more sustainable, and reduce stigma.

Use a stepped care approach: Early response includes practical help and pragmatic support, and specialized services are reserved for those who require more care.

Provide multilayered supports (i.e., work with media or Internet to prepare the community at large; facilitate appropriate communal, cultural, memorial, spiritual, and religious healing practices).

Provide a spectrum of services, including:

- Provision of basic needs;

- Assessment at the individual level (triage, screening for high risk, monitoring, formal assessment) and the community level (needs assessment and ongoing monitoring, program evaluation);

- Psychological First Aid/resilience-enhancing support;

- Outreach and information;

- Technical assistance, consultation, and training to local providers;

- Treatment for individuals with continuing distress or decrements in functioning (preferably evidence-based treatments like trauma-focused cognitive-behavioral therapy).

Notes: Taken from Watson, Brymer & Bonano (2011).

Watson et al. further state, "The primary goals of early interventions following disasters should be to promote safety, attend to practical needs, enhance coping, stabilize survivors, and connect survivors with additional resources" (e.g., Bryant & Litz, 2009; Brymer, Reyes, & Steinberg, in press). There is a growing current consensus that this type of approach, often coined Psychological First Aid, is more appropriate for children, adults, and families exhibiting distress or decrements in functioning in the acute aftermath of disasters and mass violence (e.g., Bisson et al., 2010; Bryant & Litz, 2009; Disaster Mental Health Subcommittee, 2009; Inter-Agency Standing Committee, 2007; National Commission on Children and Disasters, 2010). This is an ambitious set of goals and more planning needs to be done to ensure that these can be effectively achieved.

10. *Delivering some of these mental health services in multidisciplinary teams such as those found in integrated care settings (James & O'Donohue, 2009) or in patient-centered medical homes (O'Donohue & Maragakis, 2015).* Although consumers often favor one-stop shopping, postdisaster such conveniences and efficiencies can be particularly valued. In addition, consumers can develop a variety of needs that could be better met when interdisciplinary teams consisting of physicians, mental health professionals, social workers, dieticians, and others are available.

11. *Working with the military and other key government organizations to increase their effectiveness.* The military, intelligence communities, and policing communities have vital roles to play in preventing terrorism. Too few psychologists have been involved to see if their expertise can be used to enhance the effectiveness of these agencies. To be sure psychologists have played roles in providing mental health services to individuals in these organizations. However, it is not clear to what extent these agencies have a vision for the possible contributions of psychologists in their mission or to what extent psychologists, perhaps due to their political biases, have not been interested in aiding these organizations. For example, psychologists had strong reactions that may have not been completely rational to their role in enhanced interrogations—whose aim is to gain information to decrease the likelihood of future terrorist attacks (see O'Donohue et al., 2013, for a discussion of the ethics of this). Psychologists have been very concerned about cultural sensitivity—perhaps overly concerned given the paucity of research showing these actually matters as well as the conceptual confusions in this enterprise (see Frisby and O'Donohue, in preparation). However, there has been a somewhat surprising lack of interest on the part of psychologists in helping the military and intelligence agencies achieve their aims. This may be due to the leftist political bias of psychologists (O'Donohue & Dyslin, 1996); however, this gap needs to be noted and at least discussed because these agencies are the tip of the spear in preventing future terrorist acts, and it is in the interest of everyone to make these agencies as effective as possible.

STRATEGIES TARGETING IRRATIONAL

In this section, human beings are recognized as not completely rational agents—a premise of the cognitive behavioral approach. As such, interventions are needed to correct these irrationalities so that improved functioning can take place. Among the irrationalities that a comprehensive policy must target are:

1. *Improve risk appraisal regarding terrorism.* Tversky and Kahneman (1971) and others have contributed to our knowledge regarding how irrationalities can produce beliefs that although they may serve as "cognitive shortcuts" can also lead to false beliefs. Some of these so-called heuristical errors can be involved in risk appraisal associated with terrorist acts. For example, one heuristic, known as the *representative heuristic*, indicates that people overvalue memories that can be more easily brought to awareness. Thus, individuals may fear riding on an airplane more than riding in a car because they can more easily recall airplane disasters such as those that occurred during 9/11 than car accidents. However, the opposite is actually true: airplanes, even after 9/11, are still the safest mode of transportation. People in general are very poor at accurately understanding actual risks. A study by Lichtenstein et al. (1978) examined absolute and relative probability judgments of risk. Most people know generally which risks cause large numbers of deaths and which cause few deaths. However, when asked to quantify risks more precisely, people usually severely overestimate the frequency of the rare causes of death, and severely underestimate the frequency of common causes of death. In addition, findings indicated that accidents were judged to cause as many deaths as disease, when, in fact, diseases cause about 16 times as many deaths as accidents. Homicide was incorrectly judged a more frequent cause of death than diabetes, or stomach cancer. Interestingly, a follow-up study by Combs and Slovic (1979) counted *reporting* of deaths in two newspapers, and found that errors in probability judgments correlated strongly (.85 and .89) with selective reporting in newspapers.

   In addition, as another example, *hindsight bias* is another heuristical error, which can result in irrational beliefs about terrorist attacks. *Hindsight bias* is when subjects, after learning the eventual outcome, give a much higher estimate for the predictability of that outcome than subjects who predict the outcome without advance knowledge. Hindsight bias can cause individuals to unjustifiably criticize officials because "they should have known better" when in fact these events were not as obvious or predictable as hindsight bias now seems to reveal. Thus, postdisaster a careful assessment needs to be made between actual failures and apparent failures due to hindsight bias. More research and intervention are needed to correct these heretical errors so that citizens can make more realistic and accurate risk assessments.

2. *Educating the public the real value of actuarial prediction (also called "racial profiling") instead of politicizing this type of prediction.* Clinical psychologists have known since Meehls's (1959) classic work that actuarial assessment works better than clinical assessment. We need to have an accurate prediction of future terrorist acts. In assessing risk of future terrorist acts we need to use our best predictive models. However, there is a somewhat understandable sensitivity when demographic categories are used in these equations. People worry that the inclusion of categories simply reflects prejudice. However, fortunately these worries can be empirically evaluated. Technically, the issue is whether the use of these kinds of variables as predictors in regression equations results in the most variance accounted for—if it does, then the inclusion is empirically and statistically justified; and if it does not,

then the inclusion is not empirically and statistically justified. Let us take one quick illustrative example. When automotive insurance companies use an actuarial equation to determine the risk of a future automobile accident, they find that gender is predictive and thus it is used in their actuarial equations to determine premium rates. However, gender is predictive in exactly the opposite direction of the prejudicial societal stereotype—that is, the male gender is predictive of an increased risk of accidents. If the opposite relationship was found empirically, no doubt there would be some claiming sexism. Thus, we need to be clearheaded about whether certain demographic variables such as maleness, Arab nationality, Muslim religion, and being young are forms of prejudice or actual predictors of terrorist acts. This obviously does not mean that every individual with these characteristics will be a terrorist in the same way that insurance tables do not mean that every male will get into an accident. However, again, we need to be clearheaded and educate citizens on the value of actuarial prediction and the content of the best actuarial equations.

3. *Increased interventions to reduce the spread of prejudice and discrimination toward Muslims or individuals or Mid-Eastern descent.* Prejudice is an example of irrational beliefs—for example, inaccurate beliefs are held about all members of a group, perhaps due to hasty generalizations from the behavior of a few. There have certainly been irrational backlashes against these groups due to the terroristic activities of some. There has also been concern about the extent to which the peaceful, nonoffending members of these groups have been sufficiently outspoken about the misbehavior of other members of their groups. However, psychologists need to use their knowledge of the factors responsible for prejudice and develop programs to decrease prejudice toward peaceful Muslims and people of Mid-Eastern descent.

4. *A research agenda: Attempt to understand the conditions for the recruitment of terrorists, especially home-grown terrorists.* Terrorists are made, not born. Psychologists need to study the methods by which individuals including—or maybe particularly—children are recruited into terrorist activities—particularly suicide bombers—and attempt to see if there are interventions that can be used to counteract these recruitment methods. An additional difficulty to be faced is that it may be logistically difficult to reach these individuals as they may be poor and in Third World countries that do not have access to mass media. However, until progress is made on this problem, it seems as if a fairly steady stream of recruits may be indefinitely available and thus terrorism is a problem that will plague the West indefinitely. Psychologists understand persuasion, group think, conformity, and other phenomena that will likely be involved in these recruitment procedures.

5. *Increased commitment to evidence-based interventions such as cognitive behavior therapy's prolonged exposure for PTSD (see, for example, the IOM report (Institute of Medicine 2014) and treatments for depression and bereavement as well as a concomitant decrease to "feel good" interventions that are either ineffective or iatrogenic interventions such as Critical Incidence Stress Debriefing.* Finally, we psychologists as a profession possess our own irrationalities. We can believe in the value of certain tests like the Rorschach when there is simply no psychometric evidence to justify their use (Lilienfeld, Wood, & Howard, 2000). Post-9/11 interventions were used that subsequently were shown to have no value or even be iatrogenic (Lilienfeld). There are authoritative reviews conducted by the American Psychological Association (the so-called Chambless report), the Institute of Medicine, and the Cochrane report, which need to be

understood and utilized by mental health professionals. We owe our consumers the most effective and efficient care and of course "to at least do no harm." A clear understanding of what the evidence says regarding these issues is always owed to our consumers but particularly postdisasters such as terrorist attacks.

CONCLUSIONS

To date, there does not seem to be a coherent policy related to mitigating the psychological consequences of terrorism. This chapter argues that this should be a priority and that professional organizations need to work together and with the government to develop such a policy. This policy needs to be multidimensional given the complexity of the problem. It is argued that negative psychological states—terror—are the major aim of terrorists, so being proactive about mitigating these effects seems both necessary and prudent. This chapter suggests that psychologists and other mental health professionals have and continue to have an important role to play in this enterprise. However, it is also fair to say that it is none too clear that they are living up to the demands of this important task. Several specific suggestions, including how to mobilize psychological resources postdisaster, how to aid rational risk appraisal, and how to decrease irrational beliefs about Muslims, are also discussed. Finally, it is argued that these tasks should take place in a context of epistemic sophistication in which research and quality improvement are prioritized.

REFERENCES

Bisson, J. I., Tavakoly, B., Witteveen, A. B., Ajdukovic, D., Jehel, L., Johansen, V. J., Nordanger, D., Garcia, F. O., Punamaki, R. L., Schnyder, U., Sezgin, A. U., Wittman. L., & Olff, M. (2010). TENTS Guidelines: Development of Post-Disaster Psychosocial Care Guidelines through a Delphi Process. *The British Journal of Psychiatry*, 196(1), 69–74.

Bloom, N. (2007). SIEPR Policy Brief. 1–6.

Bonanno, G. A., Galea, S., Bucciarelli, A., & Vlahov, D. (2006). Psychological Resilience after Disaster New York City in the Aftermath of the September 11th Terrorist Attack. *Psychological Science*, 17(3), 181–186.

Bonanno, G. A., Galea, S., Bucciarelli, A., & Vlahov, D. (2007). What Predicts Psychological Resilience after Disaster? The Role of Demographics, Resources, and Life Stress. *Journal of Consulting and Clinical Psychology*, 75(5), 671.

Brewin, C. R., Andrews, B., & Valentine, J. D. (2000). Meta-analysis of Risk Factors for Posttraumatic Stress Disorder in Trauma-Exposed Adults. *Journal of Consulting and Clinical Psychology*, 68(5), 748.

Bryant, R. A., & Litz, B. T. (2009). Mental Health Treatments in the Wake of Disaster. A chapter in R. Bryant and B. Litz. *Mental Health and Disasters*, 321–335. West Nyack, NY: Cambridge University Press.

Combs, B., & Slovic, P. (1979). Newspaper Coverage of Causes of Death. *Journalism Quarterly*, 56(4), 837.

Disaster Mental Health Subcommittee. (2009). Disaster Mental Health Recommendations: Report of the Disaster Mental Health Subcommittee of the National Biodefense Science Board. http://www.phe.gov/Perparedness/legal/boards/nbsb/Documents/nbsb-dmhreport-final.pdf.

Eisenberg, N., & Silver, R. C. (2011). Growing Up in the Shadow of Terrorism: Youth in America after 9/11. *American Psychologist*, 66(6), 468.

Ehlers, A., Clark, D. M., Hackmann, A., McManus, F., Fennell, M., Herbert, C., & Mayou, R. (2003). A Randomized Controlled Trial of Cognitive Therapy, a Self-help Booklet, and Repeated Assessments As Early Interventions for Posttraumatic Stress Disorder. *Archives of General Psychiatry*, 60(10), 1024–1032.

Fisher, J. E., & O'Donohue, W. (2009). *The Practitioner's Guide to Evidence Based Treatment*. New York: Springer.

Hobfoll, S. E., Watson, P., Bell, C. C., Bryant, R. A., Brymer, M. J., Friedman, M. J., Friedma, M., Gerson, B. P. R., Jong, J., Layne, C. M., Maguen, S., Neria, Y., Norwood, A. E., Pynoos, R. S., Reissman, D., Ruzek, J. I., Shalev, A. Y., Solomon, Z., Steinberg, A. M., & Ursano, R. J. (2007). Five Essential Elements of Immediate and Mid–term Mass Trauma Intervention: Empirical Evidence. *Psychiatry*, 70(4), 283–315.

Holman, E. A., & Silver, R. C. (2005). Future-oriented Thinking and Adjustment in a Nationwide Longitudinal Study Following the September 11th Terrorist Attacks. *Motivation and Emotion*, 29(4), 385–406.

Huddie, L., & Feldman, S. (2011). Americans Respond Politically to 9/11. *American Psychologist*, 66(6), 455–467.

Inter-Agency Standing Committee. (2007). *IASC Guidelines on Mental Health and Psychosocial Support in Emergency Settings*. Geneva: IASC.

James, L., & O'Donohue, W. (2009). The primary care toolbook. New York, NY: Springer Press.

Jasen, G. (2011) Economic Cost of 9-11-Three Industries Still-Recovering. *The Fiscal Times*.

Galea, S., Vlahov, D., Resnick, H., Ahern, J., Susser, E., Gold, J., & Kilpatrick, D. (2003). Trends of Probable Post-traumatic Stress Disorder in New York City after the September 11 Terrorist Attacks. *American Journal of Epidemiology*, 158(6), 514–524.

Goenjian, A. K., Walling, D., Steinberg, A. M., Karayan, I., Najarian, L. M., & Pynoos, R. (2005). A Prospective Study of Posttraumatic Stress and Depressive Reactions among Treated and Untreated Adolescents 5 years after a Catastrophic Disaster. *American Journal of Psychiatry*, 162(12), 230–238.

Institute of Medicine report (June, 2014). Treatment for Posttraumatic Stress Disorder in Military and Veteran Populations: Final Assessment. Institute of Medicine.

Kaniasty, K., & Norris, F H. (2009). Distinctions that Matter: Received Social Support, Perceived Social Support, and Social Embeddedness after Disasters. *Mental Health and Disasters*, pp. 175–200.

Lichtenstein, S., Slovic, P., Fischhoff, B., Layman, M., & Combs, B. (1978). Judged Frequency of Lethal Events. *Journal of Experimental Psychology: Human Learning and Memory*, 4(6), 551.

Lilienfeld, S. O., Wood, J. M., & Howard, N. (2000). The Scientific Status of Projective Techniques. *Psychological Science in the Public Interest*, 1(2), 27–66.

Meehl, P. E. (1959). *Clinical vs. Statistical Prediction.* New York: Echo Point Books.

National Commission on Children and Disasters. (2010). *National Commission on Children and Disasters: 2010 Report to the President and Congress.* Retrieved from http://www .childrenanddisasters.acf.hhs.gov

Neria, Y., Olfson, M., Gameroff, M. J., DiGrande, L., Wickramaratne, P., Gross, R., Pillowsky, D. J., Neugebaur, R., Manetti-Cusa, J., Lewis-Fermandez, R., Lantigua, R., Shea, S., & Weissman, M. M. (2010). Long-term Course of Probable PTSD after the 9/11 Attacks: A Study in Urban Primary Care. *Journal of Traumatic Stress, 23*(4), 474–482.

O'Donohue, W., & Draper, C. (2011). *Stepped Care and ehealth.* New York: Springer.

O'Donohue, W., & Dyslin, C. (1996). Abortion, Boxing and Zionism: Politics and the APA. *New Ideas in Psychology, 14*(1), 1–10.

O'Donohue, W., & Maragakis, A. (2015). *Behavioral health in Patient Centered Medical Homes.* New York: Springer.

O'Donohue, W., Snipes, C., Dalto, G., Soto, C., Maragakis, A., & Im, S. (2014). The Ethics of Enhanced Interrogations and Torture. *Ethics & Behavior, 25*(5), 361–372.

Perlman, S. E, Friedman, S., Galea, S., Nair, H. P., Erős-Sarnyai, M., Stellman, S. D., Hon, J., & Greene, C. M. (2011). Short-Term and Medium-Term Health Effects of 9/11. *The Lancet, 378*, 925–934.

Pfefferbaum, B., Nixon, S. J., Tivis, R. D., Doughty, D. E., Pynoos, R. S., Gurwitch, R. H., & Foy, D. W. (2001). Television Exposure in Children after a Terrorist Incident. *Psychiatry, 64*(3), 202–211.

Silver, R. C., Holman, E. A., McIntosh, D. N., Poulin, M., & Gil-Rivas, V. (2002). Nationwide Longitudinal Study of Psychological Responses to September 11. *JAMA, 288*(10), 1235–1244.

Tversky, A., & Kahneman, D. (1971). Belief in the Law of Small Numbers. *Psychological Bulletin, 76*(2), 105.

Watson, P. J., Brymer, M. J., & Bonano, G. (2011). Post Disaster Psychological Intervention since 9/11. *American Psychologist, 66*, 482–494.

Part V
Future Considerations

14

Emerging Trends in the Prevention and Management of WMPD

Terry L. Oroszi and Larry C. James

What have we learned since the September 11, 2001 (9/11), attacks on New York and Washington D.C.? Since 9/11, a coalition of European nations has been at war in the Middle East. The world has witnessed an increase in novel weapons technology. New policies were created. The following chapter will use our history and present events to predict potential future trends.

EMERGING POLICY

A detailed discussion of prevention and policy related to weapons of mass destruction (WMDs) national policy and prevention is discussed elsewhere in this book. New threats by new terrorist groups have sprouted up all over the globe. Boko Haram and ISIS are two terrorist groups that have infiltrated our lands, our media, and more importantly the minds of our youth. Olson (2011) and Seager (2012) discuss recruitment trends targeting American youth and young adults. Olson and Seager suggest a rather uncomplicated process to identifying persons who can be radicalized to terrorism.

There is a vigilance in our nation reminiscent of the revolutionary war; however, instead of fighting redcoats for our freedom we are at war with an enemy that remains invisible until the moment it strikes. Prior to 9/11 identification, tracking and interdiction of terrorists was not a national goal; post 9/11 it has become a priority at all levels, and this defense requires all levels; it takes the whole community to combat the unknown.

The technology of CBRNE (chemical, biological, radiological, nuclear, and explosive) and WMD terrorism strategies are evolving so quickly that the United States has developed under the State Department the Office of Mass Destruction Terrorism (http://www.state.gov/t/isn/c16403.htm).

EMERGING TRENDS IN WMD TECHNOLOGY

The likelihood of a terrorist using a WMD in the future is high, according to Berry, Curtis, and Hudson (1998), three authors who surveyed 295 monographs and journals, acknowledging the potential threats of chemical, biological, radiological, and nuclear (CBRN) terrorism. A portion of the study comprised of discussion on cyberterrorism and the potential threat to the United States' information technology–based infrastructure.

It is the twenty-first century and people are blending with technology, relying on technology on a day-to-day basis, even wearing it. We are becoming more dependent on our technology. This human aspect of information technology opens doors to our enemies. They need not be technology experts; they just need to derive some basic information from the user and with a password, a birth date, or credit card security code they gain access. The proliferation of online shopping, banking, and other forms of identification detailing the personal information is all stored online and accessible to anyone skilled enough to retrieve it.

THE USE OF SOCIAL MEDIA

Terrorist groups have a presence on the Internet and are familiar with online platforms such as e-mails, chat rooms, blogs, and social media such as Facebook, YouTube, and Twitter. The Internet is now a recruiting tool for terrorist groups, and people interested in joining a terrorist group need only do a Google search to start their path to rebellion and terror. Weimann (2011) illustrates how the Internet has been key in promoting terrorism. He acknowledged that cyberterrorism has been a tool to promote suicide bombing, the killing of innocents, the killing of children and women, and the killing of Muslims. Psychology of terrorism models suggested by Banks and James (2006) asserts that terrorists use the media, Facebook, and specifically YouTube to psychologically harm millions of people around the world by broadcasting beheading and hangings.

Oppenheimer (2012) asserts that cyberterrorists are targeting the computer systems that control air traffic, military command systems, electric power grids, nuclear power plants, telecommunications networks, and financial transactions; everyone who plugs in, who accesses the Internet has potential to be a target. Now terrorists can create mass destruction without bombs or weapons.

A biological weapon such as a virus can be costly to replicate and to disseminate. Why spend so much when a highly skilled computer specialist can do the same with a computer virus? A cyberterrorist can cause mass damage to people and property with malware, hacking, and stealing data, and with a keystroke one can undermine corporations and wipe out economies. With cyber technology, terrorists recognize and can exploit fragile economic markets. There are over 150,000 viruses in transmitting on the net. Cybercrime exceeds international terrorism as a major threat (Oppenheimer, 2012).

THE SCHOOLYARD AS A NEW BATTLEFIELD

Olson (2011) and Jenkins (2001) claim that the American schoolyard is the new battleground for terrorism. American youth, as never seen before, is attracted to the life of terrorism. Olson (2011) chronicles several cases of youth radicalized by terror cells. Unemployment, broken homes, despair, and a romanticized sense of hope and prosperity make the life of a terrorist enticing to our young Americans. They can reach out to the terror cells simply by engaging in a chat room conversation.

NEW WMD MODEL

Historically CBRN agents were viewed by most as the only WMDs. The authors postulated that weapons causing mass destruction or mass psychological destruction should include, but not be limited to, firearms and cyberterror activities. James argues that the weapons used in the Fort Hood massacre caused significant psychological harm to thousands of people exposed to the attack, thanks to our media.

Danieli, Brom, and Sillis (2005), in their book *The Trauma of Terrorism*, demonstrate how terrorist attacks can cause posttraumatic stress disorder (PTSD) without the use of CBRN weaponry. Firearms, typically not recognized as a WMD, can psychologically harm millions of people viewing the attack or witnessing the tragedy, making them a WMPD.

EDUCATION AS AN EMERGING TREND

Prior to 9/11, few universities offered graduate or undergraduate degrees in national security, homeland defense, or emergency management. Now more than 30 graduate programs exist in the country offering degrees in these fields. Training in combating terrorism, the psychology of terrorism, homeland defense, and/or emergency management is now routine for law enforcement personnel, school administrators, and government officials.

CBRN^2: NANOPARTICLES, THE NEW WMD

Chemical, biological, radiological, nuclear, and nanotechnology generates the acronym $CBRN^2$, and draws attention to the potential risk of nanotechnology. Nanoparticles are literally a WMD, delivered to destroy cancer cells in mice and achieving dramatic results (Yang, 2009). Nanomaterials are currently being developed to collect and or detect WMDs (Reynolds & Hart, 2004). Nanotechnology can be a tool to help medicine, or detect WMD, but it has the potential to cause danger (de Magalhaes, 2002). Nanotechnology has become a $6 billion industry. The risks associated with nanotechnology are still unknown; however, there is speculation that the risk could be related to health and environmental issues, as well as the proliferation of WMDs. Coolidge and Freedman (2004) theorize that nanotechnology allows the scientist to build weapons on an atomic level.

INNOVATIVE POLICING

Community policing has changed as a result of the terrorism threat. Prior to 9/11 police joint task forces were rare. Fast forward 10 years and every large metropolitan community within the United States has a form of a Joint Terrorism Task force. The participants are frequently from several city police departments, the FBI, representatives from federal and state departments of homeland defense. In addition, the FBI and many local and state police departments around the country have two critical new functions in the post 9/11 world: a cyberterrorism division and a terrorism task force. Monitoring and preventing terrorism is a full-time career for many law enforcement staff around the country.

THE PSYCHOLOGY OF TERRORISM

The most powerful tool we have to combat terrorism is education. When we understand the psychology of terrorists, their tactics will lose their power. Kidnapping of women or children, beheadings, hangings, torture, or the use of CBRN agents—the fear will be replaced with a greater sense of community outrage.

REFERENCES

Banks, L. M., & James, L. C. (2006). Warfare, Terrorism & Psychology. In Bongar, B., Brown, L., Beutler, L., Breckenridge, J., & Zimbardo, P. (Eds.) *The Psychology of Terrorism*. pp. 216–224. New York, NY: Oxford University Press.

Berry, L., Curtis, G., & Hudson, R. (1998). *Bibliography on Future Trends in Terrorism*. Scotts Valley, CA: Createspace Independent Publishing Platform.

Coolidge, C., & Freedman, M. (2004). Nanofear. *Forbes*, *174*(4), 168–170.

Danieli, Y., Brom, D., & Sills, J. (Eds.). (2005). *The Trauma of Terrorism*. Binghamton, NY: The Haworth Press.

de Magalhaes, J. P. (2002). The One-man Rule. *Futurist*, *36*(6), 41.

Jenkins, B. (2001). *Stray Dogs & Virtual Arms: Radicalization to Jihadist Terrorism in the United States*. Washington, DC: Rand Corporation.

Olson, P. A. (2011). *The Making of a Homegrown Terrorist.* Santa Barbarr, CA: Praeger Press.

Oppenheimer, A. (2012). Fighting the Quiet WMD – Cyber-Warfare. *Military Technology, 36*(4), 76–80.

Reynolds, J. G., & Hart, B. R. (2004). Nanomaterials and their Application to Defense and Homeland Security. JOM: *The Journal of the Minerals, Metals & Materials Society (TMS), 56*(1), 36–39. doi: 10.1007/s11837-004-0270-8

Seager, W. (2012). *Bureau of Counterterrorism Report on Terrorism in the United States.* Washington, DC.

Weimann, G. (2011). Cyber – Fatwas and Terrorism. *Studies in Conflict & Terrorism, 34*(10), 765–781.

Yang, B. (2009). Nanoparticles Effective in Delivering Genes Targeting Angiogenesis in Cancer. *Discovery Medicine, 1*(11), 2.

Further Reading on Terrorism

Larry C. James

Banks, L. M., & James, L. C. (2006). Warfare, Terrorism & Psychology. In Bongar, B., Brown, L., Beutler, L., Breckenridge, J., & Zimbardo, P. (Eds.), *The Psychology of Terrorism*. pp. 216–224. New York, NY: Oxford University Press.

Berko, A. (2012). *The Smarter Bomber: Women & Children As Suicide Bombers*. New York: Rowan & Littlefield Publishers, Inc.

Bloom, M. (2011). *Bombshell: Women and Terrorism*. New York, NY: Random House.

Bongar, B., Brown, L., Beutler, L., Breckenridge, J., & Zimbardo, P. (Eds.) (2006). *The Psychology of Terrorism*. New York: Oxford University Press.

Borum, R. (2004). *Psychology of Terrorism*. Tampa: University of South Florida.

British Broadcasting Company (BBC). (2015). The Search for Peace: The IRA Continuity. http://news.bbc.co.uk/hi/english/static/northern_ireland/understanding/parties _paramilitaries/continuity_ira.stm

Coogan, T. P. (2002). *The IRA*. New York, NY: Palgrave Macmillan Trade Press.

Danieli, Y., Brom, D., & Sills, J. (Eds.). (2005). *The Trauma of Terrorism*. Binghamton, NY: The Haworth Press.

Foote, D. (1988). A Shadow Government: An Insider Describes the Workings of the Ira, Europe's Most Potent Guerrilla Organization. *Newsweek*, September 12, pp. 37–38.

Gerstein, D. M. (2009). *Bioterrorism in the 21st Century*. Annapolis, MD: National Institute Press.

Guillemin, J. (2005). *Biological Weapons*. New York: Columbia University Press.

Hafez, M. (2007). *Female Suicide Bombers: The Strategy and Ideology of Martyrdom*. United States Institute of Peace. Jefferson, North Carolina: McFarland & Company.

Hudson, R. (2002). *Who Becomes a Terrorist and Why?* New York, NY: The Lyons Press.

Hudson, R. (1999). *The Sociology & Psychology of Terrorism: Who Becomes a Terrorist & Why*. Washington, DC: The Library of Congress.

The Irish Republican Army Green Book I & II. (2015). http://cain.ulst.ac.uk/othelem/ organ/ira/ira_green_book.htm

Irish Republican Army. (1996). *Handbook for Volunteers of the IRA: Notes on Guerrilla Warfare*. Boulder, CO: Paladin Press.

James, L. (2015). Domestic, Radicalized, Terrorism in the United States. A paper presented at the Middletown Chamber of Commerce. Middletown, Ohio.

James, L. (2008). *Fixing Hell: An Army Psychologist Confronts Abu Ghraib*. New York: Grand Central Press.

Jenkins, B. (2001). *Stray Dogs & Virtual Arms: Radicalization to Jihadist Terrorism in the United States*. Washington, DC: Rand Corporation.

Kilcullen, D. (2010). *Counterinsurgency*. New York, NY: Oxford University Press.

MacDonald, E. (1992). *Shoot the Women First*. New York, NY: Random House.

Mangelsdorff, A. D. (Ed.). (2006). *Psychology in the Service of National Security*. Washington, DC: American Psychological Association Press.

Moghaddam, F. M. (2013). *The Psychology of Dictatorship*. Washington, DC: American Psychological Association Press.

Moghaddam, F. M. (2008). *How Globalization Spurs Terrorism: The Lopsided Benefits of One World and Why That Fuels Violence*. Santa Barbara, CA: Praeger Press.

Navarro, B. (2015). *Acts of Terrorism in the United States*. Scotts Valley, CA: Creative Space Publishing.

Olson, P. A. (2011). *The Making of a Homegrown Terrorist*. Santa Barbara, CA: Praeger Press.

Public Broadcast Station. (2015). America and the Conflict. http://www.pbs.org/wgbh/pages/frontline/shows/ira/reports/america.html

Seager, W. (2012). *Bureau of Counterterrorism Report on Terrorism in the United States*. Washington, DC.

Simon, R. (2013). *Lone Wolf Terrorism and the Great Threat*. New York, NY: Prometheus Press.

Skaine, R. (2006). *Female Suicide Bombers*. Jefferson, NC: McFarland & Company.

Slike, A. (Eds.). (2011). *The Psychology of Counter-Terrorism*. New York: Routledge.

Taylor, M., & Quayle, E. (1995). *Terrorist Lives*. London, UK: Brassey, Ltd.

Terrorism, Research & Analysis Consortium. (2015). Continuity Irish Republican Army (CIRA) Summary. http://www.trackingterrorism.org/group/continuity-irish-republican-army-cira

U.S. Army War College. (2015). *Female Suicide Bombers*. Carlisle Barracks, PA: Create Space Independent Publishing Platform.

Weschler, L. (1998). *A Miracle, a universe: Settling accounts with torturers*. Chicago, IL: University of Chicago Press.

Wright, L. (2006). *The Looming Tower: Al-Qaeda and the Road to 9–11*. New York: Vintage Press.

Wright, J. (1986). *Torture in Brazil*. Austin: The University of Texas Press.

Zubay, G., et al. (2005). *Agents of Bioterrorism: Pathogens & Their Weaponization*. New York: Columbia University Press.

About the Editors and Contributors

EDITORS

COLONEL RETIRED (DR.) LARRY C. JAMES, PHD, ABPP, is a nationally recognized expert in national security and defense issues related to the psychology of terrorism and weapons of mass psychological destruction. He is currently the President and CEO of the Wright Behavioral Health Group, LLC, and a Professor at Wright State University. Previously he served as the Associate Vice President for Military Affairs at Wright State University in Dayton, Ohio. He served as the Dean, School of Professional Psychology, Wright State University from 2008 to 2013. Dr. James completed his PhD. in Counseling Psychology at the University of Iowa and a Postdoctoral Fellowship in Behavioral Medicine at Tripler Army Medical Center. Colonel James was the Chair, Department of Psychology, at Walter Reed Army Medical Center and the also the Chair, Department of Psychology, at Tripler Army Medical Center in Honolulu, Hawaii. He was awarded a Bronze Star and the Defense Superior Service Medal. In his more than two-decade military career, Colonel James has had many deployments. Most notably, he was deployed to Abu Ghraib, Iraq, and Guantanamo Bay, Cuba. Colonel James distinguished himself during these deployments and is one of the nation's military officers who was created with putting policies and procedures in place to prevent abuses. Dr James has been active as a lecturer, teacher, military officer, and scholar. He has lectured internationally and has published five books with several others in press and he has published more than 100 professional articles, papers, and conference presentations. His book *Fixing Hell: An Army psychologist Confronts Abu Ghraib* tells the story of Abu Ghraib through the eyes of a prominent, senior army psychologist; what caused the debacle at Abu Ghraib; and what procedures he put into place to stem the abuses at this horrible place. Colonel James, a disabled veteran himself, has worked actively to develop research and training programs for disabled veterans. In particular, his work has positively affected the lives of many veterans with posttraumatic stress disorder and traumatic brain injuries.

TERRY L. OROSZI is an award-winning leader, biologist, geneticist, writer, science communicator, educator, and program strategist. Ms Oroszi has spearheaded multiple program innovations at Wright State University and pioneered many interdisciplinary programs. Ms Oroszi was the Director of the Genetic Testing Facility at the College of Medicine, Wright State University, from 2006 to 2011 and is the Director of the Pharmacology & Toxicology Masters Degree Program. Under her leadership this program has grown to be one of the most successful research programs at WSU. With the current trends in international and domestic threats, she recognized the need for expertise and readiness in chemical, biological, radiological, nuclear and explosive (CBRNE) warfare. Ms Oroszi created the first graduate certificate program on campus with comprehensive instruction from members of the military, federal research facilities, and the FBI.

In September 2013, Ms Oroszi codirected the development of the FBI-Wright State University Weapons of Mass Destruction workshop. The workshop was a multidisciplinary collaboration between the FBI, Wright State University, and community experts to offer cutting-edge information on weapons of mass destruction. Ms Oroszi is the visionary behind the proposed MS degree in Emergency Management & Disaster Preparedness, a national model of a truly multidisciplinary program involving every college in the university. Ms Oroszi began her interest in national defense, terrorism, and CBNRE when she served in the U.S. Army from 1984 to 1988 including a tour in Germany as a member of the 52nd Air Defense Artillery Battalion. Her military background coupled with her expertise as a molecular biologist has served as the foundation for her expertise in terrorism and weapons of mass destruction. Ms Oroszi received her MS in Biological Sciences from Wright State University in the Spring of 2002 and the BS degree in Biological Sciences from Wright State University in June 1998. She is currently a Doctoral Candidate in Organizational Leadership at the College of Education, Wright State University. Ms Oroszi is the recipient of numerous awards including Phi Beta Delta International Honor Society, the College of Science & Math Award for Outstanding Teaching, and the Michelle Obama Role Model of Excellence Award.

CONTRIBUTORS

R. WILLIAM AYRES, PHD, is the Associate Dean of the Graduate School and Associate Professor of Political Science at Wright State University. He has published widely on ethnic conflict, U.S. foreign policy, and international business, including the coauthored book *For Kin or Country: Xenophobia, Nationalism, and War*. He teaches courses on international conflict analysis, diplomacy and negotiation, mediation, and international relations.

BRUCE BONGAR, PHD, ABPP, FAPM, CPSYCHOL, graduated from the University of Wisconsin (with distinction) with a degree in psychology and received his PhD from the University of Southern California in 1977. Dr Bongar is the Calvin Distinguished Professor of Psychology at the Pacific Graduate School of Psychology in Palo Alto, California, and was for many years Consulting Professor in the Department of Psychiatry and the Behavioral Sciences at Stanford University School of Medicine. He also has served as a Visiting Distinguished Professor of National Security Affairs at the Naval Postgraduate School in Monterey. From 2002 to 2005, he was the founding director of the National Center on the Psychology of Terrorism. Early in his career, Dr Bongar developed strong interests in identifying the risk factors associated with suicidal behavior and other clinical emergencies, and he has remained a very prolific contributor to the scholarly literature in this area. He is past president of the Section on Clinical Emergencies and Crises of Division 12 (Clinical Psychology) of the American Psychological Association (APA). The American Association of Suicidology recognized Dr Bongar for his work by the early career achievement Edwin S. Shneidman Award for outstanding contributions to research in suicidology, and the Louis I. Dublin Award (2004) for significant lifetime career contributions to research in suicidology. In 2008, Professor Bongar was presented with the Florence Halpern award from the Division of Clinical Psychology of the APA for his distinguished contributions to the profession of clinical psychology.

GEORGE W. HEDDLESTON is the Director of Marketing and Communications for the Wright State Research Institute at Wright State University. He is the former vice president of Marketing & Communications at Wright State University. Mr Heddleston has significant national experience with the media. He has served in many major roles in the media, public relations, and communications community. He previously worked for the San Francisco FortyNiners and the Dallas Cowboys Super Bowl winning teams.

MICHELLE HOLMAN is a graduate of Tiffin University and the Advanced Technical Intelligence Center (ATIC). Holman was a member of the National Society of Leadership and Success and the Tiffin University Equestrian Team. Holman is ranked 11th in the Nation for Western Horsemanship in Equestrian Riding Competition. Holman completed a Bachelor's of Criminal Justice with concentration in Homeland Security and Counter-Terrorism. Holman completed the Ohio Peace Officer Academy in December 2014, and in July 2015 Michelle Holman has started working as a Patrolman for the Miami Township Police Department. A native of Springfield, Ohio, Holman is devoted to the safety of the community and has an endless eagerness to learn. She enjoys riding her horse, Walker, and spending time with her family and friends.

WILLIAM O'DONOHUE, PHD, is a Professor of Psychology at the University of Nevada, Reno, where he directs a free clinic treating sexually abused children and adults. He has published over 75 books and has been awarded over $2 million in grant funding.

MAJOR LEWIS M. PULLEY, PSYD, is a psychologist in the U.S. Air Force. He previously served eight years in the U.S. Army as a helicopter pilot and aviation maintenance officer. Dr Pulley has been recognized for his psychologist role in combating terrorism and mental health conditions associated with combat-related events.

VIKRAM SETHI, PHD, is a Professor in the College of Business at Wright State University. He is also the Director of the Institute of Defense Studies and Education at Wright State University.

TIMOTHY SHAW, JD, is an attorney and retired FBI agent with over 30 years of experience with counterterrorism. He is currently the Senior Assistant Vice President for the Advanced Technical Intelligence Center of Wright State University.

ELVIN SHEYKHANI, MS, is a fourth year doctoral candidate in clinical psychology at Palo Alto University. Elvin's primary research interests include suicide risk prevention within both the military and ethnically diverse populations. Elvin also conducts research on suicide terrorism as well as the psychopathology of refugees and asylum seekers postmigration.

JAMES SOTTILE is a second year doctoral student in clinical psychology at Palo Alto University. He received his BA in psychology from Bard College. Before entering graduate school, James worked as a research assistant for the Uniformed Services University of the Health Sciences (USUHS) in Bethesda, Maryland. While working for USUHS, James assisted with the Army Study to Assess Risk and Resilience in service members, the largest epidemiological study of suicide in the military to date. His current research interests include the development of mental health education programs for military service members, as well as effective therapeutic interventions for posttraumatic stress disorder.

COLONEL MARK A. STAAL is the senior operational psychologist at the U.S. Air Force's Special Operations Command. He holds board certification in clinical psychology and received postdoctoral training in aerospace human factors engineering from NASA. Col Staal has supported operations ENDURING FREEDOM and IRAQI FREEDOM on numerous occasions as a Special Operations Task Force Command Psychologist as well as a Multi-National Force—Iraq counterinsurgency strategist. He holds the rank of Associate Professor at the United States Air Force Academy and has been a guest instructor at the Joint

Special Operations University teaching Contemporary Insurgent Warfare, Dynamics of International Terrorism, and the Psychology of Terrorism.

JOSEPH TOMLINS, MS, is a fourth year doctoral candidate in clinical psychology at Palo Alto University. He received his BA in psychology from the University of Tulsa. His research interests include military suicide risk assessment, intervention, treatment, and postintervention practices. He also researches the effect culture plays on the clinical presentation of suicidal ideation and behaviors. Joseph has given multiple presentations, such as a presidential symposium on military suicide risk assessment, at national conventions such as the American Psychological Association, the American Association of Suicidology, and the International Society of Traumatic Stress Studies. Joseph also has three years' experience in clinical work. He is currently a psychology trainee at the Neuropsychology Assessment and Intervention Clinic at the VA Palo Alto Health Care System in Palo Alto, California.

CAPTAIN KELLEY J. WILLIAMS is the Associate Director of the Wright State University CBRN Defense graduate certificate program. He is a full-spectrum CBRN/WMD expert with a wealth of experience in tactical incident response and graduate academic research. Kelley is a career military officer and Operation Iraqi Freedom veteran. He served with the U.S. Army Nuclear Disablement Teams and in various assignments with the National Guard WMD Civil Support Teams. He holds Masters of Science degrees from the Air Force Institute of Technology (Combating WMD), Wright State University (Microbiology & Immunology), and Embry-Riddle Aeronautical University (Management & Integrated Logistics). He graduated from Virginia Tech with a Bachelor's of Science in Aerospace Engineering and was a member of the Virginia Tech Corps of Cadets.

About the Series and Series Editor

PRACTICAL AND APPLIED PSYCHOLOGY SERIES

The books in the Practical and Applied Psychology series address topics immediately relevant to issues in human psychology, behavior, and emotion. Topics are of a wide range, from the psychology of black boys and adolescents, to the sexual enslavement of girls and women worldwide, and living in an environmentally traumatized world.

SERIES EDITOR

JUDY KURIANSKY, PHD, is a Licensed Clinical Psychologist, adjunct faculty in the Department of Clinical Psychology at Columbia University Teachers College, and also the Department of Psychiatry at Columbia University College of Physicians and Surgeons. Kuriansky is a UN representative for the International Association of Applied Psychology and for the World Council for Psychotherapy. She is also a Visiting Professor at the Peking University Health Sciences Center, a Fellow of the American Psychological Association, Founder of the APA Media Psychology Division, and a widely known journalist for CBS, CNBC, LIFETIME, and A&E, as well as a past regular weekly columnist for the *New York Daily News*. She has also been a syndicated radio talk show host for more than 20 years.

Index